TRANSPLANTED

A Memoir of Faith and Vision
for American Muslims

TRANSPLANTED

A Memoir of Faith and Vision
for American Muslims

Dr. Mahmood Sarram

amana publications

First Edition
(1429AH/2008AC)

© Copyright 1429AH/2008AC
amana publications
10710 Tucker Street
Beltsville, Maryland 20705-2223 USA
Tel: (301) 595-5777 / Fax: (301) 595-5888
E-mail: amana@igprinting.com
www.amana-publications.com

Library of Congress Cataloging-in-Publication Data

Sarram. M. (Mahmood)
  Transplanted : a memoir of faith and vision for American Muslims / Mahmood
Sarram.
     p. cm.
  ISBN 978-1-59008-052-8
  1. Sarram. M. (Mahmood) 2. Iranian Americans--Biography. 3. Muslims--United
States--Biography. 4. Physicians--United States--Biography. 5. United States--
Emigration and immigration--Biography. 6. Iran--Emigration and immigration--
Biography. I. Title.

  E184.I5S268 2008
  305.891'55073092--dc22
  [B]
                                    2008028987

Printed in the United States of America
by International Graphics,
10710 Tucker Street,
Beltsville, Maryland 20705-2223
Tel. (301) 595-5999
Fax. (301) 595-5888
www.igprinting.com

Dedicated to
Members and Supporters of
The American Moslem Foundation and
The House of Mercy All-Muslim Cemetery Foundation

Table of Contents

Preface & Acknowledgments ix

INTRODUCTION
Falling Seeds from a Growing Tree xiii

CHAPTER ONE
The Foundations of a Boy's Life 1

CHAPTER TWO
An Opportunity and a Challenge 18

CHAPTER THREE
Overcoming Culture Shock 32

CHAPTER FOUR
Homecomings, Courtship, and Marriage 64

CHAPTER FIVE
In America, the First Time 80

CHAPTER SIX
Welcome Home 98

CHAPTER SEVEN
Resentment, Resistance, Revolution 122

CHAPTER EIGHT
Leaving Iran Again 141

CHAPTER NINE
In America Again: A Doctor ... and a Muslim 164

CHAPTER TEN
The Struggle to Build Community 179

CHAPTER ELEVEN
*A Vision for Muslims in America:
Understanding Our Heritage* 201

CHAPTER TWELVE
*A Vision for Muslims in America:
Building Institutions for Our Future* 232

APPENDIXES 251

Preface and Acknowledgments

During the past 60 years, millions of Muslims have immigrated to the United States and settled in all corners of this country. They all profess themselves as being Muslim and followers of the Prophet Mohammad *pbuh*. However, under close scrutiny, their concept of Islam varies depending upon their country of origin and their affiliation to a particular denomination. After arriving in the U.S. they have created small communities of like-minded Muslims with similar backgrounds and have developed Sunni Mosques, Shi'a Mosques, Arab communities, Iranian communities, Pakistani communities, and Somali communities, to name just a few. The host country and the general American public, however, see all of these immigrants as "Muslims" and tend to treat them as a monolithic group. The way non-Muslims deal with Muslims is strongly conditioned by images that have been created by the mass media and Hollywood films. Added to these often-distorted images are the inputs from the political developments in the Middle East during the past fifty years. In the general American mind, Muslims are associated with harsh fundamentalists, terrorists, and people who stridently oppose democracy, progress, and modernization—and who are antag-onistic to the "American way of life."

This book is a memoir of my life in two worlds: the world in which I was born, that is, the Islamic world; and the world in which I have lived during two periods of my life. I have written this book not simply to tell my own story but to bear witness to certain truths I have learned and wish to pass on to others. In particular, I wish to elucidate three major points:

• Islam is not opposed to modernization, progress, democracy, freedom, and the American way of life. Islamic teachings encourage Muslims to be good, loyal, law-abiding citizens and to become con-tributing members of whatever society they live in—in our case, the American society. The traditions of the Islamic faith undergird this statement, and the large numbers of successful Muslims in academic and research institutions, high-tech industries, and elsewhere in roles of leadership and productivity bear witness to the reality of our contri-bution.

• To become good and contributory citizens, Muslims have to adopt the current rules and ethics in social behavior that dominate public life in America. This does not mean abandoning the principles of their faith or their past tradition, but rather that they must rediscov-er and revive the original, true teachings and values of Islam in ethics and social behavior, teachings and values that are thoroughly compat-ible with American norms and rules of social behavior and ethics.

• To be successful in their new environment and preserve their reli-gious and cultural identities, Muslims must build strong community institutions reaching across various ethnic and denominational com-munities, and work to create a vibrant and unified minority within the pluralistic American society.

In writing this book, I had the good fortune of collaborating with

David W. Paul as my editor. I have often admired his talent and ability to read my mind and put my thoughts in writing. I am indebted to him for his hard work, honesty, and patience.

I also thank Dr. Mohammad Azadeh and Dr. Khalil Khalilian for their review of the manuscript and their input.

I am grateful to Amana Publications for appreciating the value of this book for future Muslim generations in the United States and for supporting its publication.

Last but not least, I would like to thank my wife Fereshteh, who tolerated my long hours of retreat in my room and gave me encouragement and support in writing this book.

Mahmood Sarram, MD
Lakewood, Washington
2008

INTRODUCTION

Falling Seeds from a Growing Tree

Not long after our family came to the United States, my teenage son Ali felt lonely and worried about what would happen to us in this new country. He was a bright, respectful boy who was earning good grades, and I could feel his pain and his sense of separation. I told him, "Ali, don't worry. You are like a tree that has been pulled up from an orchard in Iran and transplanted in an oasis. You will grow here and bear fruit. The fruits will fall down and leave their seeds in the ground, and other trees will grow. As time passes—and it will pass quickly—someday you'll have another orchard in the United States. So look positively toward the future, and you will be okay."

My response appeared to reassure Ali. In truth, however, I had my own concerns about our fate in this new homeland. I believed that our family would prosper here, and time has born out my confidence. More than two decades later, I'm proud to say that all of my children have found success in America and feel at home here. My wife Fereshteh and I have similarly prospered, and I have retired from the practice of medicine after having delivered more than 5,000 babies in the course of my career. We consider ourselves good citizens of this country—and faithful Muslims as well. Our orchard is thriving. But what about future generations?

We Muslims confront challenges in our efforts to realize the American dream. We are under constant stress because of our image in the media, and we often feel conflicted by questions of identity. The events of recent years, which I do not need to name, have intensified the stresses, and one sometimes wonders if Muslims are truly welcome in America. Those of us who have chosen to make our lives in the U.S. believe that we belong here. This country has given us much, and in return, we have much to contribute to American culture. The best way we can do this is by holding true to the core values of our religion and our centuries-old Islamic heritage.

But do Americans know who we really are?

Think about all of the news stories that flash across our television screens concerning Muslim militants. Now ask yourself, how many news stories do we read about Muslims who do good in the world? Everybody knows who Osama bin Laden and Saddam Hussein are, but how many recognize the names of Nobel laureates Orhan Pamuk, Naguib Mafouz, Ahmed Zewail, Shirin Ebadi, Abd-alSalam, Mohammad el-Baradei, or Muhammad Yunus? We Muslims hear others telling us that we are bad people, and we want to say, "No, we are good people." So many others look at us and immediately wonder if we sympathize with terrorism, and we want to say, "No! The terrorists do not represent us. The terrorists do not reflect Islam." In an interview for the Public Broadcasting System shortly after 9/11/2001, Dr. Maher Hathout, an Egyptian-American gynecologist and a prominent spokesman for the Muslim Public Affairs Council, said it well: "What [others] perceive [about Islam] is not … the real Islam. It is Islam that has been hijacked, tampered with, and project-ed according to the bias of special agendas, or just mere ignorance."

Do we American Muslims really know who we are? Have we read the works of the great poets from the Islamic tradition? Do we know about the Muslims who established the basis of modern mathematics; the scientists whose work, six and seven centuries ago, was far in advance of anything being done then in Europe; and the scholars who kept alive the philosophy and literature of the ancient Greeks at a time when those priceless works might otherwise have been lost forever?

For that matter, do we even have a thorough grasp on the fundamental principles of our own religion? It was late in my life when I came to understand that there are three core aspects to Islam:

• The Islamic worldview: concepts of God, His creations, the truth, the afterlife, and humans' responsibility for their actions on earth

• A code of personal and social ethics that grew up as Islam developed

• The ritual practices through which we approach God and express our faith

The first two aspects were central to the message of Islam and instrumental in the rapid expansion of Islam during the first two centuries after the Prophet Mohammad, peace be upon him. In the course of history, however, the third aspect, the rituals, became primary. Islam as a worldview faded into the background; ethics lost its social implications and came to be treated as a private matter. Thus it is that so many Muslims today see our religion only in terms of its ritual practices, along with dress codes and standards of sexual morality. They don't have a clear picture of the broader worldview developed in classical Islam or an understanding of the code of social ethics that is also of central importance.

The challenge for Muslims in contemporary America is to understand our core religious values, take pride in our heritage, and share the insights of our tradition with our neighbors and fellow citizens. Deep down in our hearts, Muslims feel a sense of honor and dignity, and yet our fellow Americans—our neighbors, public officials, and the mass media—do not grant us this dignity. Instead of feeling alienated and sorry for ourselves, we need to cut through the smoke and distortions, to present ourselves as the proud bearers of our heritage and also as active contributors to the wonderful melting-pot that is the American nation . If Muslims apply the totality of the teachings of Islam in our daily lives, in word and practice, our fellow Americans will appreciate us as the good people that we believe we are.

America has always been a land of immigrants. The first English, Spanish, Dutch, and French settlers were strangers in a harsh environment. The Africans who arrived in the deplorable condition of slavery, the Germans, Scandinavians and Slavs, Greeks and Italians, Irish and Chinese, Jews from Eastern Europe and the Levant—all came here as outsiders; all faced hardships. All had to ask themselves, "Who am I, now that I have left my ancestral home behind, and how do I fit in here?"

It was particularly difficult for those waves of immigrants arriving from eastern and southern Europe, and the Irish as well, around the beginning of the twentieth century. Many of them met a hostile reception from those who had come before, and struggled to make a living almost as much as they had struggled in their homelands. And yet, if it was hard for, say, Italians or Greeks or Sephardic Jews to fit into their new surroundings, it is even harder for Muslims today because our culture and historical background are more distant from the European cultures whose traditions have dominated in North America. Moreover, the surrounding culture is obsessed by what it perceives as a global war in which Muslims are the adversaries. Some doubt that we Muslims can be faithful both to our religion and to America. There are even some Muslims who believe we must assimilate by abandoning our core religious and cultural values if we are to flourish amid the modernity of the West.

They are mistaken. Our religious faith does not diminish our ability to be American patriots any more than Christianity or Judaism does. Patriotism is a value separate from religion. And nothing that is intrinsic to Islam is in conflict with the basic human qualities that have produced the West's advances in science, technology, and organizational skills. Modernity is not repugnant to Islam. On the contrary, wise Muslims see modernity as a gift of God; it is the fruit of human knowledge and creativity, which spring from God. Modernity is good.

Modernity is not the product of specific institutional forms such as capitalism. The underpinnings of modernity lie in the core values and behaviors that have arisen in the West—honesty, hard work, discipline, punctuality, love for humanity. A landmark of modernity is the general ability to organize human systems for working together in pursuit of a common goal; collaboration, teamwork, coordination—without these dynamic qualities, Western societies would still be at the level of the Middle Ages. In Islamic societies, these values and skills were undervalued and repressed for several hundred years, often obscured and discouraged by clergy and rulers, and buried by the effects of Western colonialism.

If one studies the entire history of Islam, however, one finds the same fundamental values at the heart of our tradition. They are values written in the Qur'an, honored by the Prophet Muhammad *pbuh*, taught by many generations of scholars and religious leaders, and realized in the achievements of Muslims over centuries in literature, mathematics, botany, physics, medicine, architecture, and history, as well as philosophy and theology. Our scientists' discoveries laid the groundwork for the technologies of modern Europe. Our poets and thinkers left a legacy of wisdom about the eternal questions of life, death, and the purpose of mankind's earthly existence. Islamic scholarship sprang from an intellectual tradition based on reason and the pursuit of truth, not from a dogmatic and one-sided view of the world.

It is precisely here that we find a crucial connection between our Islamic past and the modernity of the West. We Muslims are not aliens in the culture of modernity. We should not think of ourselves as soldiers in a war against modern values. However, we do need to reconnect with those qualities in our heritage that can equip us for functioning in the Western world while we maintain our identity, our religious faith, and our moral principles.

The Western world is different from our ancestral societies. One cannot deny that the religious and cultural norms of our native lands are in conflict with many aspects of the culture in which we live today. Our ancestors were taught to shun the materialism of the Westerners who came to their lands as colonialists. As a result, we Muslims developed an image of ourselves that is spiritual and even ascetic. We are accustomed to considering the material world, the world of pleasure, and perhaps even the world itself, as either unimportant or sinful. Our spiritual and ascetic self-image has set us apart from Westerners for the past several hundred years. We have clung to the image as a matter of pride and a mark of our virtue. And yet, this Muslim self-image complicates relations between the Middle East and the West, and it is an added source of difficulty for those of us who are now living in materialistic Western societies.

However, if we go back to early Islam, if we go back to the Book and the teachings of our Prophet, we discover a different approach to life, one that is not so ascetic. We see in those teachings that life is important, the world is important. God connects with us through the works of His Creation. The world is God's Creation. People are God's Creation. Pleasure is God's Creation. We must respect Creation, honor it, and preserve it. We do not live a righteous life just by going to the mosque and praying. We do not achieve salvation simply by performing the ritual acts of our faith. God calls us to live in the world He has given us, not to withdraw from it; He asks us to be a part of society, to do good works.

It is said that the Prophet Mohammad *pbuh* once passed a man in the graveyard who was praying for long hours during the day. The Prophet asked the man's companions, "Who feeds this man and his family?"

"His brother," said the companions.

The Prophet said, "His brother will earn the rewards for this man's praying."

This message, emphasizing good works and care for our fellow man, is at the heart of Islam, but it is one that has been largely lost to Muslims over the centuries.

Why were those precious pieces of wisdom lost? The main fault lies with those who assumed the role of rulers and interpreters throughout the history of the Islamic world, beginning with the khalifs belonging to dynasties who came to power during the early centuries after the Prophet. After them, the various kings, sultans, shahs, and colonial satraps of the Middle East, together with clergy selected to serve their rulers' ends, continued to interpret the Word in their own ways. Thanks to them, over time, the people of Islam forgot much of the content and the importance of the original Islamic teachings. What they remembered were the rituals and the conventions of moral behavior, dress codes, and other manners and habits that form the outer layer of Muslim cultures.

Historians have suggested that the Mongol invasion of the Islamic Empire in the thirteenth century (Christian calendar), an enormous catastrophe, also played a role in changing the practices of Islam. Mysticism became central in religious teaching, and the importance of work and material gain as an Islamic value diminished. This tendency was reinforced during the many years of modern European colonial rule.

Because so much of the fundamental message became lost or obscured, Muslims have not fully appreciated the centrality of God in human affairs and the dignity of human communities as expressed in a code of interpersonal behavior. Sometimes it has seemed as if the central lesson of our religion, as popularly understood, is God for me, not I for God; and kindness, honesty, the pursuit of social justice and collective welfare—essential points in the Islamic code of behavior—have given way to an ethos of every man, every family, every clan and tribe for their own interests.

The failure to teach the complexities of Islam remains to this day a major shortcoming in the spiritual cultures of the Middle East. In particular, the absence of religious and social ethics in the modern Islamic consciousness underlies the great problems that we see in the region today and has its reflection in the relations between the Islamic world and the West. Today, we hear much talk of bringing democracy to the Middle East, but democracy, like other elements of modernity, will not come to the Middle East until the Muslims of the region rediscover the true essence of their religion—that is, until they understand, at a deep level, the centrality of God in the world and the code of social ethics that is inherent in Islam: for it is only by understanding these truths that they can engage as equals in a dialogue with the West.

During the nineteenth and twentieth centuries, Westerners, with their own economic and political interests, moved into positions of power and authority in many Islamic countries. Under their influence, local leaders tried to teach their citizens to adopt Western ideas and patterns of behavior. Government officials reorganized institutions along functional models drawn from those of Europe or America. Public servants and businessmen adopted Western clothing fashions, often under pressure from their governments, in such countries as Turkey and Iran. (There were some obvious exceptions, as in Saudi Arabia and the small states of the Persian Gulf.)

Muslims at large rejected these efforts at changing their culture, in part because they saw that Westerners' behavior violated some of the standards by which they had been taught to live their lives as Muslims. Westerners drank alcohol, for example; their sexual behavior flouted Muslims' morals, and they seemed to value power, wealth, and the possession of material goods above all else. Western influence threatened the integrity of Muslims' religion, their self-respect, and their dignity. In the long run, neither the Westerners nor the political leaders could impose Western standards onto the citizens from above without undermining the fundamental religious values supporting society from below.

It's not that the masses of the Middle East have rejected the goals of economic development, ending poverty, and lifting their countries to positions of strength. They fear the effects of modernity, which they are unable to separate from the undesirable qualities of Western culture. They do not understand that the modernization process depends not upon specific habits and customs, but rather on the more fundamental patterns of ethics and behavioral norms that have fueled economic, social, and political development in the West—honesty, discipline, teamwork, reliability, and mutual trust.

By and large, Muslims living in America and Europe have brought with them this confusion, this false tension between modernization and the core values of their religious heritage. Many find it hard to hold onto their faith, and some have decided that the traditional values of their heritage are irrelevant here. Many others are struggling to practice their religion and live according to their traditional values, a complex mixture of Islamic core values and the cultural habits of their particular ethnic and local backgrounds, even as they feel the pressure every day to be more "modern," to blend into their surroundings and try to forget the past. But such forgetting bears an intolerable cost in terms of self-respect, dignity, and indeed, one's very sense of identity.

And it is not necessary. To be successful in the West, we do not have to renounce our own values and become carbon copies of Westerners. We must, however, open our minds to recognize those positive qualities that our tradition has in common with the West. And as it happens, some of those common qualities center on the fundamental ethics and behavioral codes that have produced the modern Western personality.

When we look closely at the Qur'an and other authoritative sources of our religion, we discover commandments and teachings that show the way. These sources teach us that as Muslims we should always tell the truth, fulfill our promises and contracts, deal fairly with others, and safeguard all goods entrusted to us. We should work hard and in a focused way, perform to the best of our abilities, create wealth, and support our families. We should give a portion of our earnings to the poor and to the public welfare. We should not be hypocrites. And we should fear no one but God.

These teachings, which constitute an Islamic code of ethics and social behavior, will come up again in the course of this book. For now, it is important to note that they are thoroughly compatible with the motivational ethics of the modern West. If we as Muslims absorb the ethics of our own religious tradition into our lives, into our consciousness and our daily practices, we will be welcomed into our social surroundings. More importantly, if we apply the Islamic social and personal ethics with sincerity and conviction, we will please God and earn salvation at the same time as we are becoming successful American citizens.

This should be good news for American Muslims in particular. It means we do not have to adopt the total package of Western habits and behaviors to become a part of America; we do not have to mimic the trends and fashions that lie on the surface of the popular culture. We can reach within our own heritage, and within our true selves, to define our identities and guide our behaviors. We can draw from the deep well-spring of our own traditions and still be a part of the rich mosaic that we know America to be.

Here in this land we now call home, we have an opportunity that exists in no other country. We have freedom—the freedom to be who we truly are; the freedom to cast aside the layers of ethnic interpretations of Islam and local cultural habits, and rediscover the core values of Islam, as described in the documented traditions of Prophet Muhammad *pbuh* and the undisputed word of God in the Qur'an. Here we are not required to accept false or distorted interpretations of the Qur'an from members of the clergy who would manipulate the truth in the service of ruling dynasties. We are free to explore our history, our traditions, our beliefs, our music, and our literature—to read books and hold discussions, to pray and practice our rituals according to the spirit of our religion. This freedom is the great gift that America has given to us.

We can wave the stars and stripes while also feeling proud of our centuries-old Islamic heritage. We can look into the mirror and see our-selves as good people, honest people, people of dignity, people deserving of our neighbors' respect. And to this new homeland, which has given us freedom and economic opportunity, we can offer something in return: our heritage, our religious history, our values, our wisdom and insights into human life. We can live out and demonstrate the oneness of God's creation, joining with our brothers and sisters of all faiths in general—and with our brothers and sisters in the Jewish and Christian faiths in particular—to express our unity as people of God and our mutual need to seek the truth together.

I personally bear witness to both the possibilities and the difficulties of this vision. I came to the West originally as a student, a temporary resident who expected to return home and live his life in service to his native land. I devoted two decades of my professional years to my homeland, but then circumstances impelled me to leave and restart my career abroad. I arrived in the United States at the age of 54, with just enough money to set up a medical practice and provide the security and comfort of a home for my family. America blessed me with success sufficient to fulfill the remaining years of my professional life and provide for my retirement. It is in my "senior" years that I now devote my time to giving back—giving back to my fellow Muslims and giving back to America.

Since my retirement, I have spent many hours reading, studying, and thinking. I have gone back to the original texts of the Islamic tradition, and I have read widely from the works of scholars and sages throughout the centuries. I have reflected on my life and on the lives of others, those whom I have known personally and those I know through books. With the help of God, and with the guidance and technical support of good, philanthropic Americans, I have established the American Moslem Foundation and the House of Mercy All-Muslim Cemetery. The purpose of these institutions is to support Muslims in the United States in safeguarding their religious heritage and to increase Americans' knowledge of Islam. It is my hope that others will learn what I have learned and join me in giving back.

These pages tell a story about a journey of discovery. The story is about a boy from a humble Iranian family who was brought up in conservative traditions and found himself, as a student in the West, confronting a culture different from his own. It is the story of a man who has striven to bridge those two cultures through committed work and dialogue, all the while struggling to maintain his own true identity as a Muslim because he knows the ultimate value of Islam for himself, his family, and the world in which he now lives.

This is my story: the story of my life and, far more importantly, the story of the wisdom I have gained in the course of my journey. My insights do not make me a prophet or sage; I simply wish to pass along what I know and what I feel in the form of a call to present and future generations of Muslims living in America and Europe. I call upon them not to lose their heritage, but to have the courage to explore it and understand it, as I have endeavored to do; to cherish that precious heritage, preserve it, and draw inspiration from it.

This book is also a call to non-Muslims: an appeal for openness, trust, dialogue, and mutual understanding. We are neighbors and friends. We are not opposing forces facing off across an unbridgeable chasm. We cannot deny that there are differences among us, but we share a common purpose on this earth: to live together as brothers and sisters, to respect and support each other, and to build a world of harmony and good by drawing from the best resources of our traditions. Together we must plant orchards to nourish many future generations.

There is no question but that Islam is in the countries of the West to stay. The problems and sensitivities arising from this fact represent a challenge that both Muslims and non-Muslims must overcome. Such problems arise from ignorance and distrust, as well as unfortunate events in the past, and it is incumbent upon all of us to engage in an ongoing, heartfelt dialogue that will lead to trust and mutual understanding. As for us Muslims who have made our home in America, we must strive to see ourselves not as a people torn between two cultures, but as a part of the American community. Our culture is a part of the larger culture, not separate from it, and certainly not alien or hostile to it. If we can demonstrate that to our fellow citizens, I have no doubt that they will respond, as Americans always have, with open hearts.

CHAPTER ONE

The Foundations of a Boy's Life

Engineer Sedehi arrived at our home in Isfahan in a dark, European-style suit. He was in his late twenties, tall and clean-shaven, and he brought with him his new wife. The young Mrs. Sedehi had on a tight-fitting dress, and, unlike my mother and my sisters, she did not cover her head but displayed her long, dark hair for all to see. The things that struck me most about her, though, were her makeup, her prominent eyebrows and her deep-red lips.

Several days earlier, I had become aware that something important was about to happen. There was much commotion in our house as my parents and siblings talked about the upcoming visit of Engineer Sedehi. He was my mother's cousin, and he had recently returned from France with a degree in engineering. He married into a wealthy Iranian family and took an excellent job working for the government in Tehran. Such distinguished guests deserved special treatment, and my family planned and debated about how to welcome them and what to serve for lunch.

We received them in the north wing of our house where the rooms were bigger, the furniture of better quality, and the carpets more plush. We all sat on chairs in the receiving room, and the adults carried on a conversation as tea and sweets were offered. I sat in the corner of the room quietly and had the feeling that no one noticed me; after all, I was only six years old. I, however, noticed everything. My big eyes and open ears took it all in: how my parents treated these guests with particular courtesy and deference; how Engineer Sedehi spoke precisely and with an air of authority; and how, when we moved into the dining room for lunch, Mrs. Sedehi sat uncomfortably on the floor with us, shifting her legs in her tight dress from one side to the other. This made me nervous, and I felt embarrassed that, like most Iranian families, we had no table and chairs in our dining room.

Engineer Sedehi had much to say about France, and he spoke about how it was to come back to Iran. He told us that he was washing his car one day, not long after his return from France—it was 1938 and very few people had a car then—and his mother was upset because she felt that a person in his position should not do such menial work; that is what servants were for.

My mother had made sure to include me in this gathering. Like all mothers, she wanted the best for her children, and she wanted me to see an example of a young man who had gone away for his education and become a success. Mother never talked to me about this, but I knew what she wanted me to learn: Engineer Sedehi was an example for me, a role model. This was my mother's dream of where I should go with my life.

It was not where my father had gone with his life. Father, who was the son of a farmer and orchard keeper, did not have the opportunity to study for a profession. Instead, he became a petty merchant in the bazaar, located in Isfahan's former caravanserai, where in earlier times caravans of merchants and their animals stopped to rest during their long journeys. Like most fathers, mine went off to work in the morning and came back in the evening, and we children didn't see much of him. He was rather distant to us. He was not without a sense of humor and would laugh when something was funny, but his eyes generally expressed the seriousness with which he took his role as breadwinner for our family. We knew he was important behind the scenes of our household and he did take an interest in our lives, but he was not one to show affection. As in most families that I knew of, our lives revolved around our mother.

There were six of us, two boys and four girls. The oldest was my brother Ahmad; then there were three sisters: Esmat, Aghdas, and Alam. I was the fifth child, ten years younger than my brother, and the baby of the family was my sister Touran, born four years after me. All of us slept in one room, close to my mother's bedroom. Ahmad was the favored child, and he lorded it over the rest of us. I particularly remember envying him his bicycle and begging him to let me ride it, but he would not. I always wished he would treat us more fairly, but that is how brothers and sisters are; they will sometimes take advantage of each other.

My strongest memory from my schooldays in Isfahan is that I received the highest grade in my class in the final primary-school certificate examination. This surprised me, because it seemed to me I had achieved the top rank without trying. My mathematics teacher, Mr. Sarrafnia, called me into his office and said to me, "You are an intelligent boy. You are capable of achieving a lot in your life. Take care of yourself and work hard." I took his advice to heart, and as I grew older I developed a love of learning and a passion for excelling.

One day as I was walking through the city on my way to school, I saw a scary sight: The central square was filled with military trucks and Jeeps. Strange men milled around the vehicles, speaking in a language that I could not immediately identify. Eventually, I recognized a few words from my English classes. The second world war was underway, and despite the fact that Iran was neutral, my country came under occupation by Soviet troops from the north and British troops from the south, determined to secure Iranian oilfields and keep the precious supplies from the hands of the Germans. Eventually, American forces came, too, and it was Americans whom I encountered in Isfahan.

No nation likes being occupied by foreign armies, and Iran was no exception. The Allies had sent our king, Reza Shah Pahlavi, into exile and installed his son, Mohammad Reza Pahlavi, on the throne. The young shah agreed to bring Iran into the war on the Allies' side. The highest government officials of the old shah's regime were imprisoned, including the national chief of police, Col. Rokneddin Mokhtari, who was much feared by the Iranian people.

At first, these foreigners with guns intimidated me, but, like everyone else, I got used to them. In fact, I came to admire them. They had money, they carried weapons, and they presented a snappy appearance. When they walked together, they moved steadily and with a smart gait that impressed me; Iranians did not walk like that. From the way the foreigners carried themselves, they seemed intelligent and very organized. Other kids began to approach them and strike up conversations, and they discovered that the soldiers would sometimes give them chocolates or a pencil. We all felt that if we talked with the soldiers, it would reflect positively on us; it would somehow make us bigger.

And so, one day I approached a soldier who was standing slightly apart from his group and tried out my English on him.

"Good morning," I said. "Do you have a pencil?"

He answered politely, "No, I don't have a pencil."

The conversation went no further. In fact, I felt embarrassed. My family was poor, and sometimes we children did not have the pencils that we needed for our schoolwork. Nevertheless, I had a sense of pride, and it struck me immediately that I had just done something unbecoming. I never again asked the soldiers for anything, and to this day, the memory shames me. To Muslims, begging compromises one's dignity. We expect to receive from God's bounty and by our own efforts; begging is an unacceptable act.

Thus my first intercultural experience left me with mixed feelings. On the one hand, I had met a foreign soldier, a young man who presented himself favorably and left me with a feeling that, by meeting him, I had expanded the horizons of my life. On the other hand, I had embarrassed myself—not, as far as I knew, in the eyes of the soldier, but in my own eyes.

The foreign troops stayed in Iran for several years, and later, when our family moved to Tehran just after the war's end, I saw some of the Russian soldiers who were occupying the capital city. There were also Americans in Tehran, in a neighborhood called Amir-Abad, encamped within a barrier of barbed wire. It disturbed me that the Americans separated themselves by means of barbed wire. Also disturbing were the stories I heard about them getting into fights and using their knives. Knife fights were something unheard-of among Iranians. Add to that the fact that the occupation forces had special legal privileges—if they got in trouble with the law, they were not prosecuted in Iranian courts, but in American military courts—and my attitude toward them soured. I came to understand the reality of military occupation, the indignity and humiliation of having one's country under the control of outsiders.

It was not until sometime later, after the war, that I heard yet another troubling story about the foreigners. During the late stages of the war, there were food shortages in Tehran. For a while, even the most basic staples, such as bread, became extremely hard to get. It was later discovered that, in those difficult days, some of the Allied forces confiscated grain from farmers, contributing to the famine in the capital city.

The Americans and the British ended their occupation before the Soviets did. The war ended in 1945, but it was not until 1947, under pressure by the United States government and the United Nations, that the Russians finally pulled out and Iranians celebrated the departure of foreign troops from our soil.

* * *

We had moved to Tehran in 1945 for economic reasons. The markets dropped severely at the end of the war, and it was a very difficult time for everyone. I was thirteen years old and had finished my seventh year of education.

For me, our move to Tehran was exciting. Tehran seemed like the center of the world; it was a big city, and everything about it was new to me. The move divided our family, however. Ahmad was still single, and he came with us, along with my little sistet Touran. However, my three older sisters had already married, and they stayed with their husbands in Isfahan. This made my mother very sad. At first, I didn't understand exactly why; she and my sisters cried together during the weeks leading up to our departure, and when the day came that we packed all our belongings and boarded the bus that would take us away, they cried again. Finally, as our bus started to move away from the people standing outside—our family members and some of our neighbors—I, too, felt their sadness for a brief moment. But it soon passed. I was going off to something better; I was going to the big city in search of my future.

Our living circumstances in Tehran represented a step down for us as we settled into a rented apartment in the southern part of the city, a low-income district. In Isfahan, we had owned our own house, a pleasant dwelling with three wings built around a courtyard with a flower garden. As in Isfahan, my father worked in the local bazaar. It was only later, after I had gone abroad, that he took a better position, as a bank employee.

Despite our family's hardships, I had the good fortune to land in Hakim-Nezami High School, one of Tehran's best high schools. There I became an achiever, ranking between first and fifth in the final exams every year. Just as importantly, I met a special teacher who helped turn my life into a spiritual journey.

It didn't start out pleasantly, however. The first time I stood up in class to speak, the other kids laughed at me because of my accent. I spoke Farsi, just as they did, but I spoke it in a southern Iranian dialect. Kids can be cruel; they will pick apart someone who is different in any obvious way.

I turned around and said to them, "What's wrong? I'm speaking Farsi just like you."

But they laughed again.

Within a month or so, I learned how to speak with a Tehran accent. To this day, I speak Farsi mainly in the Tehran dialect.

Anyway, I was eager to show my teachers and fellow students what I knew. Often, I was the first to put up his hand and answer questions, especially in mathematics classes, and proud of my ability to solve problems quickly. Later, however, I had a religious learning experience that changed me in this respect. I became more modest and less of a show-off. When teachers gave us a problem to be solved, I kept my hand down, even though I had solved it before anyone else did.

My mathematics teacher became curious about this, and one day he came around to my desk and looked at my notebook.

He said, "See, this guy has solved the problem, but he's not talking about it." He meant to make a point about my modesty.

I had learned an important principle: We need to be strong from within. We must not seek our strength in recognition by others. If we know that we are strong—truly know this—we don't become dependent on others' approval.

One of my best friends noticed this new "me." He said, "Mahmood, you are not talking so much any more."

I had in fact become refocused. I was now thinking about things that were bigger than myself.

The change had begun in physics class during my second year of high school. Our teacher, Mr. Abdol-Ali Gouya, was discussing sound one day when he digressed to the subject of eternity.

"What we do or say in the world does not disappear," he said. "Like a sound wave that grows lower and lower in amplitude, but never fades completely away, so are our actions. If we had enough perception and sensitivity, if we had instruments sensitive enough to magnify sound waves from long ago to the point at which we could hear them, we could retrieve all from the past of human history. Just think—we might actually hear the words of the Prophet, for example, in his own voice."

Mr. Gouya was a handsome man with a mustache, thick hair, and eyeglasses. He rarely smiled or laughed, but he was compassionate and kind. He was a good teacher, and we respected him a lot for his knowledge of physics. Now, however, he seemed to be reaching beyond physics.

"You are like a radio," he continued. "If you are correctly tuned, you can decipher things that others cannot hear."

The tuning of a person, Mr. Gouya suggested, takes place through human acts. Doing good deeds and refraining from doing evil, living a pure and simple life—these ways "tune" us in to those truths and realities that hold so many of the world's mysteries. By living a good life, we can see and understand things that would otherwise remain hidden from us.

What Mr. Gouya said intrigued me. My good friend, Hushang Sobati, was also fascinated. One day Hushang approached me after class and said, "Mr. Gouya said some interesting things. Let's go to his home and ask him to talk about them some more." It was quite unusual for students in Iran to go to a teacher's home, but the fatherly and caring attitude of Mr. Gouya gave us the courage to do so.

Mr. Gouya was quite surprised to see us, but he welcomed us and was happy to talk to us. We started having periodic meetings at his home. He taught us about his approach to life and told us his views about religion. His approach was similar to that of the Sufis, a sect of Muslims who look down on the material life. According to Sufis, material is ballast in one's life, an impediment to knowing God. They teach asceticism, believing that a person should eat little, stay up at night praying, and give one's money to others. This, according to the Sufis, is the way to God.

Mr. Gouya told us about some of the legendary Sufis in Iran's past, those whose wisdom flowered before and after the Mongol invasion of the thirteenth century, particularly Farid od-Din Attar and Jalaledin Rumi. He also talked about some of the early Arab Sufis, such as Jonaid al-Baghdadi and Abu ibn al-Arabi. He recommended books such as Attar's *Tazkerat ol-Olia (Biographies of the Saints)* and Rumi's *Masnavi-ye Manavi (Spiritual Couplets)*, which rank among the greatest works of world literature. These great Sufi masters taught their followers to turn their backs on earthly things and focus their lives on God.

I read about the lives of the great Iranian Sufis, as Mr. Gouya recommended. An impressionable teenager, I believed what I read and started putting the Sufi ascetic teachings into practice. I slept less and ate little. I studied diligently at school, worked hard around the house, and tried in every possible way to help others. I gave my monetary allowances to the poor. In the course of a short time, I lost a lot of weight. My family became alarmed. They did not know the details of my conversations with Mr. Gouya; they saw only that I had become more religious and was neglecting my health.

Because they trusted Mr. Gouya, they decided to seek his advice and requested a meeting with him. They brought me along. Mr. Gouya himself became alarmed when he realized what was going on with me. I had perhaps taken his teachings—and those of the Sufi masters—too seriously. He said that among the Sufis there were sometimes movements that were overzealous, and I had slipped into such an overzealous interpretation of religion. Mr. Gouya promised my parents he would help me reestablish a balanced approach to life.

He introduced me to a religious circle guided by a learned mystic, Sheikh Rajabali-Khayyat. Together with my friend Hushang, I started attending Sheikh Khayyat's sessions, held on a rotating basis in the homes of his followers, and sometimes in the Sheikh's own home. Some twenty or thirty men came to the sessions; Hushang and I were the youngest in the group. We all sat in a circle on the floor, including Sheikh Khayyat. We said our evening prayers together, and then he spoke. The host of the evening served food, and we ate together. When I told my father that we ate together at these sessions, my father said, "So you are becoming a clergyman." It was a joke, because everyone understood that clergymen always expected to be fed.

On occasion, Sheikh Khayyat would go with us on an outing. He would walk with us, and we would talk. We often called him Agha Sheikh, a title of great respect.

Sheikh Rajabali-Khayyat was not a clergyman; he was a tailor who lived in a small house in the southern part of Tehran. In his sixties at the time, he was wise, soft-spoken, and gentle, and his words showed a great understanding of the many books he had read. His followers considered him truly a man of God. He presented religion in terms of love: love toward God and love toward other human beings.

Sheikh Khayyat had no ambition to displace the Islamic clergy. Of their teachings and ritual instructions, he said that they are correct, but they tended to leave out one important thing: In all of our prayers and actions, we need to change our focus from benefiting ourselves and turn our attention toward pleasing God.

Agha Sheikh reminded us that the Prophet Mohammad *pbuh* said we must "take on the attributes of God. God is good; He is kind, merciful, and forgiving. We, too, must be kind to one another. We must show mercy and forgive those who have wronged us. Taking on the attributes of God is the ultimate goal of our lives. This is what brings us close to God. Everything else in this world and the afterlife, including salvation and paradise, pales in value when we weigh it against the lofty goal of being close to God."

He explained that God is always available to us if we seek His guidance. He will connect with us, talk to us, and show us His influence in our lives. The Sheikh told us not to underestimate ourselves.

"You all belong to God," he said, "and you should let the Spirit of God flourish within you."

He told us that, just as the Prophet had been in contact with God, so too could we obtain divine guidance. He said, "If you wake up in the middle of the night, look up and speak to God. He notices you; He will hear you. You can talk to God. He cares for you."

As Sheikh Rajabali-Khayyat described Him, Allah is a personal God who requires no intercession. Yes, He is the Almighty, All-knowing, All-powerful One; and yet, we can approach Him directly. He is not an angry God; He is a God of gentleness and great love, a caring God who is active in the center of our lives.

Sheikh Khayyat taught us about the importance of self-control (*taghwa*). Through self-control, he said, a person becomes the master of himself. The Sheikh was not an ascetic, however. He did not belittle the pleasures that God gives us in life, and he accepted the need to enjoy them. A good Muslim, he said, may have worldly possessions as long as he realizes that he does not own them. All things belong to God, who entrusts material possessions to us to use for the welfare of mankind.

"You can have the entire world," the Sheikh said, "as long as you acknowledge that you are merely the world's custodian, caring for it as God's possession. But if you consider even the skin of an onion to be yours, you are mistaken."

Thus, we learned, it is incumbent on us to recognize who is the ultimate Owner of the world and the hereafter. If we understand that, we understand His will; we grow close to Him and become worthy of standing before Him on the Day of Judgment.

I attended those sessions two or three times a week for two years. I never had a clear sense of how the others in our group were progressing in their enlightenment and spiritual strength. Everybody listened, but what we each took away from the lessons was very personal. As for me, Sheikh Rajabali-Khayyat had a profound impact upon my thinking. He taught me much about the nature of God, and he taught me that religion is a steppingstone to higher achievement. It is not something imposed upon us; it is a road that we can be shown, a path to a higher dimension of being—the *Serat-o-al-Mostaghim*, the "straight path," mentioned in the Qur'an: the way of the Truth.

Certainly, Sheikh Rajabali-Khayyat opened me to a new dimension of religion—new to me, at least. For Iranian Muslims, religious training was at that time, and still is, mainly ritualistic: You pray, you fast, and you read from the Qur'an. There was very little instruction in religious ethics. I learned the rituals from my mother and from our nanny. These were a normal part of my life. Aside from the ritual practices, the concept of God bewildered me. Once when I was six or seven years old, I was walking with a friend, and we started talking about God. We talked for a little while about what God was, but we really had no understanding of what, or whom, we were talking about.

I knew that I was a Muslim, because there were also Christians and Jews in our community, particularly after we moved to Tehran, and I knew they were different from me. The Christians never went to the mosque; they had their churches. Jewish merchants came to our house and sold goods to our mother—antiques, fine cloth for sewing dresses, and other things. When it came time to put together my sisters' dowries, there was a lot of business with the Jewish merchants. I made no judgment of them. We had no animosity toward them, and we did not consider them inferior to us. Sometimes while making his rounds, one or another merchant would sit down with my mother and drink a cup of tea. In any event, I wasn't aware of why Jews and Christians were not like us, that is, how and why our religions differed. And a part of the reason was that, prior to my instruction by Sheikh Rajabali-Khayyat, I didn't really understand Islam. It was because of Sheikh Rajabali-Khayyat that I began to understand the true fundamentals of my religion.

* * *

At one of Agha Sheikh's sessions, he announced that we would meet again the next evening. I turned to the person sitting next to me and said quietly, "I can't come because I have an exam coming up and I have to study." At the moment, it felt as if I were betraying the cause.

But the man next to me said, "Do not worry. Pick up your books, and do your studying. Go and do your job—that is your prayer."

He had in fact grasped the core of Rajabali-Khayyat's teaching: being a good person, serving others, doing your work in a disciplined and ethical way—this is how we move close to God.

I took that advice to heart. The next evening, instead of attending the Sheikh's session, I studied for my exam. It felt like praying, and when it came time for the exam, I passed with flying colors. I continued to work hard in my studies and, eventually, got the top score in Tehran's citywide final high school examination. My academic success, together with my ever-growing sense of God's presence, gave me enormous self-confidence. I believed that I was on the path to the great Truths of life, and that hard work and disciplined study would take me toward my destiny.

My particular career path started to become clear while I was still in high school. At that time, the education system was divided into primary school, high school up to the eleventh grade, and one final year for university preparation. Only a small minority, probably less than 10 percent, entered universities, so every parent dreamed of having at least one child who would enter a university. I was fortunate to qualify for the university-preparatory program. That final year of secondary school offered a choice of three tracks: natural sciences, literature, and engineering. I wanted to take the engineering track and become an architect. My parents realized that I showed great promise, and my father had discussions with my uncle and others about my future.

One afternoon, as my father, my brother, and I were coming home from the bazaar, I told them I wanted to go into the engineering program and become an architect. They both came down on me, saying, "No way! You are not going to become an architect. Don't you see all the architects around us who don't have jobs and are poor? Go and become a doctor. You'll do much better." They pointed out the example of a doctor we knew, who attracted a lot of patients and, in a year or so, bought a nice house.

At home, my mother seconded the idea. She said, "I hope you will become a good doctor and make a lot of money."

There was nothing I could do in the face of strong parental opinions on the subject. In Iran, what the father says goes. To this day, I have not forgiven him for making me choose the natural-science track and becoming a doctor. I believe I could have been a fine architect. This is not to deny that I was a good doctor, lived an interesting life, and prospered. However, I regret that it was not I who made the decision about my profession.

I think this aspect of Iranian customs is wrong. Here in America, I have happily accepted the idea that children should be respected more, and that their parents should take their wishes into account. We can help our children, and guide them, but they must find their own identity as they mature.

* * *

Because my transcripts were exceptional, including my rank in the citywide final examination, I entered the Alborz School, a prestigious high school in the northern part of Tehran, for my college-preparatory year. An American Christian missionary had founded the Alborz School, but by the time I attended, it had transferred to the Iranian Ministry of Education. It was unique among the schools in Tehran. In contrast to other high schools, which were in buildings that were often shabby, the Alborz School was located on a twenty-acre campus. The buildings were well constructed and airy, and the classrooms were spacious and well furnished.

The school selected the best students from all over the city and divided them into classes according to their grade-point averages. The class I was in was a powerhouse. Our teachers were almost desperate in teaching us, because the students were so fast at grasping things. They liked us and enjoyed teaching us, but it was difficult for them to stay ahead of us. We all did well on our final examination, and when we also took the university entrance exam, most of us qualified.

I did as well at the Alborz School as I had at Hakim-Nezami, ranking first in my class and fourth in the entrance examination for the medical school of Tehran University. As it turned out, financial difficulties would keep me from studying medicine in Tehran, but for the moment, it appeared as though my future course had been set.

* * *

I believe that the important things in life happen in stages. It's like climbing a stairway, opening a door, and entering a room filled with surprises. When you've absorbed all that the room has to offer you and are ready to move on, you climb another flight of stairs and open another door. In other words, life is not a steady line; you have to create greater capabilities of perception before you can acquire a greater consciousness of God. You have to be able to tolerate the mysteries of life and bear up in the face of truths that might at first seem overwhelming.

There are truths so profound, so overwhelming, that the knowledge of them can destroy a person if he or she is not ready to receive them. For example, if I know that I'm going to die two days from now, I'm not going to carry on my life in a normal way. This knowledge is so powerful that it will interfere with my existence, change my behavior. It may plunge me into despair and immobility. On the other hand, if I am prepared for it—that is, if I am prepared to accept my imminent death—I might draw on my inner strength to make peace with my enemies, gather together one last time with my friends, make sure my will and all financial matters are in place, and pray to God for my salvation and the well-being of my family.

Thus, for certain forms and levels of knowledge, you have to be strong enough before God will grant you such knowledge. This is how it is with prophets; they go through trials until they become firm in their convictions, and then they are given the command to go out and teach and do good deeds.

As I ended my secondary education at the Alborz School, I took with me enough knowledge to step up to the next level of education, the next stage of my life journey. Whatever I thought my future would be, my knowledge was limited. Doors began to open, but I could not see exactly what lay in the rooms behind them.

CHAPTER TWO

An Opportunity and a Challenge

On a sunny day in October 1950, a group of teen-age boys entered the gates of the Marble Palace in Tehran and were shown into the famous Hall of Mirrors. It was a place of magnificent beauty and grandeur, with crystal chandeliers and curtains woven from threads of gold. Hundreds of master craftsmen had been brought in from all of Iran's provinces to create this building, the finest of the shah's luxurious homes. The boys stood in a line, and the shah, wearing a dark, European-styled suit, entered the room with his retinue of officials and bodyguards. The Minister of Education, Dr. Jazayeri, introduced the boys to the shah, who shook hands and spoke personally with each boy. None of them had ever been inside this palace before, and all were keenly aware that such an audience with the shah was a great honor.

I was one of those boys, and after I returned home from that event, my proud father told everybody he knew that his son had met the shah. For my part, I had been very conscious of being in the presence of power, and I was impressed, although not intimidated. I knew that there was a power in the universe much stronger than this earthly prince. Later in my life, I would come to understand that the shah ruled over a system that was cruel and corrupt, and that most of his subjects bitterly resented his efforts to westernize Iranian society. For the moment, however, I made no judgment of the man, his wealth, and the circumstances of his position. My overwhelming feeling was amazement that I, a poor boy originally from the provinces, was suddenly catapulted into a place where I was shaking the hand of the shah. Many, many times I had walked past the outside of the Marble Palace wondering what was going on inside, without a thought that I might one day be invited in, and now here I was, in my own, modest clothes, as if fortune were smiling on me.

How I got to this moment is a story about the culmination of my scholarly efforts to that point, a story of discipline and hard work, but it is also a story of how I passed through a time of agonizing doubt and soul-searching. My life was at a crossroads, and with God's help, I had to make a pivotal decision.

* * *

At the end of my year at the Alborz School, I applied to take an examination that would qualify me for admission to the medical school of Tehran University. It was the custom for students to study together, and I teamed up with my friend Ahmad Ourandi. We met outside, on the green campus of the Alborz School, with our textbooks to discuss our readings and quiz each other. Because I had done so well in school, I did not worry about my success in the exam; I assumed that I would pass it and enter the university.

It was a written examination, given in two sessions. There were questions on various subjects, including chemistry, biology, mathematics, and English. They were aimed at testing how well prepared we were for the rigors of a university education. As it turned out, the Alborz School and, before that, Hakim-Nezami High School had made me ready to go on. At no time during the exam did I lose my confidence, and when the people who evaluated the tests compiled the results, my confidence was justified. I qualified easily.

Now, however, I had to confront a harsh reality: my family's financial situation. Times were hard in Iran for some years after World War II. My father had lost his job in the bazaar and was unemployed. It was all we could do to afford rent, food, and other necessities. In high school, I earned a small amount of money through private tutoring and gave some of my income to my mother to help buy food for the family. Our being poor was not a matter of shame; a great many people had difficulty making ends meet, and all were conscious that we were in the same boat. Still, the pressures would only increase if I attended the university. The cost of tuition was not so high, but neither was it insubstantial, and I would also need money for books, not to mention clothes and food while I continued to live at home. My parents would have done anything to help me further my education, but, knowing their financial situation, I did not see how I could expect them to support me, as well as my sister Touran, who was in high school. My parents never told me I could not attend the university; it was my own judgment that I should not inflict the financial sacrifice upon the family.

I contemplated joining the Army, because there I would be housed and fed. I didn't want to join the Army, though; I could not stand the thought of joining any organization that required my submission to its authority and rules. I even considered taking a job in the bazaar to feed myself.

Then my friend and study-mate, Ahmad Ourandi, told me about a recent announcement by the Ministry of Education. The government was offering a number of scholarships to study medicine in Europe, and there would be a competitive examination for the scholarships. Ahmad, whose family was as poor as mine, saw it as a golden opportunity for us both. He planned to enter the competition and urged me to join him. I hesitated, fearing that my religious beliefs would weaken if I went abroad and lived among non-Muslims. Ahmad continued to push me, however, and eventually I agreed to sit for the examinations, uncertain about what I would do if I were accepted.

The government exams were three times as hard as the Tehran University exams. They took about six hours and included an oral exam in Farsi. Some of the questions were intentionally misleading—trick questions in mathematics, in which the propositions were stated incorrectly so as to test our ability to recognize the discrepancies. Aside from those trick questions, which caused me some frustration, I had little difficulty with the tests but felt exhausted by the end. My approach was to take it all as an exhilarating challenge.

Of course, the scholarships were considered very desirable, and many wealthy and powerful people wanted their children to be chosen. The person in charge of the exams, Dr. Mosahab, had been a government scholarship recipient earlier, and he conducted the exams with complete integrity. Dr. Mosahab, the head of the Higher Education Department in the Ministry of Education, made sure that people were not chosen because of their social standing or family connections. Those who succeeded were the best-qualified students, and many were from families of modest income and status. The guiding principle was that the money used to support the scholarships belonged to the elderly and disadvantaged among Iran's citizens, and that it would be upon the shoulders of these chosen students to pay back their debt to society by returning to their homeland and applying what they learned during their European studies.

Thus, at a time when corruption was widespread in Iran, Dr. Mosahab stood firm, in effect saying, "We want to do the right thing. These are the people of whom we are proud; they are intelligent students, worthy of representing us in their studies overseas, and they will bring back skills that our country needs."

Sending students to study in other countries was not new; government support had enabled Iranian students to study abroad as far back as the nineteenth century. That early program, however, took place without long-term planning and operated sporadically. In the early twentieth century, the government took steps to systematize a program of scholarships abroad with the purpose of promoting modernization. The first batch of students was sent to Europe in 1924. Following the accession of Reza Shah Pahlavi (1925–1941), the program accelerated; eventually, the government sent 100 students each year to study medicine, mathematics, natural sciences, and engineering—but, interestingly, not the social sciences, art, and culture. By 1931, there were 1,200 Iranian students in Europe, some of them studying at their own families' expense. The government-sponsored program then disappeared for some years, but with the opening of several new universities in the provinces of Iran after World War II, the country faced a severe shortage of qualified teachers. Dr. Jazayeri, the Minister of Education whom I met during my visit to the Marble Palace, was a government scholarship student during the 1930s and saw the solution of the problem in reviving that program to train future teachers for the provincial universities in Europe. Thus it was expected that those chosen to study abroad would return to Iran to play important roles not only as medical and scientific professionals, but also as faculty members in the growing university system.

I was at home on a summery morning when the doorbell rang. It was Ahmad. He had learned the results of the government exams, and he had a sad expression on his face.

"I didn't qualify," he said, "but you did. Congratulations."

The news excited me, but it also shook me. It brought to a head the conflict that had been growing within me. Within the religious circle of Sheikh Rajabali-Khayyat there were a number of people who disapproved of the modern, secular educational system which had been brought to Iran from Europe and America by missionary schools and, later, more systematically by the government of Reza Shah, the father and predecessor of the shah whom I met. Parallel to this modern educational system were the traditional, religious schools that had existed for over 1,000 years. The proponents of the traditional system in the religious seminaries believed that modern, secular education was a threat to Islamic values. Sheikh Rajabali-Khayyat did not teach distrust of modern education—he, in fact, received his medical care from a physician trained in Europe—nor did all members of his circle interpret the Sheikh's teachings in this way; the discussions that took place within the circle focused on religious questions, particularly the human struggle to become close to God, and did not directly concern politics or questions of everyday life. The participants, however, came from a diversity of backgrounds—laborers, shopkeepers, military officers, university professors, students, and others—and interpreted the Sheikh's teachings in a variety of ways. Among the participants, one could often hear or perceive the idea that attending modern schools and pursuing a career such as government administration would damage a person's faith. Some went so far as to express the opinion that men should abandon secular education, renounce the modern professions, and live lives of simplicity, as in the case of one young man who dropped out of high school and took a job in the dairy owned by another member of the circle. According to this mind-set, even being exposed to people of other beliefs ran a risk; indeed, most Shi'a ayatollahs at the time admonished Muslims to wash their hands and their clothing before prayer if they came into contact with Christians. Going to Europe, living within a Western society, and being educated by non-Muslims was the ultimate danger to which someone could expose himself. At the very least, one would encounter obstacles to saying one's prayers and staying in touch with one's fundamental beliefs; at worst … well, it was disturbing to think of the consequences.

During the time when I was attending Agha Sheikh's meetings, I was naturally influenced by this way of thinking, which ran counter to what my family kept reminding me: that public life and its amenities are good and desirable, and that I should study hard, be competitive, go to a university, and become a doctor or an engineer. Engineer Sedehi, my mother's cousin, had paved the way, suggesting to us that studying in Europe and becoming a professional was something that every young man in our family should strive for. I now had an opportunity to achieve the dreams my parents had for me.

Engineer Sedehi's example, however, was exactly what I feared. According to his own father, Sedehi was a pious young man as a youth, but soon after he arrived in Europe, he stopped practicing his religion. When we met him in Isfahan, he was not even saying his daily prayers.

My mother expected nothing less than Engineer Sedehi for me, and I very much wanted to please her. My father, too, had great hopes and dreams for my future. On the other hand, the thought that like Engineer Sedehi, I too would desert my religion frightened and discouraged me.

Thus it was that, at the tender age of 18, I found myself at a fork in the road. The decision confronting me had far-reaching consequences. If I followed one fork, I would be choosing my faith, my deeply held religious values, and I would stay in Iran—but at the risk of greatly disappointing my family and provoking their anger. If I took the other fork, I had the chance of a lifetime to go abroad at the expense of my government, study at a great university, become a successful physician and university professor, and enjoy a comfortable life with all its amenities—but I risked losing my religion and my soul.

I was by no means naively opposed to all things Western; indeed, I had great respect for the achievements of European science and technology. I had learned the names of Western scientists and honored the Europeans' application of reason to all fields of education. I longed to be trained in their methodologies of experimentation and critical observation, learn the healing arts, and return home to serve my people. But could I spend years studying abroad and still hold tight to the faith that I had worked so hard to develop, and that I hoped would guide me through the rest of my life?

None of my family was present when Ahmad brought me the news of my success in the government exams, and I could not bring myself to tell them right away. The tension within me was almost unbearable, and I forced myself to go to sleep early that night to escape it.

In the morning, I headed to the home of my trusted mentor, Sheikh Rajabali, to share my dilemma and ask for guidance. Agha Sheikh received me with kindness. I sat in front of him and poured out my internal turmoil. I could feel the heat of my tears on my cheeks. My mentor listened to me carefully and then opened the Qur'an to seek guidance. He read some beautiful verses, but his advice seemed noncommittal. He understood, though, how difficult the road in front of me was.

He looked at me, and then glanced back at the open page of the Qur'an. I could see in his face his reluctance to take a position on my question. He quoted a verse from the Qur'an: "There is no turn of events or any power (in the world) except through God" (*La howla wa la ghowwate ella be-Allah*). And he prayed that God would guide and support me in my decision.

Finally, he said to me, "God will be with you, wherever you go. He will not forget you, nor would He lead you astray. He will protect you and help you find the way."

I felt some relief, as I left him, but not yet confident that I knew which fork of the road to take.

I still could not talk to my father about the decision. Instead, I prayed and agonized for several more days. Finally, I broke the news to both parents as we were finishing our breakfast one morning.

"I passed the government exams," I said, "but I have decided not to accept the scholarship to study in Germany."

My father's face registered alarm, and before he could respond, I rushed out of the house. I avoided him for most of that day, and when we were together again, he made the argument that I was not qualified to interpret religion and did not have the knowledge to make such an important decision. He expressed his worry that my religious zeal might be impelling me toward a decision that would in fact be contrary to the teachings of the Qur'an, and he persuaded me to seek the counsel of a respected clergyman in our local mosque, Ayatollah Kamarei.

My father took me to the mosque, where we found the ayatollah sitting in his place of worship. At first he seemed aloof, but he listened carefully to my concerns and my father's expressions of frustration. To my surprise, he proposed a solution that, on the surface, seemed too simple to believe: I should change my followership (*taghlid*) and adopt the followership and teachings of a Lebanese grand ayatollah whose attitude toward Christians and Jews was one of greater leniency. Then

I could feel free to associate with non-Muslims, and as long as I remembered my own religious indoctrination and practiced the values of Islam, I need not fear that living in a Western society would destroy my faith.

This was a revelation to me. Since I was 15, I had been a follower of Grand Ayatollah Seyyed Hossein Borujerdi of Qum, whose leadership I had chosen because my father had suggested him to me. Among Shi'ite Muslims, people customarily follow the teachings, value system, and rituals handed down to them by the grand ayatollah of their choosing. A grand ayatollah is an ayatollah who is the most learned man among his fellow ayatollahs and has earned great respect among them because of his piety and self-control (*taghwa*) and his wisdom in sacred and juridical matters, as well as his ability to instruct people in the conduct of their daily lives. Only a small number of ayatollahs become grand ayatollahs; generally, they are men in their sixties or seventies and have been in religious circles for decades. When a Muslim of the Shi'a denomination becomes the follower of a grand ayatollah, he seeks to emulate that leader in both religious matters and personal conduct. (The word *taghlid* is often translated as "emulation.") The ayatollah's writings and *fatwas* (legal pronouncements) become a central source of guidance to his followers. It is not quite accurate to compare the grand ayatollahs to the pope in Roman Catholicism, but in a certain sense, Shi'ite Muslims hold the grand ayatollahs in a similar degree of veneration. One major difference is that the College of Cardinals, the highest-ranking body in the church hierarchy, chooses the pope, who has authority over all Roman Catholics; the Catholic masses have no input into his election. In contrast, Shi'ite Muslims can choose their personal leader from among a number of grand ayatollahs, making the choice from below, so to speak. A Muslim is not bound to the same ayatollah forever but can change his *taghlid*, using his own judgment and the recommendations of informed clergy.

Moreover, the grand ayatollahs are known to hold differing positions on some questions of scriptural interpretation and human conduct. Grand Ayatollah Jabal-Ameli lived in cosmopolitan Beirut, populated by Shi'a and Sunni Muslims, as well as Druze, Christians, and a small number of Jews. Ayatollah Jabal-Ameli saw people of all backgrounds mixing in the streets of Beirut every day; they conducted business and made friendships with each other, were invited to each other's homes, and even married across the faiths. Grand Ayatollah Jabal-Ameli accepted Christians and Jews as "people of the Book" and saw nothing wrong in the fact that Muslims associated with them.

This revelation washed over me like cleansing water. By changing my *taghlid* to Ayatollah Jabal-Ameli, I was free to follow my dreams and study in Germany. From that day on, I felt a change in myself. My future was filled with possibilities, and I felt free to embrace life fully. At the same time, I vowed to honor the basic beliefs and rituals of Islam wherever I would be. I would perform my prayers regularly, fast throughout the month of Ramazan, and avoid drinking alcohol. To this day, I have remained true to that promise.

* * *

Those of us who shook the hand of the shah in his Marble Palace had been chosen to represent our country abroad, to study in foreign universities and learn skills that would help our fellow citizens as we developed our careers back home, and to become valued and productive members of our communities.

Toward the end of the audience, the shah gave a short speech to us. He said, "Go and learn. Study the subjects you will be taught in your universities. Learn science well, and bring home the skills of your profession. But study also the people with whom you will be living. Keenly observe their social system and their ways of organizing their life, for here in Iran, we can profit from their example."

That advice, to learn the modern way of life from the Westerners and bring it back to Iran, did not strike me as unusual at the time because it was compatible with the prevalent assumption among Iranian intellectuals. They, as well as the shah, really believed that Iran had to become like the West in order to develop and modernize.

In retrospect, I find it revealing that the shah did not tell us that we were representatives of a great and ancient culture; he told us to go and learn from others. He might have said, "Find the richness of your past, and build the new Iran on the basis of that." At the time, I was not conscious that his admiration for Western values was a slap in the face to our own rich heritage. This would become apparent to me years later, after I returned to my homeland and experienced many disappointments in my efforts, as a doctor and educator, to bring modernization to Iran. The shortcomings of the shah's pro-Western attitude would be exposed in the 1970s, when the long-simmering frustration of the masses produced social, political, and religious unrest that ultimately boiled over into revolution.

In the meantime, I prepared for my great adventure. Everybody at home was excited for me. My sisters came from Isfahan, and the whole family saw me off at the airport for my early-morning departure. I flew Air France on a propeller plane—all passenger airplanes were propeller-driven then—first to Beirut. There were thirteen in our group of students, and the airline took good care of us; we were well fed, and we were taken into an airport reception room to wait for our connection. From Beirut, we flew to Geneva and, the following day, continued on to Stuttgart.

All of this was new to me. I had never before been outside of Iran, never flown in an airplane. In the Beirut airport, I saw a banana for the first time in my life. We landed in Geneva after dark, and for the first time I stayed, together with my fellow students, in a hotel, the Hôtel de Famille. On the way into the city by bus, I had a mild disappointment. I expected to see high-rise buildings and glamorous people, as I had seen in movies and postcards. What I saw, however, were buildings and people not much different from our own in Iran. The city appeared cleaner, though, and the people moving about in the streets seemed more serious and orderly than Iranians.

In Stuttgart, representatives of the Iranian Legation received us. To our surprise, the head of the Legation made it clear that he did not consider it the Legation's responsibility to help us enroll in a German university, find living quarters, or get settled in any other way. We were on our own. Fortunately, it was easy at that time to get into German universities. Together with a good friend of mine from high school, Mohammad Tahbasian, I decided to apply to the University of Göttingen.

It took us sixteen hours by express train to travel to Göttingen, and we arrived in the middle of the night. We stayed in a hotel and dashed out early in the morning to look up some Iranian students who were already studying there. They took us to the University's *Auslandsamt*, the office for foreign students, and the man in charge helped us enroll and find a place to live. In postwar Germany, housing was in short supply. A stringent postwar law restricted each family to a number of rooms equal to the number of family members and required that any extra rooms be rented out. I was fortunate to find a room for myself in Pension Behler at No. 17 Lotze Strasse, where I also received my meals, all for DM150 (about $40) per month.

And so began my experience abroad. I plunged into my classes knowing no German; I had to learn this new language by immersing myself in the academic environment. It was not easy at first, but I was not intimidated—I was young, and as far as I knew, there was no problem in the world that I could not solve. It took me about six months to feel completely comfortable in my new surroundings. I received letters from home every week, and that helped by reassuring me that my family was all behind me. I became almost fluent in German within those first six months; I could speak it well, read books, and follow my class lectures. I felt that nothing could stop me from embracing the world and making it mine.

* * *

Now, many years later, I look back at those crucial days and feel strongly that God was indeed with me, showing me the way and giving me the courage to make the right decision. The fork that I chose started me on the path to a life that would not have been possible if I had stayed in Iran. In Germany I gained more than a professional education; I learned to observe others and think independently, to be self-critical, and to look inwardly at my beliefs and values while surrounded by people who had very little knowledge of Islam and sometimes seemed hostile to it. I remained true to my beliefs. In fact, contrary to my worst fears during those days of doubt and indecision in the summer of 1950, I became a better Muslim as a result of my exposure to the West and the freedom I experienced.

CHAPTER THREE
Overcoming Culture Shock

D
espite my country's rich history and deep culture, which should have given me strength as I entered a new environment, I felt intimidated and insecure upon my arrival in Germany. I did not understand my anxiety at the time, but it probably had something to do with the long exposure of Iranian society to Western colonial attitudes and the effect of that exposure on our cultural self-esteem. Our own national leadership told us, time and again, that we needed to be like the West if we wanted to be a part of the modern world.

In my youth, I did not think very often about those larger cultural questions, but I did think a lot about science. The fact that the Islamic world had developed the most advanced science of the Middle Ages was not sufficiently instilled in our consciousness, either at home or by our teachers, public officials, or religious leaders. The preponderant message we received was that everything good comes from Europe. I knew that the most advanced science of my era was being discovered, developed, and practiced in Europe and America.

In my secular, Western-oriented high school, I came to revere the names associated with modern science: Galileo, Newton, Pasteur, Planck, Einstein—these were superhumans; these, to me, were pure, faultless men who devoted themselves to science and were above the frailties and vices of ordinary men.

In Germany, I breathed the air of the great modern scientists. I passed by the house in Göttingen where Max Planck, the Nobel prize-winning physicist who founded quantum theory, lived out the last years of his life. I walked the corridors of the building where Adolf Windaus had won a Nobel Prize for his pioneering work on Vitamin D. Later, in Freiburg, I spent my externship and wrote my doctoral thesis in the Ludwig-Aschoff-Haus, the home of the University of Freiburg's Department of Pathology, named after Prof. Ludwig Aschoff, the co-discoverer of the atrioventricular node in the human heart, also known as the Aschoff-Tawara node, about which I had learned in high school. And while I was studying at Freiburg, Prof. Hermann Staudinger, who worked next door in the Chemistry Department, received a Nobel Prize for his work on synthetic fibers.

During my first semester at the University of Göttingen in 1951, I attended the lectures of Professor Josef Goubeau in Windaus-Haus, the home of the Chemistry Department, named after Prof. Windaus, the Nobel Prize winner, whose statue stood in front of the building. Naturally, I associated Prof. Goubeau with the great traditions of his science and his university, and I listened attentively to every word he spoke from the podium of the Windaus-Haus amphitheater. He performed chemical experiments right there, in front of us, with the help of two young assistants dressed in white coats and looking always very serious. Prof. Goubeau's assistants were devoted to him and to their science, and they, like he, lived in a world of pure scholarship— or so I assumed. I wanted to be like them.

One day, I went into the laboratory to get something from one of Prof. Goubeau's assistants. He greeted me cordially and pulled open a drawer in his lab table to look for the item I had requested, and while his drawer was open, I got a glimpse of some photos. It happened to be during Fasching, that period just before the Christian time of Lent, similar to Mardi Gras, a time of formal dances and wild parties, and the young assistant's photos showed him partying with half-naked girls, laughing and in sensual poses. I was shocked. I had never seen such photos before, let alone such photos of somebody I knew and respected.

It was my first lesson in the real world of scientists who are also humans. I would eventually learn that even the most esteemed professors, they whom we called "*Chef*" (Chief), were susceptible to vices, that even they might enjoy drinking beer and were interested in sex. My mind simply had not envisioned that a serious professor of chemistry or physics or anatomy, or his assistants, also has a side to his life that is sensual and pleasure seeking. I came to realize that in Western culture, the two seemingly contradictory tendencies of the human personality exist side by side: that which values and dedicates a person to serious work and that which impels him to the pleasures of play and, yes, sexual relations between men and women—something with which I was not yet acquainted.

In time, I came to realize that this experience was all about duality in the spheres of human life, the difference between one's public and private spheres. In the West, society tends to keep the public and private spheres of people's lives separate. The private sphere is considered a sanctuary; one's private behavior and opinions are the concern of the individual himself as long as they do not spill over and affect his public life. Thus it is that a person's religion, political views, personal habits, marital status, and so on are not presumed relevant to his professional standing; one does not choose a physician because he or she is Christian or Jewish, and one does not consider the family life of a shopkeeper a factor in one's buying habits. Iranian culture, and Islamic culture more generally, approach the question from a different angle, and the margin of separation is not so sharp. For example, a physician who is known to be religious will more easily gain the trust of his patients, and a merchant who visits the mosque regularly is presumed not to cheat his customers.

In any case, I stored this experience in my mind and spent many moments contemplating it.

* * *

In Göttingen, I took regular classes for pre-med students, with no special preparatory work and no language instruction. At first, I did not understand all that the professor was saying. It was at times discouraging, but, in my youthful enthusiasm, I endured it. The fact that German is a perfectly phonetic language—that is, it is spoken exactly as it is written—made it easy for me to learn. During lectures, I wrote down the words that I did not understand and looked them up in the dictionary when I got home. People tend to use a limited speaking vocabulary, and it helped that much of the professors' vocabulary centered on technical language. Just one or two months into the class, I could understand the lectures reasonably well, and by the end of the semester, I was having no difficulty at all.

It also helped that my friends and I were able to keep our sense of humor. One day, my friend Ahmad Hasanein burst into my room laughing and said that he had heard a rooster speaking the same language as Iranian roosters.

There were approximately 200 students in my classes, of whom all but a few were Germans. The foreign students were mainly Iranians, plus a few Arabs and an occasional Swede or Norwegian. Not all were preparing for medical school, for the pre-med curriculum drew in students from other fields as well. For example, biology students would also take physiology classes, and students in the nursing program would take anatomy classes. The program was more tightly structured than it usually is in the United States, but more liberal than in Iran. In other words, we were not bound to the content of our textbooks, lectures, and assigned lab work; we could read and explore concepts outside of the textbook and then discuss what we found with our teachers.

The professors were German *Herren* (gentlemen) and very conscious of their status. The *Ordinarius*, the head of a department, had tremendous power; he had, for example, full authority over the hiring and firing of assistants. Faculty members were in no way answerable to the student body. Respect was assumed, and we students knew that it was not in our interest to cross the "Herr Professor." The strict hierarchy of power and decision-making was not new to us Iranians, but we were surprised that this hierarchy was incorporated in the organizational management of every unit in society. The same relationship of "Chef" and employee was seen in small grocery stores and large government offices. It was interesting to us that the Germans accepted and respected this hierarchy as a fact of life.

I recall a moment when one of my professors was writing on the blackboard and the chalk fell from his hand. I expected him to bend over and pick up the chalk. The professor, however, kicked the chalk away and took another piece from the tray—the idea of bending over in front of students was beneath his dignity. It was the job of his assistants to bend over and pick up the chalk.

Sometimes this loftiness could become overbearing. One evening early in my Göttingen years, a widely regarded professor by the name of Hans Heinrich Schaeder, whose field was Persian Languages, invited a group of us to his home. In the course of our conversations, one of the Iranian students politely corrected his pronunciation of a Persian word.

"Excuse me, Herr Professor," the student said, "but this is how we say that. ..."

Professor Schaeder jumped on him. "Are you criticizing me?" he said, angered that the student had the boldness to challenge him.

Over and over I witnessed such professorial egotism, such an unwillingness to accept criticism even when wrong. The professors believed they were the best in their field and did not abide criticism or questioning of their work, as if it would have destroyed their reputations to err on any fact or matter of interpretation. There was an aura of competition hovering over the head of everybody at each level of the academic hierarchy. Professors would compete with each other for publications, recognition, and prizes; assistants competed to earn the favor of the Chef.

The Chefs were quite fair, however; they appreciated their assistants' good work, discipline, and reliability. Professors were unforgiving of mistakes, but at the same time they were very supportive and protective of their good assistants. The concept of mentoring was strong, and Chefs trained their assistants as protégés for the day when there would be an opening for a university *Ordinarius* position or chief of a city hospital.

Toward students, professors could be stern and even arrogant, but they could also be very kind. They truly cared about our learning. And they certainly presented us with the opportunity to learn at a level I had only dreamed of. There was a professor of physiology named Hermann Rein who was studying the causes of hypertension: pioneering work in the study of adrenaline and nor-adrenaline, alpha-receptors and beta-receptors. Prof. Rein had hypertension himself and eventually died from it. I was fascinated by him, so hard working and serious in his research and teaching, but also fatherly. I remember him saying that his goal in life was to solve the mystery of hypertension in humans. He was the head of a big Institute of Physiology, where a visiting professor by the name of Allela, from the University of Turin, was performing experiments on dogs. Prof. Allela once showed me how he had his animals hooked up to wires so he could record the blood flow in the heart muscles and the effect of various drugs on the blood flow. This was pure science, something out of my imagination about the West and Europe.

One day in class, a professor of biochemistry was lecturing about a part of the metabolic pathway known as the Krebs cycle, and he told us of new discoveries that had been presented only two weeks earlier at an international conference. In Iran, what I had learned about the subject was based on translations of outdated books. Another professor, Erich Blechschmidt, had his own, original theories about the mechanical (pull and push) forces in embryo development; the reason we have limbs, he argued, is because of the growth of cells within the embryo that push matter out—it's not genetic, he said, it's just mechanical. Professor Blechschmidt's ideas were very controversial, but for me it was exciting to see that somebody could depart from the conventional wisdom and challenge the reigning ideas without suffering rejection and dismissal. I also remember Professor Loeschke from the Department of Physiology, who told us to follow our own interest and concentrate on studying the subjects that we liked the most. We should study other subjects in order to pass the exams, he said, but he advised us to give our hearts, and put most of our time, into the field that most excited us.

That was the norm in Germany. The system encouraged original thinking, thinking for yourself. This atmosphere could not help but influence me. What I had studied in Iran was twenty or thirty years behind the times, and now I was learning from people who were in the forefront of medical science. The drive to be on the cutting edge of progress was something that has stayed with me ever since. I became passionate about new ideas and theories, always eager to learn something new.

It was customary in Germany that a student did not stay in the same university throughout the entire course of his study; most moved on to another university. The assumption was that a student learns more if he is exposed to more professors, each contributing his own knowledge and perspective. In reality, many students moved because they wanted a different cultural environment, or they wanted to be closer to the mountains for skiing or at the seashore for sailing, or whatever their particular interest was. I chose to go to Freiburg after completing my $2^{1/2}$-year program of pre-med studies because of the weather. Göttingen, in the province of Lower Saxony, is stuck in what the locals call a *Regenloch*, or "rain hole." When I first arrived there, I did not see the sun for 40 days. Then I was walking in the streets when it suddenly poked through the clouds and shone on me. I stopped in my tracks and started laughing without knowing why, like a crazy person. One generally becomes accustomed to the climate wherever one lives, but I never liked the weather in Göttingen. I had come from a country with a lot of sunshine, and I was constantly missing it. Freiburg is farther south, the climate is more agreeable, and that is what drew me there for four years of medical education.

Maybe it was my own frame of mind, but Freiburg seemed more open than Göttingen. There was not only more sunshine; there was more color, more joy. Freiburg was a predominantly Roman Catholic city, with a beautiful cathedral. Its people were more outgoing and friendly; Protestant Göttingen had not only the climate but also the temperament of the North, serious and reserved.

This is not to say that university life in Freiburg was less intense; on the contrary. The University of Freiburg, and its medical studies, traced their history back to 1547. The university's hospitals were very large, and the faculty had a long tradition of excellence in advanced research, as the examples of Aschoff and Staudinger testify. Numerous faculty and students of Freiburg have received Nobel Prizes, and many renowned scholars in diverse fields have passed through the university. A few examples are the Renaissance-era theologian Erasmus of Rotterdam, social-science greats Max Weber and Hannah Arendt, philosopher Martin Heidegger, economist Friedrich von Hayek, and the first Chancellor of the post-war Federal Republic of Germany, Konrad Adenauer.

My time at the Ludwig-Aschoff-Haus was a particularly formative period for me. The chairman of the Pathology Department and the Director of the Aschoff-Haus was Professor Franz Büchner, a hard-working, ambitious gentleman in his sixties. Prof. Büchner was an excellent teacher with a stern look and a serious personality. He accepted me as his doctoral candidate and gave me the assignment of studying the effect of hypoxia on heart muscles. On the first day of my work, I was given a key to the institute with permission to come and go as I pleased at any time, day or night. I had use of the library and various other institute facilities. I felt greatly honored by this trust. All of a sudden, I was a member of a scientific team.

I worked there in my spare time, sometimes into the late hours. Among the assistants, there was a kind of competition over who would work latest and who would turn the last light off. Some assistants worked until 1 a.m. and came back again at 7 a.m. Their dedication challenged me, and I learned not to mind working while others slept. I had close daily contacts with assistants, and they helped me. One day I was reviewing an article on a subject in pathology written by a prominent professor. I read a sentence and told the assistant that I thought that the statement was false. He was taken aback by my critique but pulled himself together and said, "Keep up your critical mind all your life." That pleased me; his encouragement has stayed with me throughout my life. Eventually, the result of my work was published in the journal *Beiträge zur Pathologie* under the title "*Azelluläre Nekrose der Herzmuskeln*" ("Acellular Necrosis of the Myocardial Muscles").

I felt that my professors were close to the truth, that they were searching for certainty through their work. At the same time, I still believed in my religion and supernatural forces, including the presence of God in my life. I believed that the ultimate truth lay with God, and Islam shows us the way to the truth. At first, this presented a dilemma in my mind: On the one hand, I believed in science and technology, and on the other, I held onto my original belief in Islam. How could both paths lead to the truth?

My friend and classmate, Ali Rasekh-Afshar, was also concerned about these questions, and while he and I were studying in Göttingen, we invited Prof. Blechschmidt for tea after dinner one evening to ask his opinion. Ali and I admired Prof. Blechschmidt for his passionate way of teaching and his originality in research. What we wanted to ask him was this: We were accustomed to finding the truth through our religious leadership and our religious texts, and we believed that these sources of wisdom could lead us to the truth. When we spoke about anatomy, physiology, biology, and medicine, we didn't talk about why we were studying it, and our teachers didn't seem interested in the question of whether they were pursuing the truth as an overarching construct; they didn't talk about whether you can find such truth through science.

Professor Blechschmidt graciously accepted our invitation. He sat and talked with us for about two hours. We asked him questions about the way to finding the truth, and how science and technology deal with the claim of religion that the truth can be discovered only through religious experiences. We posed to him the proposition that one could not find the truth through the study of science, but only through religious inquiry, prayer, and revelation.

"You are wrong," Prof. Blechschmidt said. "We scientists are also seeking the truth, but our instruments—observation, experimentation, and deduction—are different from yours. The truth is not "revealed" to us by prophets and spiritual leaders; instead, we try to *discover* truth by using our mind and the methods at our disposal. Science does not compete with religion in finding the truth; it just approaches the subject from a different angle. Humans are constantly struggling to find the truth, and we must use both religion and science and technology in that struggle."

Prof. Blechschmidt's explanation gratified me because the two disciplines were both precious to me, and I had hoped to find a way to reconcile them. Once again, as when I had struggled with the decision to come to Germany in the first place, I felt comfortable with my path. I did not have to choose between science and technology, on the one hand, and my religion, on the other.

* * *

Pension Behler, my first place of residence in Göttingen, was a family-run guesthouse where I had a small room and took my meals together with other guests. People tended to stay there for extended periods of time, and it was always a pleasure to share their company. Among them, for example, was the former German ambassador to Japan and Visiting Professor Allela, who introduced me to his experiments at the Institute of Physiology.

The Behlers—husband, wife, and two daughters—managed their establishment in a very professional way and took good care of me. My room was always clean, and the meals were hearty. One time, however, I was served *Bratkartoffel,* fried potatoes containing bits of bacon. Mrs. Behler knew that, as a Muslim, I did not eat pork, and generally she was conscientious about not serving it to me. This time, apparently, she forgot and cooked the *Bratkartoffel* as she normally did. I wasn't aware of it until toward the end of the meal, when I noticed the small pieces of meat. I asked if it was bacon, and the Behlers were very apologetic when they realized their mistake. As for me, I became so upset that I went up to my room and just slept; I couldn't sit and study or make conversation with others that evening—I had kept the dietary rule for so long, and now I had slipped. It was as if I had lost my virginity.

I lived with the Behler family for about a year, and then I moved out because, since I was not only sleeping there but eating there also, I was feeling isolated from the other Iranian students. I rented a room in another household, in the Arndtstrasse, and later, another room in the Herzbergerlandstrasse, and now took my meals with other students in the Mensa, or cafeteria. Besides giving me more social contact with other students, this arrangement forced me to learn how to take care of myself, that is, without the Behler family to look after me. It was an important step for me, a boy who was, step by step, becoming an adult in a world much wider than that of his childhood.

My life in Göttingen was simple, but not without its small pleasures. I went to classes during the day and studied in the evenings. I bought a bicycle and enjoyed riding it. On weekends I went walking in the woods, sometimes alone and sometimes with friends. Kee See, a small lake near the Pension Behler, provided another walking route, as well as a place for swimming in the summer months. Once Ali Rasekh-Afshar and I hitchhiked from Göttingen to Munich, a journey of more than 500 kilometers each way, to visit the science museum there.

Freiburg, too, had its attractions. It was a bigger city than Göttingen, and it was within an easy bicycle ride of Kaiserstuhl, a beautiful region known for its vineyards. Switzerland and France were also nearby. With friends, I went often to Switzerland and occasionally to France. From the German side of the Rhine River, we could see the ruined bunkers of the Maginot Line. In Switzerland, we could buy real coffee and good chocolate, and smuggle them into Germany. These items were a rare extravagance in Germany, which was struggling to recover from the economic devastation of World War II. Coffee drinks were made of roasted barley, which was called "Mukufuk." It tasted horrible and made the smuggling more appealing.

In fact, my financial circumstances were not bad at all. My monthly stipend of DM 420 (about $100.00) from the Iranian Embassy was more than what most German students lived on. The money made my travel possible, and it enabled me to buy an Agfa camera. I became an avid photographer; every weekend I took snapshots, and every Tuesday I picked up my photos from a shop in Königstrasse. I enjoyed sharing my photos with friends and sent copies to my parents back home. Photography became my hobby and brought me closer to nature, as I roamed the forest and countryside with my camera.

For all of my four years in Freiburg, I rented a room from the Gehrig family at Zasiusstrasse #100. It was a wonderful room with a private entry, something that was rather uncommon at the time. The house was close in to the city but also near a forest, where I could go for walks in nature. The family consisted of a father, a mother, and a daughter. They were kind and generous, and whatever rough edges I had—for I was still not very skilled at dealing with people—they put up with me.

I was fortunate to have that room, and I got it in a way that taught me another of life's important lessons. I had gone home to Tehran after my graduation from Göttingen, and when I returned to Germany I brought another Iranian student back with me. His name was Ebrahim Hashemian, and he became my best friend. He was a shy boy who was tied closely to his mother, and I could tell that he would need my encouragement to get settled in, so we went house hunting together in Freiburg. We looked at a number of rooms and didn't like them, and then we found that room in Zasiusstrasse. It was a big room, with a bed, a couch, and everything one needed, and I badly wanted it. However, I held myself back and offered Ebrahim first claim to it because I knew he would not find anything else as good.

I said, "Ebrahim, you take this room."

He hesitated, looked around the room again, and said, "No, I do not like it and I don't want it."

I never understood exactly what it was about the room that didn't appeal to him, but I gladly took it. I have always felt that my moment's act of kindness, offering Ebrahim the room that I really wanted, was rewarded. I learned from this that if you help someone in a moment of need, if you restrain your own desire or greed and give the advantage to others, life will, in turn, be kind to you.

As for Ebrahim, he eventually found a room in the home of an Italian princess who had become dispossessed of her family fortune and was living in Freiburg. And there he had an experience from which I drew another lesson. Ebrahim was fussy about what he ate; he was used to his mother's cooking and did not like German food.

The princess became impatient with him about this, so she sat him down in front of her and said, "Listen, I'll tell you a story about myself. I was a princess from a prominent family. At one time we had wealth, we had palaces, and we wanted for nothing. One morning our maid put my breakfast in front of me, and I said 'I don't like it.' She told my mother that I wouldn't eat my breakfast. My mother said, 'Take it away.' She did, and I didn't eat. At lunchtime, I was hungry. The same food appeared on the table before me—the breakfast I had not eaten. Again, I refused it. The maid's instruction was the same, and so she again took the food away. In the evening, I was so hungry that I couldn't resist the food, and I ate it. Life is like that—you have to take it as it comes."

I generally took life as it came, and it was not always easy or smooth. Along with the many good experiences I had with the Germans, there were also negative experiences, moments when I became aware of prejudices and stereotypes about my culture. People from the Middle East are sensitive to cultural slights, and I was quick to pick up on the tone of a person's comments or the insensitivity of someone's remarks.

One time in Pension Behler, a guest was spreading butter on his bread, and he asked me, "Do you have butter in Iran?" The idea that we might not have butter seemed ridiculous to me. I understood from the man's question that he considered my country so backward that we didn't know how to make butter.

On another occasion, a guest at the table asked me about camels: Did my family own one? Had I ever ridden one? Perhaps these were innocent questions, but they underscored for me the level of ignorance among the people with whom I was living—that they had no idea of the size and sophistication of Tehran, Iran's capital and largest city, and that they probably thought all Iranians were nomads and rug merchants. Of course, the level of knowledge in the West about Iran today is higher than in the 1950s, and such conversation would be unimaginable.

These seemingly trivial incidents were the mark of simple people, and one might forgive such insensitivity on their part; however, I occasionally encountered an equal degree of tactlessness on the part of educated persons. For example, I met a professor, an Orientalist, as the Europeans used to call those among their numbers who had an interest in the Middle East, who became the editor of a local news-paper, the *Göttinger Tageblat*. He had spent some time in Iran as German cultural attaché before World War II, and he spoke a little bit of Persian. One day he invited a few of us Iranian students to his office, where he had a collection of souvenirs from our country, including the wedge-shaped black flag with writing about Imam Hossein, the martyr from Karbala. This flag has a religious signifi-cance for Shi'ite Muslims; it is customarily carried at the front of religious processions, but in the professor/editor's office, it was being used, along with his other souvenirs, as decoration. It dawned on me that those objects were ours, they meant something to Iranians—and this man was using them to impress people, to show them how sophisticated he was: He had been to the Middle East, a land suppos-edly of mystery and intrigue, and he had artifacts to prove his world-liness. It seemed that he even believed he would impress us with his sophistication, but we, on the contrary, realized that he was displaying one of the traits Middle Easterners most resent about the Orientalists: that they look upon us not as normal human beings with our own, rich culture, but as subjects of interest and exotic "others," people who are emotional, superstitious, and not rational.

The Germans were by no means the only Westerners who saw other cultures in terms of stereotypes and prejudices, and I am aware now that when these attitudes showed their face to me, I might as well have experienced them in France, England, or the United States. They struck me as "German" attitudes at the time, however, because I first discovered them in Germany.

As far as the German students were concerned, they treated us very cordially. As it happened, however, I was one of the very few Iranian students who developed close friendships with some of them—lifelong friendships in several cases. During the semester holidays and on other occasions, German friends invited me home with them to Hanover, Hamburg, Bremen, and Bremerhaven. Those whom I got to know best tended to be the sons of professors or physicians. To this day, I am still in contact with several of them, particularly Hans-Jürgen Meyer, who became a professor of ophthalmology at the University of Göttingen and chief of the Marian Hospital in Osnabrück, and Hans-Ulrich Gottesleben, also an ophthalmologist, who, along with his wife Dr. Inge Gottesleben, practiced ophthalmology in Freiburg until the time of his retirement a few years ago.

After our graduation ceremony at *Göttingen*, the German students organized a celebration at a *Jugendherberge*, a youth hostel that they rented for the occasion. As their ancestors had done for centuries, the students bought a keg of beer, put on *Lederhosen* (leather shorts), boots, and hats with a feather in them, and rolled the keg ceremoniously up the hill, singing and shouting, to the social hall of the *Jugendherberge*. There they carried on, long into the night, until the last one dropped.

A day or two before the party, my friend Hans-Jürgen Meyer said to me, "You should come."

I had an idea what the party would be like, and I said, "No, I don't drink beer."

He said, "That doesn't matter. We'll serve you apple juice."

I was open to that, because I wanted to be a part of the crowd. The *Jugendherberge* was nestled amid the woods outside the city, a pretty place. The students set up tables and served food. We sat, talked, joked, and sang together. Eventually, they started getting drunk.

Some of them urged me to join them, saying, "Come on, and celebrate with us."

I again resisted. "No, I really can't. It's against my religion."

They respected my position on this, and I did not drink beer with them.

At a certain point, however, one of my friends told me, "It's time for you to go." He had overheard someone making a comment about my beard, and my friend was concerned that others, losing their inhibitions to the alcohol, would start saying things that might insult me.

My friend was very sensitive about that. He said, "You know, in Germany, if you insult somebody about his body features, he can challenge you to a duel."

Even in the 1950s, it seemed, such antiquated attitudes about personal honor survived, often associated with the *Burschenschaften*, student fraternities of a particular kind with their roots in the nineteenth century. One of our respected professors had a deep scar on his face, a mark that he carried with honor and pride. Some of the students at the party were *Burschenschaft* members, and my friend worried that drunkenness might drive one of them to goad me into doing or saying something that would provoke the worst in them. By this time, people had started dancing on the tabletops, and one couldn't be sure that the situation would remain under control. And so I left the party.

The party was a good illustration of my ability to relate to my German classmates. I felt included, but only up to a point. I felt sorry for myself that I couldn't drink beer, because I wanted to be a part of the larger student community, but my culture, my identity, and, most importantly, my religious convictions kept me apart. And yet, there was a vitally important message in this experience. Even though we Muslims cannot drink alcohol, we can come and sit with others, be their friends, celebrate with them. We do not have to change our lifestyles or violate our religious customs.

This is a reality that I consider fundamental; a truth that I believe must be understood by all in the Muslim community as well as those who do not share our religion. We are all members of a larger world community. We need to respect each other's culture and system of values, and make peace with those whose faith and daily practices are different from ours. To be able to do so, we as Muslims must first honor our own values, put our own faith into practice, and stand firm on the principles we bring with us into our current lives.

* * *

Foreign students naturally seek out their co-nationals wherever they are, and that was certainly true of me in Germany. However, one of the biggest shocks upon my arrival in Göttingen was to find that many of my fellow Iranian students had given in to the temptations of which I had been afraid at the time I decided to go abroad. Like Engineer Sedehi, they had strayed from their religion. A lot of them had also fallen into bad personal habits, drinking alcohol, going to parties until late at night, getting involved with sex, sleeping in late and missing lectures. It was not uncommon to meet one or two of these students staggering into the *Mensa* at lunchtime, saying, "I just got up." Such students would later on continue their lifestyle after returning to Iran; some of them took prominent positions in the government, becoming poor role models for the younger generation.

A part of the problem was the relatively loose structure of the educational system in Germany. A student could matriculate in Medicine and not show up in classes, except perhaps for the practical classes; the professors did not take roll, did not grade students on class participation, and gave very few exams. In fact, the only hard-and-fast requirements for graduating in the pre-med program were that a student take prescribed semester classes and pass the qualifying exam given at the end of two and one-half years. Iranian students had difficulty adapting to this loose system, and many—at least in their first semesters—did not develop the self-discipline required to keep up with their studies in the absence of tight schedules, programmed assignments, and frequent tests. Most of them eventually made the adaptation and managed to catch up with what they neglected in the early part of their education, but some did not. It was, indeed, a kind of educational-system culture shock; those who had problems were like people spun around in a circle and then released to stagger their way back to stability.

Generally speaking, these were also the students who suffered most from homesickness, or *Heimweh*, as the Germans call it. They would cry and sometimes become physically ill, and it took them months to get over their misery and feel comfortable in their new habitat.

I was fortunate to find a handful of friends in Göttingen who did not fall victim to culture shock. I missed my family, and it was always a great joy to receive a letter from home every Tuesday, but I never cried or lost time away from my studies because I was unhappy.

It took me some time, however, to find companions who shared my concern for religion. At first, I thought I was all alone with my strict behavior and my adherence to Islamic rituals. I had grown a short beard as a sign of my faith, and this brought upon me some ridicule and pressure from my fellow Iranians to shave the beard. In fact, I believe to this day that I was the only man in all of Göttingen, Muslim or German, who wore a beard at that time. I resisted the pressure to shave it off, and in time, I met a few other Iranians who were practicing Muslims.

Ali Rasekh-Afshar was the first of these likeminded cohorts. Ali was originally a student at an Islamic seminary in Qum who switched to pre-med studies and came to Germany on his own expense to study. Early on in our friendship, Ali defended me against the criticisms of others by arguing that religion is a private affair and everybody is entitled to his beliefs. Ali and I were joined by Kazim Mostafid and Karim Ghiassi, and, still later, Ebrahim Hashemian. We formed a close circle that banded together for prayer meetings and supported each other among the larger Iranian student community. We sat together in class, had lunch together, spent holidays together, went walking together, and we lent money to each other. (Ironically, Ali Rasekh-Afshar, the erstwhile seminarian, became a non-practicing Muslim later in his life.)

In Freiburg, I discovered a larger group of Iranian Muslims who were determined to practice their faith. In contrast to our experience in Göttingen, we were now respected and accepted in the Iranian circles; we were not struggling to hold onto our religious beliefs. We met every week in the evening to study the Qur'an and discuss religion, and we were as close as brothers. Outside of our meetings, however, we didn't talk much among ourselves about what it was like to be Muslims in our present environment. Religion for us was private, and our priority in the world where we were living was to get an education and prepare for our future. We wanted to remain what we were, Muslims, and to this end our friendship and mutual support were vital to us, but we never lost sight of our goal to gain an education and return to our country as skilled professionals with a gift to share.

Some of us tried to organize an association of Iranian students, intended purely to uphold our national identity in Freiburg. There were students from Sweden, and there were Mormons from America—we saw them together in groups all the time, and we felt that we wanted to be together, too. We tried to organize several times, but things always came to a standstill after a few meetings. People started arguing with each other, unable to come together around defining a basic direction or purpose. Somebody would propose an entertainment program of some sort, and another would say, no, we should study the Qur'an. We didn't have the experience in high school of building student bodies; it didn't seem to be in our blood, or at least we weren't accustomed to the discipline of compromise and pulling together for the common good—a problem that continues even today among Iranians, and Muslims in general, in America—and, as a result, our efforts fizzled.

Thus, despite my close friendship with a small number of fellow Iranians, I, along with my friends, felt the same marginality that I had experienced in Göttingen. We all had the sense of being visitors in Germany. Some of this feeling was probably due to our knowledge that we would eventually leave, but the fact was that, no matter how well we got along with our German classmates and regardless of how comfortable we were in our temporary home, we were outsiders.

Of course, we felt this especially at times when the university was closed for holidays. Christmas, for example, was a time when the Germans gathered together with their families to celebrate their rituals, give gifts, and have feasts. The German students went home, and I stayed in the Pension Behler or in my room at the Gehrig residence in Zasiusstrasse. Christmas music filled the air, the town was aglow with decorations, and people flocked to the stores to buy presents for their loved ones. I became depressed during Christmas time, longing to go home, join my family, and receive love and companionship from them. But Christmas would pass, students would return, and my academic routine would keep me occupied. We had no resentment about the Christmas holiday itself—Jesus was our prophet, too—and we saw a lot of similarity between how Christians expressed their religion and the way we did. This was especially true in Freiburg, where the Catholics marched in their processions and carried icons in front of crowds walking solemnly through the streets: that was similar to what we were used to in Iran. But it was *their* holiday and *their* celebration; they were having fun surrounded by their families, and we were a long, long way from ours.

Another of my regrets was that I did not connect with a girlfriend. When you do not have a girlfriend, you are very aware of others who do, and of course, people all around me in Göttingen and Freiburg were falling in love and enjoying each other's company. It's not only a matter of one's sexual needs or desires; it's also the need for the special kind of companionship that having a girlfriend provides. For a man, women friends are different from male friends; they have a different role in the mind of a man, especially when you're young. I longed to be able to buy a gift and give it to a girl. I wanted to go out, buy flowers, and give them to someone. I suppose that's natural; that's a need every man has. When you're a child, you first have your mother, then your sisters, and your aunts, and eventually you have someone in your life to whom you can transfer all these feelings. Love is a beautiful thing, and you miss out on a lot if you don't have it.

Later on in life, I often asked myself why I was so strict with myself; why did I avoid becoming involved with a girlfriend? The only thing I can think of is the unrealistic attitude of our religious leadership, their lack of understanding about young people and their needs. Instead of adapting religious teachings to reality, they forced their interpretation of religion upon reality and took satisfaction when they saw people giving expression to the superficial dogmas of religion. This problem persists very much in Iran today. Young people do not get guidance from the authorities for their real-life concerns, and therefore they find haphazard solutions, sometimes with disastrous consequences.

In Germany, about 20 percent of my classmates were women. This was different from my experience in Iran, where boys and girls had been segregated in high school, but it did not strike me as strange. Iran was a more secular country than it is today, and there was nothing that stopped boys and girls from talking to each other outside of school. The women I met in German universities were intelligent and professional, but they were also gentle, not aggressive; they did not seem to feel a need to assert masculine qualities to succeed in school or pursue their future careers. If a woman were a friend of yours, she would be caring and concerned about you, and would help you in the problems of everyday life. I was not shy about meeting women students and studying together with them sometimes, but no particularly strong feelings developed between us.

If I had to do it over again, I would try harder in the social context, to make more friends, women as well as men, Germans as well as Iranians. It would be healthier, and more in accord with the standards of a good Muslim, to connect with the people, and not isolate myself so much. And yet, I cannot deny that, all things considered, my years in Germany were good years. My education prepared me well, and I thank God that He gave me the determination and the discipline to apply myself wholeheartedly to my studies.

* * *

The German education system required two exams in Medicine. The first, called the *Physikum*, took place after two and one-half years, that is, at the end of the pre-med course. The second was the *Staatsexamen*, the final exam that we took after the four-year program of medical studies. The state gave the universities' medical schools the authority to examine students and grant them a license to practice medicine. Passing the *Staatsexamen*, therefore, qualified you to practice in Germany.

The exams were given orally, with one professor examining four students at a time. The professor would direct a question to one student, and if he or she didn't know the answer, the professor might turn to the next person and ask the same question. This method of testing, a face-to-face confrontation with the esteemed Herr Professor, might seem intimidating to someone accustomed only to written exams, but it was a long tradition in German universities and most students did not falter under the questioning.

My final exams at Freiburg, the *Staatsexamen*, comprised sessions with two professors on each subject. Ludwig Heilmeyer, chairman of the Department of Internal Medicine, conducted the first of my two sessions in internal medicine. Prof. Heilmeyer was one of the Old Guard, the remnants of the Third Reich, and it was rumored that he was harboring a man in his laboratory who had been involved in some of the atrocities associated with human experimentation during the Hitler era. However, Heilmeyer himself was highly respected for his professional work and had edited a book that was a standard reference book in internal medicine. He was responsible for attracting a substantial amount of funding to the university, and, accordingly, he was very influential.

My friend Hans-Ulrich Gottesleben was with me in the group that faced Prof. Heilmeyer, and poor Ulrich had a lot of difficulty with Heilmeyer's questions. Several times it happened that Ulrich didn't know the answer to a question, but then Prof. Heilmeyer asked me the same question and I would answer it correctly.

At one point, Prof. Heilmeyer turned to Ulrich and said, "It's a pity that the foreigner is better than you."

I exploded. "What's wrong with being a foreigner?" I said.

Heilmeyer realized I was angry, and he said, "Oh, no, no, no, that's not what I meant …" but, in fact, his remark betrayed a lingering tinge of the "master race" ideology that had so poisoned German society during the 1930s.

When we met with him again the next day to continue the internal medicine exam, Heilmeyer said, "I expected a reaction from the Iranian community after you left, but nobody has said anything."

Institutionally, the Federal Republic of Germany was very sensitive about the legacy of the Third Reich and determined to wipe out the worst vestiges of the past. Prof. Heilmeyer apparently feared that I would express my anger among the Iranian community and we might stage a protest or start a proceeding against him. I did not do so, of course.

I did well with Prof. Heilmeyer and went on to my second examiner in the Polyclinic Department of Internal Medicine. It was late in the afternoon when he started his questions. He went on and on, way beyond the normal hours, as if trying to find the outer limits of our knowledge, and finally he said, "I don't understand. There is one among you who deserves the highest grades, and I don't know why Professor Heilmeyer has marked him down."

There were four grades—1 (the highest), 2, 3, and 4 (the lowest), and Prof. Heilmeyer had given me a 2. The other professor gave me a 1. When all grades were calculated, I came out second in my graduating class. I have wondered ever since about Prof. Heilmeyer's grade, and whether that kept me from being first in my class. It didn't matter, really. Finishing second in my class was quite a distinction, and I took it as a great honor.

Nevertheless, the fact that even a towering and respected professor might penalize a student who confronted him taught me that it is human nature to be sensitive and protective of one's interest. What is amazing to me, though, is that in the West, such a confrontational reaction is considered natural and even explainable. In contrast, in Iranian society people accept unfair and abusive responses because they have no choice. They rarely resist when their superiors treat them unfairly, but it is not because they accept such treatment as justifiable. Iranians understand that protecting one's self-interest is natural, but they do not consider it justifiable.

For six and one-half years, my studies in Germany had concentrated on medicine and all the coursework required to qualify me for medical practice. I had always been interested in a wide variety of subjects and sometimes wished I could have continued to pursue other things, as I had in high school. In Göttingen, my curiosity drove me to look around for somebody who worked in a field closer to spirituality, and I discovered astronomy as an extracurricular interest. At the university's Astronomical Institute, I connected with a professor by the name of Heffner, a genial man who took walks in the woods with me and talked about his science.

"Human knowledge of the universe is forever expanding," he said to me one day. "The frontier of space exploration is widening over time, and we don't know where the end is. We see no sign that we are getting closer to the limits of the universe."

"What do you mean by 'getting closer to the limit'?" I asked.

"Do you notice how, when we walk through the woods and see the end of the woods coming, the light changes? We don't see that in the universe. Astronomers cannot observe a changing of the light at the outer limits of what we can see today. That seems to suggest that the universe is limitless."

His answer impressed me and puzzled me. It sounded like a scientific description of eternity, a theological concept. We continued our discussions, talking about reality beyond life: what it is, what we can and cannot know about it. Prof. Heffner introduced a new dimension to my thinking about the universe, about eternity, about the place of humans in it, and about God.

That was one of innumerable ways in which my world opened up. From my early days in Göttingen to my final exams in Freiburg, my life was an expanding universe. The young boy who had seen his first bananas in Beirut was now a different person, a young man with a growing awareness of the world. The boy who had a passion for learning discovered that he had the ability to excel in the advanced scientific environment of modern Germany, and, with the help of God, the anxious young Muslim who feared losing his faith amid the temptations of the West found the strength to withstand the pressures around him and hold fast to the truth.

The atmosphere of the German universities, where people were challenged to push against the frontiers of knowledge, opened my eyes and encouraged my own spirit of inquiry. Yes, my professors were renowned experts in their fields, but they were not infallible. I had witnessed their human frailties and was beginning to understand something elemental about human nature, that the wisest among us could err and that the purest soul could be tempted into taking a wrong turn on the road of life.

In retrospect, I recall one particular experience in Freiburg that illustrated my growing ability to question. A professor from the University of Athens, a specialist in diabetes who was visiting in the

Department of Pathology, was performing some experiments with cats. The animals' caretaker showed me the lab and explained that the cats were being injected with a hypertonic glucose solution in the abdomen to see the effect on hyperglycemia in their pancreatic cells. The caretaker showed me scratches on his arms.

"In the beginning," he said, "the animals would attack me when I opened the cage. In time, however, they became scared of me, and when they saw me, they crawled into a corner of the cage and would not come to me. Eventually, their legs became paralyzed and they lay in the corner of their cage with fear in their eyes."

Something about this struck me as wrong. I felt sorry for those cats and questioned the morality of treating animals in this way. Eventually, I looked into the precepts of Islam about caring for animals, and my doubts were confirmed. The Qur'an teaches that our cattle, horses, donkeys, and other animals are gifts from God. According to Islamic jurisprudence as described in *Usul-e-Kafi*, one of the most authoritative Hadith collections (traditions and sayings of Mohammad *pbuh,* and his progenies for Shi'a), such animals are entitled to proper food and a decent living place, and they should not be overworked. If an owner does not take proper care of his animals, they can be confiscated and sold to someone who will. I have taken this lesson about animals to heart, and while I know that a great deal of medical progress has been made possible because of experiments using animals, I am a strong proponent of humane treatment for laboratory animals—and all animals, for that matter.

I believe in the Islamic concept of *fetra*, the inborn quality that God gives every person as a guide for his or her life, and although I may not have been precisely conscious of it at the time, something was moving me toward realizing my *fetra*. God gave me the power to choose my course and led me to Germany on a path that eventually took me elsewhere—to America, back to Iran, and once again to America. In geographic terms, that may seem like a crooked path, or at least a path with abrupt twists and turns, but for me it was the Straight Path promised in many verses of the Qur'an. It was a path that led through many more experiences, some of them difficult; to still more revelations on the journey of my life's calling.

Life does not give us all of the answers at once, and at the time I was completing my education in Germany, there was still some confusion in my mind. Looking forward to my return home, I was convinced that incorporating science and technology into the religious and cultural framework of Iranian society was both achievable and desirable, but I had no clear concept of how it would be done—and certainly no inkling of how difficult the challenge would prove to be. It did not yet occur to me that bringing Iran up to speed with Western technology would collide with social forces rooted in rigid patterns of thinking. I had reconciled my religion with my life in science, but I would still have to learn that my own transformation was not easily passed on to my countrymen.

And, in terms of my personal development, there is an unhappy note about this juncture in my life. A professor in the Department of Obstetrics and Gynecology at the University of Freiburg liked me and invited me to work with him as his assistant. The position, which carried a salary, was very competitive, and it was an honor to be asked. As it happens, nobody in my life had ever impressed upon me the importance of keeping a promise. I gave the professor my word that I would accept the position, and I broke my promise when I got the opportunity to come to America instead. This has haunted me ever since, especially in light of what I subsequently came to appreciate about the core values and behaviors that have underpinned the great progress of Western culture—and the fact that these same values and behaviors lie at the heart of Islamic tradition. They are a part of the covenant that God made with man at the beginning of Creation, and the prophets and their disciples promulgated the same values. Over time, however, Islamic clergymen restricted their teachings to focus on rituals and underemphasized the importance of adherence to Islamic ethics and basic beliefs. This was the shortcoming of Islam as I received it during my childhood, and given what I now know and feel about life, I would tell my children ten times, "If you make a promise, you must stick with it, come hell or high water."

It is interesting to think about how my life would have evolved had I kept that promise: I might have stayed in Germany and become a *Dozent* (a habilitated professor), and then I might have taken a permanent position in Germany; or perhaps, at that point, I would have gone back to Iran. But this is idle speculation.

What happened instead was that I applied for an internship in the United States. During my entire time in Germany, everybody talked about the U.S.; that was where the real excitement was, they said— major breakthroughs in cardiovascular medicine, heart surgery, and other startling advances in medical science. Many of our books were translations of texts written in the U.S. Because I felt so passionately about being in the forefront of knowledge, America beckoned. I was quick to leave Germany behind in order to take one more step forward.

There was a second factor urging me to cross the ocean. Political developments in Iran after the fall of the Mossadegh government in 1953 had for the first time brought significant numbers of Americans into the thick of politics, the economy, education, and scientific life in my home country. It was not hard to see that the U.S. was going to have a big influence in the years to come, and I sensed that American-trained professionals would have their pick of jobs in Iran.

The decision about my next step had everything to do with my own longer-term future.

Not knowing exactly where to go, I applied for an internship program in obstetrics and gynecology at a small, church-related hospital in St. Louis, and I was accepted. Thus it was that, in June of 1957, I boarded a ship at the port of Le Havre, France, landed in New York, and traveled from there by bus to the Midwest. My view of life was far more complex and nuanced than when I first left Iran. If Germans could be arrogant and sometimes insensitive, they also exhibited qualities I admired—their rational thinking; their spirit of hard work, discipline, thoroughness, punctuality, and honesty; their goal-orientedness and their ability to focus on their job. I learned from the Germans to respect authority—to follow my boss's instructions without letting my own willfulness get in the way—and not to challenge that authority unless I was sure I had a better alternative. And I learned how to plan ahead before taking action, even if it was only for a bicycle ride in the country.

In addition to all I learned about medicine and all the practical skills for living, I took away the invaluable lesson that, because of my early religious training and with the help of God, I had within myself the strength to live outside my home culture, among non-Muslims, without compromising my convictions. This strength prepared me for the period of my medical residency—and my first experience in America.

CHAPTER FOUR
Homecomings, Courtship, and Marriage

I arrived home on a sweltering August evening in 1953 after a journey that took nearly a week by train from Frankfurt to Istanbul and Baghdad, and by bus from Baghdad. At the Iranian border, my heart swelled at the sight of my country's flag on the top of a nearby mountain, but my mood changed several hours later when I stepped off the bus in Tehran. It was with some difficulty that I found a taxi, and the ride to my parents' home took me through streets filled by a strange silence. I knew there had been a coup d'état, but I did not understand the implications for my country.

It was my first first time back in two and one-half years, and my parents were beside themselves with joy to see me. However, they quickly expressed concern that I might not be able to return to Germany. Iran was under martial law following the overthrow of the popular Prime Minister, Mohammad Mossadegh; the military were in control, and many people feared that they would close the borders. From Germany, I had written to my parents asking them whether or not I should make the trip, but my father's letter advising me not to come hadn't reached Göttingen before my departure.

Later in the evening of my arrival, I dropped in to surprise my brother Ahmad, who had married in 1950 and was living with his wife and two-year-old daughter in a rented home near my parents. He, too, had a worried look on his face, wondering what I was doing in Tehran in such uncertain times. The three of them were at the dinner table, and I could not help noticing that their meal consisted of just one cooked egg, bread, and water. The economy was in tatters because a British embargo had brought oil exports to a halt. Both Ahmad and my father were unemployed, and it made me sad to see how poor they were.

We spent several hours discussing what was happening in Iran, with Ahmad filling me in on the details of the immediate past weeks. The government was in the hands of military forces loyal to the shah and supported by other elites who opposed Mossadegh's reform programs. While in Göttingen I had read the news that Iran had nationalized the operations of the British Petroleum company in Iran and about the oil embargo, but the details had largely escaped me. Iran seemed far away, and my studies kept me so busy that it was hard to pay close attention to the events back home. The main effect that I felt, along with other Iranian students, was that our government stipends were cut off because of the economic impact of the embargo, and we had to find other means of financial support. The German universities provided some limited assistance, but I went out and found a job in an aluminum factory; it was hard work and, naturally, competed with my time for studying, but I managed. Now, upon returning to Iran, I was able to piece together the political events that had brought about my financial difficulties—and came to understand just how serious the situation was.

The political unrest reached back to the 1940s. During World War II, the occupying Allied armies forced the elder Reza Shah to abdicate, fearing that he was moving his country too close to Nazi Germany. He was replaced by his 20-year-old son, Mohammad Reza Shah, who reigned up to the time of the Islamic revolution in 1979 except for the brief Mossadegh interlude. Reza Shah (1926-1941) had alienated many with his secularization policies and his use of police and security forces, and when his son succeeded him, Iranians rejoiced in what appeared to be a new era. The young shah was educated in Switzerland, and he was intent on transforming Iran on the model of European democracy. During the first decade of his rule, political parties flourished and there was relative freedom of expression.

Meanwhile, Iran came under wartime occupation by armed forces of the Soviet Union and Great Britain. The Soviets, who occupied northern Iran, had their eye on gaining access to the Persian Gulf and wanted eventually to export communism to the entire country as well. To this end, they supported the left-wing Tudeh Party and, following the end of the war, set up a separatist, pro-Soviet state in the Iranian province of Azerbaijan. Under international pressure, especially from the United States, the Soviet army left Iran, and with U.S. support, the shah's forces suppressed the separatist movement in November 1946. The Tudeh Party was forced underground after being blamed for a failed attempt on the shah's life in 1949, but it reemerged in 1951, the year when Mossadegh was elected Prime Minister.

Mossadegh, the leader of the progressive National Front, began putting in place elements of a social revolution that caught the imagination of a large following. His government attempted to reform the tax structure and abolished the centuries-old feudal agricultural system. Legislation in March 1951 nationalized the British-owned Anglo-Iranian Oil Company, the controlling interest in Iran's petroleum industry. The British reacted by imposing an all-out embargo that crippled the Iranian economy.

At the beginning, the United States attempted to mediate between Iran and the British. President Harry Truman sent W. Averell Harriman as his special envoy to find a compromise solution to the conflict. Harriman did not succeed, but his efforts left many Iranians optimistic about American support for their cause; after all, they reasoned, the United States itself had been born out of a revolt against the British. Ultimately, however, the Americans disappointed the Iranian masses. In 1953, the new President Dwight D. Eisenhower and his Secretary of State John Foster Dulles allowed the British to persuade them that Mossadegh had ties with the Tudeh Party and posed the threat of allying his government with the USSR. Those suspicions were unfounded, but the Cold War environment and the Eisenhower administration's sensitivity to communism blinded the U.S. to the subtleties of Iran's politics. The Eisenhower administration joined in plans with the British to remove Mossadegh from his position.

In August of 1953, shortly before my arrival, the swirling political pressures forced the shah into exile, but within the same month he returned, thanks to the military coup, which was aided by British and American intelligence services. Mossadegh was tried and convicted of treason; he spent three years in prison and the rest of his life under house arrest.

Parallel to the secular political forces were the religious people, the Islamic community and especially the leading clergy, who had been unhappy about the forced secularization of Iran since the early years of the elder shah from the 1920s on. The religious elements had felt humiliated by the presence of foreign troops during the war, and they, like most others, suffered greatly from the poor economy.

Opinions within our extended family were deeply divided. One of my mother's cousins, Engineer Porushani, who was a privileged, pro-Western member of the shah's government, harshly criticized Mossadegh and rejoiced in his overthrow. On the other side, Engineer Sedehi, whose French education had left him with progressive political views, wore a sad expression on his face, and spoke cautiously and indirectly of Mossadegh's overthrow as treason. The faces of people in the streets of Tehran expressed concern and shock. There were elements in the society who stood to gain from the coup d'état—landowners, pro-British politicians from Iran's southern provinces, and those who blamed the economic hardships on Mossadegh—but, by and large, the masses saw the coup as a defeat, a terrible blow to the dignity and self-respect of all Iranians. People could not believe that their democratically elected government could be so easily toppled by men they considered no good. In a poignant moment, I was walking past the building of the *Majlis* (Iranian Parliament) one day when I encountered a little boy waving the flag of Iran and chanting "Either death or Mossadegh," a slogan he had picked up from demonstrating crowds.

My conversations with ordinary Iranians revealed a welter of confusing and disheartening factors. The economic hardships, the interference of foreigners, the machinations of the communists, and the disenfranchisement of the military during the Mossadegh period had large parts of the population perplexed. The position of the *Ulama*, the Islamic religious leaders and juridical scholars, only seemed to add more confusion. The masses lacked clear information and had no organizational connection to the political groups, and therefore they felt powerless to defend the revolution they had supported. The door was open for the old guard and the military generals to take total control.

Prior to this time, the shah had ruled in a relatively democratic fashion, allowing the *Majlis* to legislate, and he did not attempt to interfere when Mossadegh was elected Prime Minister. Upon Mossadegh's downfall, however, the shah assumed a greater degree of power. The *Majlis* lost its independence. Fearful of political opposition, the government set up a secret police organization, the SAVAK. (The letters stand for the Farsi words for Organization for Intelligence and National Security). The SAVAK quickly earned a reputation for spying on citizens and brutality against those considered enemies of the regime. American political influence in Iran grew; U.S. leaders saw the shah as a vital Cold War ally and turned a blind eye to the regime's repressiveness. Before Mossadegh, the Iranian masses had hated the British for their economic dominance and their political meddling. In time, they would also come to see the U.S. unfavorably; for now, however, they were willing to give the Americans the benefit of the doubt, holding to a glimmer of hope that it would be better to work with them than their experience with the British had been.

Daily life in Tehran returned to normal, albeit now in a mood of resignation. The mass media spared no effort in condemning the deposed government and praising the return of the shah to the throne. People continued to suffer from high unemployment, and in time, the growth of the SAVAK's power made all afraid to speak their opinion openly or gather in groups that might make the secret police suspicious of them. Iranians withdrew into their private lives, disillusioned by politics and thankful that they at least had their extended family ties to keep them going.

The forces of opposition would rise up again, but not for a long time. Throughout the 1950s and 1960s, and lasting into the 1970s, the monarchy's power was supreme. Contacts between progressive religious leaders and intellectuals who opposed the government's policies took place under dangerous conditions. Many citizens were imprisoned or executed on suspicion of political crimes. In time the opposition forces, joined by the more conservative elements of the religious community, would assert themselves and bring about another revolution.

At the time, I did not fully understand the nature of the conflict underlying the various political groups' positions. Years later, I came to realize that they were fighting over fundamental questions of national identity, Iranian traditions versus a Eurocentric concept of modernity, and secular versus religious values. Our Western-educated shah had wanted to see Iran develop economically and politically along the lines of Western capitalism. Over the years, his regime deployed large numbers of European- and American-trained intellectuals and technocrats in government planning bureaus, industry, and the country's universities. The members of this elite enjoyed great privileges of wealth and power, such that the masses came to resent them, along with the countries and foreign corporations they represented.

Mossadegh and his political allies also wanted to see Iran develop a modern system, but they believed that the best way to modernize was to break away from dependence on outside countries and develop social and economic structures based on a new model that took better account of Iranian realities. Mossadegh understood the psychology of his people and their pride in the country's rich cultural and religious heritage. He offered them a leader who would restore their dignity and self-respect. His time in office was short and turbulent. The political balance of power shifted from one side to the other, and when the shah emerged supreme, he took revenge on Mossadegh.

Over and against both the government's policies and the Mossadegh approach were the conservative religious leaders who looked askance at modernization but were not yet organized into a political force capable of challenging the powers that be. All of these conflicts would come to the forefront twenty-five years later.

I stayed in Iran until sometime in November. To my relief, the police created no difficulty as I left the country. I returned to Germany saddened by what I had seen but happy to have had the opportunity to spend those two and one-half months with my family. In Germany, my monthly stipend resumed and I was able to begin my studies at the University of Freiburg. The political realities at home faded into the background.

It was another six years before my next trip home. In the meantime, I earned my doctorate in Freiburg and went directly from there to America for my residency. What took me back to Iran in 1959 was an important event in my personal life—and, as it turned out, a disappointment. It had to do with a young woman.

During my time in Freiburg, I met a number of female students from Iran. We would see each other in the *Mensa* (cafeteria) and at parties, go on trips together, and celebrate each other's birthdays—all in groups. We did not date, but we were of course keen observers of each other; boys looked at girls and evaluated them in their minds, and vice versa. One girl whom I saw more often was a sister of one of my closest friends. She and I developed a friendship that grew stronger over time and became something more than a friendship. I took a lot of pictures of her in Freiburg's botanical garden and enjoyed giving them to her as a gift. One afternoon she invited me, along with some others, to her apartment for coffee and *Kuchen* (cakes). We both knew that we cared for each other, but we did not talk directly about it because we were not sure that our relationship was serious enough to talk about and we did not feel comfortable exposing our feelings on the question of marriage. In Iran this is a task for an intermediary.

Just a few weeks before my departure to the U.S., a mutual female friend told me that the girl had a positive feeling toward me and urged me to explore it before I left Germany. After that, the girl and I saw each other more frequently. We took a trip to Zürich together and stayed in separate rooms of a hotel. We talked late into the night, said "good night" to each other, and slept in our own rooms. We promised each other to get married as soon as I settled into America and could bring her with me. Telephone calls between Europe and America were expensive, but we remained in contact by writing frequently. She was studying dentistry, and I made some initial inquiries about the possibility for her to transfer to an American dental school. More than a year passed, but then we both returned to Iran during summer vacation with the intention of getting married.

As was the custom, I traveled to her city, accompanied by a male member of our family, to ask her father's permission to marry her, and he gave it to me in a formal meeting. However, a more serious meeting had to take place before we could proceed to marriage: members of both families had to iron out the details of the marriage contract. That meeting took place in Tehran, and my father and my brother Ahmad were present. Before the meeting, my mother made it clear that she was not pleased with the proposed match; she had some reservations about the young woman's age (24) and did not consider her beautiful enough.

The prospective bride's grandfather, who represented her in the meeting, boasted continuously about the high social standing of the bride's family. He appeared contemptuous of my family almost to the point of being disrespectful. My father became angry and blue in the face, and we left without reaching agreement. After the meeting, Ahmad took me aside and advised me strongly against the marriage. My father had known the girl's family earlier and felt that the values and aspirations of our families were not a good match because they were more secularly oriented than we were.

I felt torn between my family and my personal feelings. I loved and respected my family and, like them, I was also hurt by the haughty attitude of the girl's grandfather. I wanted to trust my family's judgment, and at the same time, I wanted to marry the girl. She and I continued to plead our case, but both sides were opposed to it and we could not budge them. I returned to the U.S. disappointed and angry with my family and myself.

I was now 27 years old and living alone in a room on the top floor of the University of Chicago Lying-in Hospital. I ate mostly in the hospital cafeteria and occasionally in a restaurant, usually alone. After work I often walked, again by myself, along the shore of Lake Michigan just to kill time, returned to my lodgings, and sat on the couch in the residents' lounge watching television until the late hours. I became listless, and my work at the hospital suffered.

An Iranian friend of mine who was interning in another Chicago hospital had married a beautiful Iranian girl, and they often invited me to their home. Seeing how happy they were together intensified my feelings of loneliness. More and more, I had the urge to get married and build a family. I expressed this to my father in several letters and asked my parents to look for a suitable wife for me. This is how it was usually done in Iran at the time.

The process took a few months, and my parents suggested several prospective brides. It was not easy for me to choose among them, because the information I got from my parents was mostly about the girls' families. From the girl herself, I would sometimes receive a photo of the type that students have made as an attachment to their diploma. I did not find most of them attractive. Finally my father sent me a photo that impressed me favorably. The girl's name was Fereshteh. My father wrote that her family was modern, but also religious. They had a very good reputation in the bazaar, and their son was studying in England. My father added that I did not have to marry her if I decided not to, but he urged me to come to Iran, at least, and meet her.

Once more, I made the long trip back to Tehran, in the winter of 1961. A friend of my father's confirmed the honesty and integrity of Fereshteh's father and added his judgment that our families shared common values in life. Fereshteh's father, Kazem Naghshineh-pour, was a self-made man. He was the eldest son in his family, and he had started earning money at the age of 14, when his father died, to support his younger siblings. He became the director of a power plant. Later, he developed modern agricultural projects in the southern province of Khuzestan and, still later, joined a group of entrepreneurs who started a shipping company to move oil and other goods between Persian Gulf ports. Fereshteh's mother, Kiandocht, was from a more educated family that had descended from an aristocratic line. She was principal of a girls' school when she married Kazem, and she was fond of reading or reciting poems aloud.

All I knew about Fereshteh and her family sounded favorable, and I went to meet her with a positive attitude. Ahmad and my father accompanied me to the family's home in the afternoon. There I met my wife for the first time, a young and beautiful girl. I gave her a sweater I had bought in Chicago, a gift that she kept and wore for a number of years.

After that, Fereshteh and I met alone several times. Once I took her to the restaurant at the airport, where we sat and talked seriously. She said that all she expected from me was to be a kind and loving husband, and I readily agreed. I do not remember what kind of wife I asked her to be, but all in all we had a good, positive conversation. She was willing to marry me and come with me to America, leaving her parents behind, and that, together with her beauty, convinced me.

One more issue remained. Traditionally, it was customary to negotiate a marriage gift, or *mehr*, before the bride's family accepts the groom's marriage proposal. The gift, given to the bride by the prospective husband and/or his family, may be in terms of land, a home, stocks, gold coins, cash, or other goods. If the gift is real estate, stock, or other property, it is usually paid at the time the marriage contract is signed; often, however, the gift comes in the form of a promise to the bride, especially if it involves cash or gold, to be paid later. It is customary for the bride's family to insist on a value for the gift as high as possible. The promise represents a way for both families to ensure that the husband does not divorce the wife for frivolous reasons, because the gift must be paid in full at the time the divorce occurs. The downside of this custom is that the *mehr* imputes a material value on the bride and implies how much the groom and his family are willing to commit themselves to earn the acceptance of the bride's family.

This gift is real, and the bride has every right to demand it. The custom of a very high-priced marriage gift, however, was already frowned upon at the time of our marriage, and I was sensitive about it. I proposed a marriage gift of a value not to exceed the annual income of a doctor; as an educated, progressive man, I wanted to set what I considered a sensible precedent of one year's income as a standard for the marriage gift. When I made this proposal to Fereshteh's father, however, I was startled by the look of dismay on his face. He refused the offer at first, but then he engaged an intermediary to accept the proposal on his behalf.

Having resolved this momentary hitch, we moved ahead quickly, and in the end, I chose my wife and married her within two weeks. Contrary to custom, our marriage ceremony was a simple one, with only the nearest family members attending. It took place in Fereshteh's home just a few days before we left for America.

Getting a passport in Iran was not easy, and it often took months; Fereshteh's mother had had the foresight to apply for Fereshteh's passport long in advance. After our marriage, we applied to the American

Embassy in Tehran for her visa, and that came through in only a few days. We were ready to begin our life together in the U.S.

On the night before our departure, I stayed with my parents and Fereshteh stayed with hers. It was a wintry day in February 1961 when we boarded an airliner and headed to America, with a stop in London to visit Fereshteh's brother. As we approached Chicago, Midway Airport was closed because of a snowstorm. We flew on and landed in Omaha, Nebraska, where we waited for several hours until we could be flown back to Chicago.

My friend Ahmad Fatahi-poor greeted us upon our arrival and gave us the key to our apartment. Just before leaving for Iran, I had applied to the University of Chicago's housing office and secured a two-bedroom rental unit. I also bought some second-hand furniture from a local family who had placed an ad in the newspaper, and Ahmad had graciously moved all the furniture into our apartment during my absence.

Fereshteh adapted well to life in America. She took English classes in a high school from a Japanese-American teacher, Mr. Kamagei, and she supplemented those lessons with a class at the downtown YMCA. She rode the "El" (elevated train) every day with such confidence that I did not worry about her alone in the big, new city. Within a few months, she was speaking English with proficiency. As it happened, I was making my rotation in the cytology laboratory under Dr. George Wied, an immigrant from Vienna and a pioneer in diagnostic cytology and the screening of female organs for cancer. Fereshteh was interested in getting some lab training, and Dr. Wied got her a fellowship to train with him as a cytotechnician. She fitted in easily, sometimes working late hours in the lab when I was on call. Her stipend was more than my salary, and we lived in modest comfort for the rest of our stay. We were able to save enough money to purchase a new Chevrolet for $2,400.

Fereshteh and I now joined a circle of other married couples who formed the basis of our social life in Chicago. We visited each other, went on picnics in nice weather, and occasionally took group trips for a weekend. Looking back now, I regret that we did not take greater advantage of the many opportunities at the university and in the city to enrich our lives through cultural and educational pursuits, but we were young newlyweds with our work, our studies, and our friends—and, before we eventually returned to Iran, we gained a new member of the family, our daughter Manya.

Our marriage was an arranged marriage, something that is alien to most Americans. Arranged marriages as they existed at that time are now mostly a matter of the past in Iran, but for centuries, they represented an institutional form that fit the needs of our culture as those needs were understood. Modern people, especially Westerners, tend to view the role of parents in arranged marriages as intrusive and dictatorial, perhaps even arbitrary; however, parents in traditional societies have always wanted the best for their children just as do parents in modern, Western societies.

In traditional societies, the extended family represents the environment in which children grow up and develop their personalities, communication skills, habits, and value systems. Everything about the child's character is presumed to reflect upon the whole family, especially when it comes to matters of public behavior and morality. Divorce and promiscuity, for example, are black marks on the extended family. In this environment, there is very little information about women outside the family; to the extent that children attend schools, boys and girls rarely mix enough to get to know each other's character, and parents caution their offspring not to get too close to other children lest they be the children of families who do not share their values. The level of peer pressure and conformity that describes American classrooms was unknown in our traditional society; the family was the overwhelming force molding the character of their children. It was assumed that the best way of predicting how a young man or woman would behave as a marriage partner was the reputation of his or her parents and other adult relatives.

Of course, family wealth and social standing were additional factors figuring in the suitability of a marriage partner. Here again, parents wanted the best possible partner for their children. They considered it crucial to have accurate information about the material well being of a prospective partner's family and sought such information from the bazaar, banks, and other financial entities.

Oftentimes, families would hire a matchmaker, a professional person who could gather the necessary information and determine a suitable match between a young man from this family and a young woman from that one. Another source of information might be daily household workers who would report their impressions of the people for whom they worked.

Families considered it important not to have divorce within their ranks. Even if they took every precaution in identifying a suitable partner for their child, there was still a possibility that the marriage might go wrong. The elders in the family had a responsibility to help young marrieds stay together, and the younger couples did not want to disappoint their parents. Love for their children further contributed to the stability of their marriage. Both men and women did their best not to disappoint their parents or to tear apart their home through divorce; women especially were taught to be patient and tolerant in order to preserve their marriage for the sake of their children.

Thus it was not a simple matter to find the appropriate partner for one's child. A good marriage, by the definition of the traditional society, resulted from diligent efforts by both partners' families. This is not to say that children in Iran were coerced into marriage; on the contrary, Islamic jurisprudence considers forced marriages to be null and void. The reality of arranged marriages was much more subtle and complex; the typical arranged marriage was one like mine in which the families did their best to make a suitable match but left the final decision of "yes" or "no" up to the children.

In my case, the result has been a marriage that is stable and full of love. Fereshteh and I have been married now for 46 years and have produced three children, all of whom hold doctoral degrees and are accomplished professionals. We are a happy family.

CHAPTER FIVE

In America, the First Time

I n the mid-1950s, Iranians pictured the United States as a place of generous, freedom-loving citizens; a land that accepted people from around the world with open arms; a land of hope. Few of us understood yet the role of American intelligence in the coup d'état of 1953. Eventually, Iranians' opinions would change as the U.S. became more and more associated with the increasing repression of the shah's government, but at the time I chose the location for my medical internship and residency, America still enjoyed a great deal of respect among us.

Studying in Germany, I had come to believe that the United States was the right place for me to complete my training. By then I had enough self-confidence to believe I would find a satisfying training position almost anywhere. I was not aware then that, in addition to university hospitals, there were also private and community hospitals with approved internship and residency training programs, and I did not have any means to evaluate the differences in type and quality of training among those institutions. I only knew that it was difficult for foreign graduates to be accepted in the university hospitals for training. In the spring of 1957, as my graduation from Freiburg approached, I read a notice announcing that a hospital in St. Louis was accepting applications. I really wanted to be at one of the most prominent hospitals, and preferably one connected with a major university, but I did not have any contacts in those institutions. So I applied to Missouri Baptist Hospital (MBH), assuming that my application would be accepted, and it was. I did not know that MBH was just a small community hospital. Coming from Freiburg's large, advanced hospital complex with many active research programs, I was soon disappointed and regretted not taking the position I had been offered in the Obstetrics/Gynecology Department at Freiburg. Nevertheless, I decided to proceed with my internship training at MBH; I did not have the courage to go back to Germany and ask to be reaccepted there.

As it turned out, there were some good things about my situation at Missouri Baptist. I was immediately accepted as a member of the medical team and expected to function as such. This was unlike the situation in German universities, where medical students have little direct contact with patients during their medical training. In contrast, medical students in the U.S. get a lot of hands-on experience in hospitals, participating in diagnostic procedures and the treatment of patients. Interns work under the supervision of the senior residents and attending staff. If I had interned at the University Hospital in Freiburg, I would have worked at the lowest level, taking my orders from the Chef, but at Missouri Baptist, I jumped into the excitement of taking calls and was directly responsible for the care of patients. As an intern, I did not carry all the responsibilities of the senior medical staff, but the working environment was such that I did not feel like an underling.

The fact that I had studied medicine overseas, in a different hospital culture, meant there were many procedures and routines I had to learn. The attending physicians and nursing staff were aware of the shortcomings of interns coming from overseas and were supportive in helping us to learn the routine. My learning process progressed quickly, and in no time I gained full confidence in myself. In addition, of course, all of my training and activities required me to function fluently in English. I had studied the language in high school, but it was still difficult, at first, to understand spoken American English. The attending physicians and the nursing staff were understanding and patient. They were ready with help and advice about everything.

Nevertheless, in spite of all the help and support I got in the initial phase of my training at MBH, I came to realize later, when I moved on to other places in the U.S., that the medical profession carried a certain prejudice toward "foreign graduates" that was not easy to overcome.

In any event, after a few weeks at MBH, I recovered from the initial shock of working in a small institution and began to discover the thrill of practicing medicine. The atmosphere was quite informal; the staff, doctors and nurses alike, were friends with each other and interacted with joy and humor. I came to appreciate this working atmosphere the more I realized how much it differed from that in Germany, where the philosophy of "because the Chef said so" operated at all levels. For example, in Freiburg there were certain nurses close to the Chef who had his complete confidence and took advantage of their status in dealing with the other doctors. A lower-level doctor did not dare to get on the wrong side of the head nurse in the operating room. She was the only one who would scrub and help the Chef with operations, and the rest of the staff paid her almost as much deference as they did the Chef himself. On the other hand, the informality of the hospital culture in America sometimes led to questionable circumstances. Nurses often had their eyes on young doctors—or on older doctors who were rich or powerful—and occasionally, a doctor and a nurse would be caught in a compromising situation, something that was unheard-of in Germany.

The majority of the house staff at Missouri Baptist were foreign-educated, and I believe this was a factor in the hospital's positive environment for the interns and residents who came from overseas. One physician I particularly respected was Dr. D.J. Verda, an immigrant from Czechoslovakia who told us that he had only $50.00 in his pocket when he disembarked from the ship in New York. Dr. Verda had a way of taking those of us who were foreign and younger under his wing; he empathized with us because he, too, had gone through the experience of adjusting to life in America. He taught us the art of surgery, for example, and gave us advice on a number of professional matters. Interestingly, he himself had not had specialized training in surgery, but at that time community hospitals permitted general practitioners to perform surgery, and Dr. Verda, who was very skilled and knowledgeable in a variety of procedures, actually performed more surgeries than the specialists at MBH. Dr. Verda became a role model for me. He showed me why America is said to be "the land of opportunity." He maintained two offices and had a busy practice. His example convinced me that it was possible for someone to come to America, work hard, succeed, and still be kind to his junior colleagues. I told myself if he could do it, I can, too.

One day Dr. Verda drove a few of us in his plush, red Lincoln Continental to a conference in another hospital. He showed us his name posted on a wall there in a list of donors to the hospital's construction fund. This was my first introduction to the concept of philanthropy, and I began to see the importance of generous giving to the common cause, a phenomenon that is well developed in America.

It was in St. Louis that I bought my first car, a green 1951 Dodge. I paid $200 for it and drove it with pride. I kept that same car for almost the entire time of my stay in the U.S. Having a car gave me a sense of mobility and independence. It was exciting to be able to pick up and go whenever I had free time, and I enjoyed traveling around in the wide Missouri countryside. Of course, the car was also available for social activities. My income was modest by American standards, but I had money enough to take a nurse out to a popular drive-in hamburger stand and go to the movies. In those days, a hamburger and a Coca-Cola cost only 25 cents and would be served up to the car window by high-school girls who worked as waitresses. I remember also a scenic road in Forest Park, called Lover's Lane, and I did not miss the opportunity to take my girlfriend there occasionally.

In a word, I became an adult during this time—a man with a profession, a member of a medical team, and a guy who owned his own car. Despite these marks of success, however, I did not want to stay at Missouri Baptist Hospital to complete my residency training; I was restless and wanted to move on to a more advanced hospital setting. In particular, I wanted to find a residency position in obstetrics and gynecology at a teaching hospital, and so I began to look around for new opportunities during the second half of 1958.

I chose obstetrics and gynecology (ob/gyn) as a specialty because it combined two aspects of medical practice, internal medicine and surgery, that appealed to me. During my internship at MBH, I learned to love surgery. At the same time, I was also good at treating patients in the medical wards. Surgery is a well-defined, concrete action in medicine that shows immediate results. Internal medicine is more of a problem-solving discipline, requiring a more refined intellectual imagination. I chose ob/gyn because it has both of those aspects.

My challenge was to overcome the medical community's prejudice against graduates of foreign medical schools. I knew I was at a disadvantage in competing for highly desired residency positions. However, I asked one of the attending physicians at MBH for a referral. He kindly recommended me to Willard M. Allen, Chairman of the Department of Obstetrics and Gynecology at Barnes Hospital of Washington University in St. Louis. Dr. Allen met with me and offered me a one-year research assistantship in his endocrine laboratory. It was not a residency position, but I accepted it, hoping that after the year of laboratory work Dr. Allen would accept me into the ob/gyn residency program.

In the meantime, I had also applied to the University of Chicago Lying-in Hospital. A few weeks after I accepted Dr. Allen's offer, I received a letter from Chicago accepting me immediately into their residency program. This new opportunity delighted me, and once again, I made the same mistake I had made in Freiburg: I broke my promise, declining the research assistantship with Dr. Allen. To this day, I feel bad about that decision. It was the last time I ever broke any promise.

The Chicago Lying-in Hospital had been built during the 1930s, thanks to donations from the local business community, and it quickly became a leading institution for the care of women. The hospital's first chairman, Professor Joseph DeLee, wrote a book on obstetrics that became a classic in the field. He came to America with a European background and established a top-heavy administrative system. He was influential among his colleagues because of his powerful personality and organizational skills.

I arrived in Chicago on the first of January 1959, and was received by a member of the hospital administrator's staff. I was given a room in the residents' quarters and two white coats with my name on them. Next morning I arrived on the patients' floor and got my assignment. The residency program at the Lying-in Hospital followed a so-called "vertical" structure, in which the same number of residents moves up to the next level each year during the entire duration of the residency program. A first-year resident would be assigned to a team upon his arrival, and he would stay with the same team during the entire time of his residency program. Thus, for the next three and one-half years, I learned my professional skills by working with a team headed by Dr. Charles P. McCartney.

Now I entered yet another new environment and had to adapt to a philosophy and working style that I sometimes found challenging. My colleagues at Missouri Baptist had helped me become a part of the team there, but at the University of Chicago, the demands of team-work and collaboration rose to a higher level. The team leader in the residency program, who was typically a faculty member at the rank of associate professor, had the power to make decisions about the assignments and training, and a new resident needed to please him in order to be promoted. Interpersonal relationships were an important factor in acquiring the favors of the team leader.

Earlier, my experience at the University of Freiburg had made me intellectually oriented toward research, in both laboratories and clinics, and instilled in me the value of independent critical thinking. The overriding purpose of my team assignment at Chicago, in contrast, was to render efficient and high-quality medical services to the patients; research did not represent a major part of the hospital's mission—and was not a central part of my training as a resident.

This institutional culture, with its strong focus on patient care, came as a surprise to me. I had assumed that American universities' medical schools, like those in Germany, would be primarily research-oriented. As I was quick to learn, most American schools gave top priority to patient care; special institutions like the National Institutes of Health and the National Laboratories carried the tradition of doing research in America. If I wanted to conduct research at Chicago Lying-in, I had to do it on my own time or else take a sabbatical leave and work at the Argonne National Laboratory, which was affiliated with the University of Chicago.

My attitude and orientation set me apart from my fellow residents. Most of them wanted to finish their residency and leave the university for private practice, where they expected to earn a lot of money. My ambition, on the contrary, was to remain within the academic environment. I wanted to teach, pursue science through research, and organize departments and institutions back in my home country. I had the feeling that the "powers that be" in our department did not appreciate my attitude.

In addition, I was not one for stroking my supervisor's ego. Dr. McCartney's favorite students seemed adept at engaging him in conversation during coffee breaks, among other things, and this was something for which I had little talent. As a result, I was not one of his favorites. It seemed to me that Dr. McCartney placed little value in his residents' ability to think and that his only concern was for us to perform our routines. And even though there were times when I stayed at work by myself and did research for him until late at night, he never went out of his way to thank me or tell me I'd done a good job. There was nothing wrong with the way Dr. McCartney taught us the skills and techniques of our profession, but it disturbed me that he seemed most interested in cultivating us as his "disciples."

Finally, the routines I was assigned often bored me; I wanted more of a challenge and felt a bit marginal because of my outlook. Nevertheless, I persevered and finished my residency with success.

By this time, of course, I had married and knew I would not be returning to Iran alone. As I considered my future, I thought about conversations I had had in Freiburg with an Iranian friend named Farrokh Hushmand. Farrokh got me interested in Nemazee Hospital, located in his hometown of Shiraz. The hospital was founded in the late 1940s by Mohammad Nemazee, whose U.S. -based Iran Foundation provided seed money, and the U.S. Agency for International Development (AID) played an important role in creating a state-of-the-art medical institution that quickly gained a reputation for excellence. Later, Nemazee Hospital became affiliated with Pahlavi University of Shiraz as its main teaching hospital. About a year before the end of my residency, I inquired about a position there, realizing that it would be a highly desirable place for me to start my work in Iran. It took some months for the possibility to develop.

I was ready to return to Iran, but one thing gave me cause for hesitation. Several Iranian friends had recently been back home, and when they returned to Chicago they told discouraging stories about the difficulty of getting work. They reported that only members of the "1,000 families"—that is, the most elite families in Iran, those closest to the shah and his inner circle —were finding it easy to get a good position at a university or in the hospitals of the national Ministry of Health. These reports made me nervous about returning, and I began to think, what if my social background and lack of political connections excluded me from achieving my professional goals, despite all my years of education abroad? I even thought of staying in the U.S., entering a Ph.D. program in endocrinology, and postponing my return to Iran.

As it happened, Fereshteh became pregnant a few months before I finished my residency. At the time, I was caring for a beautiful Iranian woman in the maternity ward named Pari Ghaffari, who was married to a Spanish count from the Canary Islands. This was not her first baby, and each time she came due, she traveled to Chicago to give birth in the Chicago Lying-in Hospital. When I asked the count why they came so far, he explained that he was worried about the future of the world; he considered the U.S. to be a safe haven in a turbulent time, and he wanted his children to have American citizenship and an American passport, which they would be entitled to if they were born in the United States. To the count, his children's American citizenship would serve as a kind of insurance against turmoil elsewhere in the world. That gave me an idea. I persuaded Fereshteh that we should stay in the U.S. until our baby was born, just in case we might some-day wish to have the option of returning permanently. My residency at the Lying-in Hospital ended in July of 1962, but I was able to secure a new residency for six months, this time in surgery, at the Woodlawn Hospital in a suburb of Chicago.

In addition, I decided to take the Washington State Medical Board's examination for physicians and surgeons. That way, I would have qualifications for employment in hand should the need arise. Washington then was one of only five U.S. states that allowed non-citizens to take the board exam. I did not know anybody there, but I was familiar with the reputation of the University of Washington's School of Medicine, and particularly that of Dr. Russell de Alvarez, who was then the head of the Obstetrics and Gynecology Department. I thought the University would be a good place for me to work if I were to stay in the U.S. I flew out to Seattle in the spring of 1962, sat for the exam, and passed it. I was now a physician licensed to practice medicine in the State of Washington.

In the meantime, my application to Nemazee University bore fruit. To my good fortune, the faculty at Nemazee Hospital, perhaps because of a strong American influence within its board of directors, was chosen not because of their political connections but because of their qualifications.

As it eventually turned out, those decisions about taking the Washington board exam and extending our stay in Chicago were wise. Our daughter Manya was born with U.S. citizenship. Years later, when we decided to immigrate to America, Manya was able to apply for permanent residency status for us, and it was granted. In the meantime, I had made sure to keep my Washington medical license alive by paying the renewal fee every year. When we did come back to the States, I could immediately open a practice and start working.

At the end of 1962, my long period of education and training abroad drew to a close. Before we went home to Iran, our little family took a road trip across the U.S., driving all the way from Chicago to San Diego, then back across the Southwest to New Orleans and, from there, to Washington, D.C. and New York. All along the way, baby Manya drew the attention of people in the motels and restaurants where we stopped, and we felt warm and comfortable about allowing strangers to pick her up, take her around, and rock her in their arms. In today's environment it would have been unthinkable for us to let a stranger carry our baby to the back of the restaurant, but at that time, we did not worry about it. In at least several places, the proprietors even volunteered to wash and sterilize her baby bottles.

The years that I spent in America helped form my outlook on life as much as the years I spent in Göttingen and Freiburg. For a young man who had grown up half a world away, America was a land of many new realities, a dynamic society of material plenty and limitless opportunities, or so it seemed. I admired the uncomplicated mindset of the Americans I met, and I was touched by their kindness and helpfulness. There were many moments prior to my marriage when I felt isolated, but the generosity of Midwesterners did much to comfort me and reassure me that I was among good people. Some invited me to their homes during Christmas and Easter holidays. They gave me gifts and cards for my birthdays, and I took trips with them.

Another quality that impressed me about Americans was their

genius for organizational and management skills, which seemed to extend to every aspect of life. The level of sophistication in systems and procedures was something I hoped to take back to Iran and apply, however I could, to my profession. In America, I saw that sophistication first and foremost in medical care, because that was the area of my professional interest, but it was also obvious in supermarkets, traffic and road systems, and hundreds of other applications—even in the planning of social gatherings.

Any foreigner living in the U.S. cannot help being struck by how Americans truly value healthy competition and admire winners. Americans take pride in good work and have a passion to excel among their peers, and they show this by giving their winners rewards and recognition.

There were also some qualities to American society that disturbed me. Materialism permeated the culture, and class-consciousness kept people divided. It seemed wrong to me that there were so many poor people in a nation with so much wealth. In particular, the concept of medical care for indigent patients puzzled me; I had not realized there were Americans without medical insurance. In Germany, all patients had some kind of insurance and were treated equally irrespective of their insurance plans. (This is not to deny that, typically, the chairman of a medical department in Germany would also have the privilege of treating private patients whom he would charge directly for his services.) In America, indigent patients received treatment as a form of charity. The maternity wards at the Chicago Lying-in Hospital took some indigent patients, and, in addition, the Hospital also ran an obstetrical clinic in the Stockyard district where residents treated patients without charge. Some other institutions offered comparable services; for example, the Presbyterian Hospital in Chicago ran a home-delivery service in which residents delivered babies in patients' homes. These services were characterized by good supervision and tight organization, and the quality of care was quite similar to that received by private patients.

Especially striking was the division between white people and African-Americans at that time. At Missouri Baptist Hospital, the dining room for African-Americans was off in the back of the building, separate from the main dining room. St. Louis was traditionally a borderline city between North and South; whites did not disguise their prejudices, and blacks appeared not to question their second-class status.

Even in Chicago, a northern city, racial discrimination was the norm in many aspects of community life. At our hospital, members of the medical staff and nurses were diligent about maintaining high standards of treatment for all, but nevertheless, the wards in our hospital were segregated. Outpatient care was carried out in two separate offices, the east office for private patients and the west office for indigent patients. In the west office, residents took care of patients under the supervision of the more senior medical staff. In the east office, senior medical staff carried out the medical care and residents were observers. The in-patient care was also segregated. The second and third floors were for indigent patients and the fourth floor, for private patients. Interestingly enough, if a white woman were married to an African-American, she would be put in the ward with African-Americans, and not with white patients.

I will never forget the reaction of my superior one day just outside the open doorway of a room in one of the wards for indigent patients. Inside the room was an African-American woman who had recently given birth and appeared haggard, with uncombed hair and no make-up, and for some reason, she was standing on a bed.

My superior turned to me and said, "I hate blacks."

His words left me speechless. I had grown up understanding that all people were equal in the eyes of God, as my religion had taught me. Racial prejudice was something shocking to me.

After Fereshteh joined me and took up her training at the hospital, we often ate together in the staff dining room. At the University of Chicago, whites and blacks did not eat in separate dining rooms, but they nevertheless rarely mixed. On several occasions, I entered the dining room and spotted Fereshteh sitting at a table with African-Americans. Being sensitive to the norms of our environment, I discreetly pointed out to her that it was not customary for a white woman to sit with non-whites and urged her to respect the custom.

"But they are so nice to me," she said. "Why shouldn't I sit with them?"

She did not understand the deep historical reasons behind the custom and the intentions of my urging. I felt uncomfortable, being in the position of trying to impose upon her a behavior that I, too, thought was not right.

In all honesty, I must admit that it was hard for me to reconcile those attitudes of racial prejudice, so common in the U.S. at the time, with the fact that Americans were generally good-hearted people, ready to give to others and keen to devote volunteer efforts to so many worthy causes. And here was a quality that eventually made me think hard about my own culture and its sense of values.

In Chicago, I learned that the impulse to philanthropy was not restricted to special individuals but was a widespread sense of obligation, shared by a great many people in all walks of life. I learned about grass-roots movements, voluntarism, endowments, and the notion of giving back to the community. I learned about the importance of people in American society—the concept that one does not live only for oneself and one's family, but that we all have a responsibility to look out for one another in whatever ways we could. The very idea of community, in this sense of people working together for the collective good, made a big impression on me.

I had not been brought up with these ideals, and at the time, they struck me as new, or at least foreign to what I knew. Later in my life, as I investigated the backgrounds of my culture and the Islamic religion, I discovered that the concept of charitable giving to public institutions and other forms of private and public generosity were in fact fundamental values. The many endowments existing in the Middle East, as well as the mosques, cemeteries, orphanages, bridges, and other public institutions—even public baths—are witness to the Muslim tradition of philanthropy, our long-held value of giving and providing for the good of society. These values are expressed in the Islamic concepts of *waghf*, *sadaghah*, and *isar*. For a number of reasons, however, these virtuous habits and norms of behavior were not promoted during the most recent centuries by the governments and the religious leadership of the Islamic world, and they fell into neglect. (See Appendix C for a discussion of *waghf*, *sadaghah*, and *isar*.)

The political system of the United States reflects the nation's competitive spirit and the power of people in shaping the public face of American society. For me, it was a particularly exciting experience to live through the campaign and election of John F. Kennedy to the presidency in 1960. Kennedy was a youthful, vigorous leader, and his victory manifested the optimism in American society at that time.

Americans respect humanity, value social justice, and set great store by individual and public opinion. These ideals, I discovered, are also inherent in the heritage of Islam, reaching back across the centuries to the early period of Islamic history. That heritage is a source of common ground, giving me utmost confidence that American values and Islamic tradition are thoroughly compatible.

When I returned to Iran in 1963, it was a true homecoming. I had completed my education and training, and I was ready to transplant my career back to my homeland. I was now a well-trained physician, full of self-confidence and eager to become an agent of change in my own country. I saw myself as a technocrat, like my distant relative, Engineer Sedehi. My country had paid for my education abroad, and it was my ambition to repay my debt: to work for my people and help Iranian medicine make up for lost time in the progress of modern science. Wealth did not interest me; I only wanted to make a difference. And unlike most of my cohorts who returned home thoroughly secularized, I was still a practicing Muslim who valued and cherished his ancestral culture, and believed that modern science and technical progress were compatible with the Truth of Islam.

In my heart, I was also still an Iranian. I took home with me my Iranian wife and our baby daughter who was Iranian by heritage but part-American in her citizenship. Although I was not conscious of it at the time, I, too, was part-American, or at least part-Western—in my professional standards, my approach to knowledge and work, and my outlook on many aspects of life. While my long sojourn in the West had strengthened my character, the ways in which my intellectual development had changed me would eventually cause me to cast a critical eye on many patterns of my own society.

Fereshteh and Manya flew back to Iran from Chicago in February 1963, a week or so ahead of me. I had little to do in the meantime except for making sure that our Chevrolet Impala was properly shipped home. With my wife and baby now gone and my residency finished, I quickly got bored and felt the painful irony of loneliness amid crowds of people in a big city. Just before my own departure, I found myself alone in Washington, D.C., and decided to take advantage of the opportunity to visit the Jefferson Memorial. I had read about Jefferson, his leadership and especially his intellectual contribution to the foundation of American democracy. I pictured him as a spiritual, humane, liberal-minded man who loved freedom, and I very much wanted to see his memorial.

It was a cold, winter day, around sunset, and I was the only person wandering the memorial grounds. I was immediately taken by the sight. The small building, which was modeled after the Pantheon in Rome, is a beautiful work of architecture, and the imposing statue of America's third president is itself moving. However, it was when I started reading the inscriptions on the Memorial walls that I had the most profound reaction. They were quotations from the Declaration of Independence and other seminal documents that Jefferson had written, and they included these words:

"I have sworn upon the altar of God eternal hostility against every form of tyranny over the mind of man. ...

"We hold these truths to be self-evident: that all men are created equal, that they are endowed by their Creator with certain inalienable rights, among these are life, liberty, and the pursuit of happiness ...

"I am not an advocate for frequent changes in laws and constitutions, but laws and institutions must go hand in hand with the progress of the human mind. As that becomes more developed, more enlightened, as new discoveries are made, new truths discovered and manners and opinions change, with the change of circumstances, institutions must advance also to keep pace with the times."

While reading Jefferson's words, I felt drops of tears fall from my eyes. I could not stop them. I don't know if it was the words and the ideas they represented, or the realization that I was leaving the United States after my years of internship and residency, my marriage and the birth of my first child, but suddenly I felt overwhelmed by emotion. I have always remembered and respected those words of Jefferson's.

They expressed the ideals to which I returned twenty-two years later, when I left Iran permanently.

I did not stay long in Washington. I drove to New York in time to drop off my car for shipping to Iran. Finally, I packed my bags and left America.

CHAPTER SIX
Welcome Home

I returned home to Iran filled with enthusiasm for repaying my debt to the country that had sent me abroad for thirteen years of first-rate medical training. A secure position awaited me, and I happily began my work as an attending physician in obstetrics and gynecology at both the Nemazee Hospital and another hospital in Shiraz, the Saadi Hospital. Fereshteh and I, along with Baby Manya, settled into a villa within a compound that was originally built to house the American physicians who served on the Nemazee Hospital's attending staff in its early years.

An American advisory board, based in the U.S., had helped set up the new hospital's departments and establish a school for training the nursing staff. The board included, among others, Dr. Charles A. Janeway, then Professor and Chairman of the Pediatrics Department at the Harvard Medical School, and Dr. Nicholson J. Eastman, Professor and Chairman of the Department of Obstetrics and Gynecology at The Johns Hopkins University School of Medicine. I felt proud to be following in the footsteps of such distinguished physicians, and excited to play a role in developing what we all expected to be a first-class hospital in Iran, modeled after the most progressive and dynamic teaching hospitals in America.

The hospital's evolution in the late 1950s and early 1960s coincided with an ambitious project, championed by the shah, to develop a high-level academic institution aimed at training teachers for Iran's universities. The shah had discussed his idea during a visit to the United States and engaged a team of specialists from the University of Pennsylvania to develop a detailed plan. The shah's government approved the team's recommendations and began applying them to the University of Shiraz, with the support of the Pennsylvania team, and the university was renamed Pahlavi University (after the family name of the shah). The existence of a first-rate hospital next door to the university's medical school made for a natural marriage, and soon the Nemazee Hospital became affiliated with Pahlavi University. Hospital staff were given academic appointments and invited to teach students and train residents in both Nemazee and Saadi Hospitals. Thus it was that I became a professor in the university's medical school—a position that I felt honored to occupy. It seemed to me that I had the ideal job, and I saw myself as an agent of change, helping Iran's attempt to catch up with the West in medical science and healthcare delivery.

The Nemazee Hospital was clean, well organized, and supplied with state-of-the-art medical and surgical equipment. It was originally envisioned to treat private and paying patients, and it attracted affluent patients from a wide area both within and outside of Iran, especially the Persian Gulf States.

Saadi Hospital, in contrast, was a much more modest institution. It had been the major teaching hospital of Shiraz University previously, and it catered to many indigent patients from the community and surrounding villages, who were treated by medical students and resident staff. The Saadi Hospital was financed from the meager budget of the university's medical school and lacked the private-foundation resources that made the Nemazee Hospital into such an advanced facility by the time of my arrival.

Of course, I was not the only Western-trained professional in Shiraz. A sizable contingent of fresh, young intellectuals had returned home to start their medical practice, take engineering jobs, and pursue other advanced career paths. Some of them took positions in the newly established faculties of Pahlavi University, such as the engineering, agriculture, and other departments.

Those of us who came back from America received the red-carpet treatment. The government and all the people looked to us as the cream of the crop. Anyone who could speak with an American accent was special. Young men who wore the style of jacket then considered fashionable in America, with two slits on the sides rather than one in the back (European style), were immediately recognizable. Those who had bought their jackets in Europe were appreciated, too, but we who had trained in America were the "golden boys" among Iran's newest physicians and technocrats.

My career in Shiraz started out well. Nemazee was run much in the fashion of an American hospital. The concept of institutional care for patients was new in Iran, and Nemazee Hospital showed the way for physicians in other parts of the country. We pioneered the routine of the annual check-up in Iran, for example—something that was in vogue in many other parts of the world. Patients from Tehran flocked to Shiraz for their annual check-ups. Soon the practice was adopted in other cities, as physicians and clinics strove to keep their business local.

I immediately felt at home in my work. In a certain sense, it seemed like an extension of my Chicago residency. I found it easy to communicate with my peers and knew that they respected my professional skills. I had a great deal of freedom in my teaching assignments and patient care, and felt that I had the full support of my institution as I practiced medicine and taught students according to the standards to which I had grown accustomed. I enjoyed caring for my patients and took delight in the opportunity to train students and residents.

With many of my peers, the younger members of our faculty and hospital staff, I shared lofty professional goals. First and foremost, we wanted to teach students and residents the newest medical knowledge and professional skills—but more: we wanted to change their attitude toward the care of their patients and focus their attention on the results of their work. We wanted them to be responsible for the outcome of their medical care and participate in the pains and joys of their patients. Within our profession, we wanted to de-emphasize monetary gain as the driving motivation and instill in our colleagues the humanistic goals of our profession's traditions. We wanted our students and residents to be conscious of the rights of patients and become their advocates. And for at least the first couple of years, I felt we were making a difference; I felt myself a part of something big.

Our tasks in Shiraz fitted into a national mission that was not new. Ever since the early part of the twentieth century, our government had sought to bring modernization to Iran and to make our country prosperous. By and large, educated intellectuals and technocrats believed that the policies of the government and the practices of our developing educational, scientific, and healthcare institutions were on the right course, even if progress sometimes seemed slow and followed a path of many ups and downs. I was no exception to this prevailing opinion, believing in the grand mission and accepting the assumptions of the national program.

There was a definite esprit de corps among physicians, especially those of us trained in the U.S. Our medical school was known around the world, and our Department of Obstetrics and Gynecology was one of the strongest units within the school. In fact, our department, along with that at Tel Aviv University in Israel, was one of the two best gynecology departments in the world outside the United States. Our students had the highest rates of acceptance for international students taking the worldwide exam to qualify for a residency in the U.S, the Educational Commission for Foreign Medical Graduates (ECFMG) examination.

Fereshteh and I were frequently invited to evening parties within the Nemazee compound and in the circles of prominent personalities in the city, where we met and dined with such notable people as the governor, the commander of the army division in Fars, and the head of the Justice Department. I was surprised and thrilled to be in such company, but at the same time I was at a loss with them; I did not speak their language of politics, power, and privilege—and I guess they were also at a loss with me. Fereshteh, however, quickly found her way in the social life of Shiraz. In many ways, we began to enjoy the lifestyle of the upwardly mobile; soon we had a servant and a nanny, and we hired a cook for our parties.

Despite all the benefits of my position, it did not take long for me to become aware of a certain tension within our ranks between the mostly-younger physicians who were newly appointed to Nemazee Hospital and the "old guard" who had previously held teaching staff positions in the Shiraz University Medical School. The younger group identified themselves with Dr. Torab Mehra, the head and administrator of the Nemazee Hospital; the older group identified themselves with Dr. Zbih-o-lah Ghorban, the founder and then-current head of the Medical School, and Dr. Suratgar, the previous chancellor of Shiraz University. Usually, the two groups treated each other with a kind of cordial distrust, but at times it erupted into open warfare that spilled over to the academic staff and paralyzed the university.

The discord among us reached the attention of persons in the Ministry of Education, the Ministry of Court in Tehran, and eventually the shah himself. These officials eventually grew so concerned about the future of Pahlavi University, their academic crown jewel, that they decided to appoint a skilled, top-level administrator as the chancellor of the university with full authority to put an end to the rivalries and bring peace to the institution. The job fell to Iran's former Prime Minister, Assadolah Alam. Beyond re-establishing peace, Alam's mission was to bring about reforms throughout the university and advance it to the standards of the best in American higher education.

It was a worthy idea, and Alam meant well, but his methods soon became disruptive. Alam brought with him the traditional culture of the government in Iran, with a top-heavy management system and many bureaucratic channels that were all administered and controlled by a few trusted people at the top. Centralized decision-making brought to an end the autonomy previously enjoyed by the departments and other university units. The chancellor's office and the various deans assumed a degree of power that they had not had before. If we wanted something for our department—to create a new faculty position, requisition office furniture, order equipment for the hospital, or almost anything else—we had to seek support in the office of the Vice-Chancellor and Alam's chief of staff, Amir Mottaghi, and then wait for a decision before we got what we wanted. In many circumstances, however, it was unclear exactly who was the official responsible for making this or that decision.

As time went on, confusion turned into disillusionment, and disillusionment into inertia. The entire university system fell victim to a kind of paralysis that was especially deadening to those of us who were American-trained, young, enthusiastic, and active with new ideas. We had no patience for bureaucratic games, no taste for the kinds of corrupt power plays that began to dominate our lives; we wanted to accomplish great things, bring our profession and our country up to the highest standards—and we felt thwarted. When our ally, Dr. Mehra, resigned from his position as chief hospital administrator, it signaled that the situation had taken a serious downturn. Dr. Mehra was a highly capable, American-trained physician whose ambition was to make Nemazee Hospital the best medical institution in the Middle East, and now he had succumbed to forces beyond himself.

Nevertheless, I continued to work hard. I expected my students and residents to meet the highest standards of learning and practice, and I gave my best to my patients—including a large number of indigent patients whom I treated. In fact, the vast majority of my patients and many of my students came from the ranks of the urban and rural poor. Compared with people from the more affluent and educated classes, I found the people from the lower socio-economic classes generally honest and sincere, grateful for my services and willing to follow my instructions without questioning my judgment.

Eventually, however, the institutional atmosphere deteriorated as Chancellor Alam's authoritarian methods took their toll on my daily life. What had begun as a dream job turned into a nightmare. The university and the hospital no longer seemed to provide an atmosphere in which my department could achieve the kind of progress I wished to see. The environment became increasingly oppressive to me, especially since I was not being fairly compensated for my efforts. Despite the fact that I worked as a full-time professor, my income, at best, was barely adequate to support my family as it grew to include three children. I was unable to save money for the future or buy a home. Doctors at Nemazee Hospital were aware that physicians in private practice earned considerably more money than we did. We tried to introduce a plan that would enable us to treat private patients at designated times after hours and supplement our salaries with the receipts from such patients, but the hospital staff turned this plan down, despite our warnings that, if this opportunity were not available, Nemazee would eventually lose its medical staff to private practice. In these circumstances I lost my enthusiasm, and my idealism gave way to the realities of life. I had to be mindful of my responsibilities toward my family and my desire to provide for their future, and so I looked around for a new opportunity, hoping for one that would provide me with challenging work and higher pay. I found such an opportunity at the University of Isfahan. I hoped the academic and professional climate would be better there.

Thus it was that, in 1967, our family moved to my town of origin, beautiful Isfahan. There I took a part-time position at the university and, contrary to the situation in Shiraz, was permitted to set up a private practice. I settled into my new life quickly, teaching students, training residents, and carrying on a reasonably successful practice of my own. At the same time, I did not neglect the obligation I felt toward the community, and so I gave a great deal of service to indigent patients at the university hospital. I became very active in the Department of Obstetrics and Gynecology, and my career advanced when a new Chancellor of the University, Dr. Ghasem Mo'tamedi, appointed me to the position of Vice-Dean of the Medical School.

Dr. Mo'tamedi's appointment as chancellor had resulted from a major change in the laws governing the administration of universities across Iran. Previously, the administrative bodies of the universities at all levels were elected from within the university; that had been true since the inception of the University of Tehran in 1913. Departmental heads elected the dean, and the Council of Deans would nominate three candidates for the chancellorship, from among whom the shah would appoint one. The system was changed around the time of my return from Chicago; thereafter, chancellors were appointed directly by the shah and the chancellors appointed deans. Thus, academic faculties lost a lot of their power.

Chancellor Mo'tamedi had been trained in the U.S. and, following the Americans' pattern, he tended to stay out of our way at the beginning. As faculty within our own departments, we had a fair amount of self-determination. At least, that was the situation immediately after my arrival in Isfahan. To my great disappointment, however, the situation turned gradually in the same negative directions I had experienced in Shiraz. The same pyramidal power structure developed into a highly authoritarian system of university governance. To make matters worse, there was no effective procedure for expressing grievances, and the university administration discouraged and sabotaged every attempt by the faculty to set up such a system. For example, if we were experiencing delays or difficulties in requisitioning supplies for the hospital, or if a faculty member felt he was being treated unfairly in the process of promotions, we had no instruments for seeking a just resolution—no ombudsman, no committee to hold a hearing on our case, and generally no channel through which to reach those at the top of the pyramid who reserved for themselves the power to make judgments. If a person did manage to voice a complaint with his superior, nothing happened.

The administration steadily became more rigid, and after five or six years, Chancellor Mo'tamedi's real attitude became clear. His loyalty was to the shah, and he interpreted every issue that arose not exclusively in terms of the university's interest, but also in terms of how the Iranian government saw things. For example, he once complained to me that when he went to Tehran to meet with the shah's sister,

Princess Fatima, who was the head of our university's Board of Regents, he had to spend much of his time justifying his decisions and undoing the supposed damage caused by staff members' complaints to the princess. And whenever the princess came to Isfahan to visit the university, Dr. Mo'tamedi required professors and administrators to leave their jobs and go to the airport to welcome her. To Dr. Mo'tamedi, every policy, every decision, had relevance to his position within the larger political system. As he grew more and more dictatorial, a joke that went around the faculty referred to our institution as the "University of Isfahan Affiliated with Dr. Mo'tamedi." Professors felt he no longer fully supported them or respected their decisions, and morale declined throughout the university.

Once again, as in Shiraz, those of us trained in the freer environment of the West became frustrated. We continued to work hard in our teaching and our medical practice, but the institutional atmosphere kept us feeling inadequate and stymied us in our efforts to do our best work. It was especially disheartening to see the climate of subservience and toadyism develop in the relations between the top university officials and the officials of the shah's government. The latter, of course, were in a position to bestow financial favors upon the university—or to withhold them. I had first seen something of this syndrome early in my career in Shiraz, where the evening parties provided a way of gaining the favor of officials; the guest lists for these parties became a kind of entry card for the politically ambitious, and university people could enhance their standing with public officials by inviting the latter to their homes. I did not approve of such behavior then, recognizing it as a shameless effort to curry favor, but it was not until I had lived and worked in Iran for some years that I fully understood how demeaning and harmful this behavior was to the system in which I worked. Others did not seem to mind these relationships with the superiors and dignitaries because they felt that it was a part of our culture. And it worked—the dignitaries took notice of those who showed up and those who treated them with particular deference, and they returned the compliments by showing more trust in those people. It was a perpetual and self-feeding habit in Iranian custom.

Dr. Mo'tamedi carried his self-advancing behavior to an extreme. More and more, he isolated himself from the rest of us. He himself gradually became alienated from the university community and focused his attention toward Tehran. Shortly before the Islamic Revolution, he moved to the capital to work on the political staff of Prime Minister Amir-Abbas Hoveida.

Dr. Mo'tamedi's evolution from a skilled, democratically oriented administrator to a self-interested dictator fit a pattern that was by now, unfortunately, familiar to me. In Shiraz, Chancellor Alam, the shah's close friend and confidante, had also failed in his efforts to keep his university on the dynamic course with which it had started and, instead, turned it into an institution that resisted change and discouraged progress. He himself expressed his frustration with the university's stagnation in his 1966 commencement address.

Slowly, I became aware that the problem lay not only in the political and administrative structures of our institutions, but also in the undercurrents of Iranian society more broadly speaking. People wanted to be recognized and respected by others, even if the respect was superficial. Beginning in the mid-1970s, it grew clear that the malaise we felt in the university was shared by nearly everybody in Iran, rich and poor, educated and less educated. All had lost trust in the government and were hoping for a major change in the political system.

Change, however, can be frightening. Everybody in Iran wanted progress, modernity, democracy, and social and economic justice, but people were afraid of change, especially if they themselves were expected to change. Patients wanted the most modern medical services, but at the same time, many of them resisted any personal responsibility required by such services and hesitated to follow the directions given to them by the attending physician. If he recommended taking a certain drug or undergoing surgery, they often had to consult others in the circle of their family and friends before they would agree to the doctor's suggestions. They wanted to get well, but they did not have enough trust to implement the recommendation without consulting others first. It is true that they had no recourse if the physician was negligent, but their cautious approach stemmed primarily from a basic lack of confidence in people outside their families, even people they knew to be experts.

The other side of the coin was that once the credibility of a physician was established in public, people would trust him or her blindly and follow his recommendations religiously. Word of mouth was important, as people tended to trust their family and friends who recommended a doctor with whom they had had a good experience.

Doctor/patient trust is always a sensitive issue, but it was especially so in Iran, compared with my experience in the United States. First-time visits were particularly difficult, as patients were often unsure about how far to trust the attending physician. For example, it often happened that a patient came to my ob/gyn office presenting herself with general complaints and vague symptoms unrelated, as it turned out, to what she really wanted to be treated for. She might complain of lower abdominal pain, or just feeling unwell. I would have to go through an investigative process to get to the bottom of the problem. It was known that I had a substantial practice dealing with infertility, and in such cases it would become apparent to me in the course of taking a detailed history that, in fact, the patient was coming to me because she had been married for a long time without producing any children.

One time I asked a patient, a younger woman, why she had not told me straightforwardly why she came. She did not reply. Her mother, who was accompanying her on the office call, said, "Doctor, if she said she was infertile, her husband would divorce her."

Generally, younger women seemed shyer than older women. A young woman, typically one who was recently married, would walk into my private office behind her companion (usually her husband or her mother) and defer to that companion to respond to the doctor's medical questions. Older women, from the age of 40 or 50, that is, after their children had grown up, often tended to walk into my office ahead of their companion, and the companion (usually the husband) would be the timid one. It eventually occurred to me that this phenomenon, which I saw mainly among lower class, less-educated Iranians, signaled a change in the relationship between husband and wife over the span of their married life. In the earlier years of marriage, the husband is the dominant person in the family. He lives his life as he chooses and is often absent from family life. The wife takes care of the children; she feeds them, clothes them, takes them to the doctor and to school, and so on. Thus the children grow up with their mother. As the years pass, their father typically becomes less socially attractive to his circle of friends and co-workers; eventually, he spends less time with them and more time at home. There he discovers that, over the years, mother and children have grown close and the mother has in fact become the dominant player in the household. She might even treat her husband with contempt and disrespect, consciously or unconsciously, in revenge for many years of suffering earlier in their marriage. The husband now finds that he has to live by her rules, so to speak, and when he accompanies his wife to the doctor's office, he enters timidly and, in a sense, begs the doctor to give his wife good care so she will become healthy and normal again, and treat him with respect and kindness in his old age. Thus, older women who came to me for treatment did so as the established authority figure in their household.

In any event, as I learned, it was one thing for me, a physician with the advantage of a Western education and a modern mind-set, to offer my knowledge and skills to the service of the broad population of my community; it was another thing for those whom I served to understand and accept the nature of modern medicine. Modern medicine depends on not just prescribing a magic pill for whatever ails the patient, but, at the basic level, a high degree of candor on the patient's part so that the physician can achieve an informed, accurate diagnosis. This, in turn, must be followed by sufficient trust to accept and follow the doctor's instructions. Cultural taboos and reticence on the part of patients are not helpful to this relationship.

And still, despite the challenges, I took much satisfaction in treating my patients. Most of them accepted me and trusted me, and were loyal and honest in their dealings with me. Whenever I delivered a baby or helped a patient recover from an infection or any other ailment, I understood why I had entered the medical profession, and why I continued to stay and work in my home country. The problems in my institutional life faded into the background whenever a patient left my office with a smile and a thank-you, and whenever I witnessed the immediate love of a mother holding her newborn infant close for the first time.

One thing that surprised me about my work in Iran from the very beginning was the challenge of teaching amid a student culture that was unlike what I had gone through in the West. I constantly had to remind myself that the structure of learning among Iranians was different, that the students had developed habits and expectations different from those of German and American students. Students had to be taught a sense of responsibility for their actions, and they also had to be taught the importance of teamwork in the medical environment. If I wanted to teach the skills of surgery, for example, I had to be constantly aware of these differences. While performing surgery in Chicago, I had relied on the nurses and assistants around me to know, and even anticipate, my every move. If I needed a scalpel, a retractor, or scissors, I had only to say the word and reach my hand out—and the tool would be in my hand instantly. In Iran, I had the hardest time teaching residents that if you have a retractor in your hand, no matter what happens, you must not let go of it. When I asked the nurse for scissors, the resident assistant would look at the nurse, reach for the scissors, and let the retractor fall. Teaching the most fundamental things became something for which I first had to retrain myself, in a way, in order to train my students and residents.

An incident that took place at the University of Isfahan sheds some light on another facet of the learning culture with which I was dealing. As in medical schools around the world, students were required to gather in the hospital for grand rounds and discussions of patients' conditions and progress. I met with my students at 8 a.m., a time that I made perfectly clear to all. It seemed that the students, however, were not quite sure that eight o'clock really meant eight o'clock. One day a student came running in at 8:15. We had already begun, of course, and his late arrival caused a short disruption.

The student excused himself, saying, "I'm sorry I'm late."

I said, "Okay, let's continue with the rounds."

We did so. At the end of the rounds, the student approached and asked me to cross out the mark next to his name on my register, signifying that he had been absent for the rounds. I said, okay, I would just put a notation next to his name that said he had come late. He insisted that I should cross out the mark entirely so his record would be unblemished. We spent some uncomfortable minutes arguing about the matter before he gave it up, and I suspect that he never quite understood why I could not grant him the favor of removing the mark beside his name.

It was a moment that typified the difference between the personal habits of discipline and professionalism that I had learned, and a certain syndrome that I have come to realize exists deep within the behavioral patterns of Iranians. It's not that Iranians are incapable of personal discipline and behaving according to norms Americans take for granted in their professional life; it's that, over the centuries, Iranians have become conditioned to these ways of behavior, these patterns of orienting themselves to their work, that run counter to the expectations of a modern society.

The student was conditioned to thinking it would be an easy thing for me to forgive his tardiness that morning because forgiveness is a big element in the Iranian ethos. In some respects, this is an admirable trait; certainly forgiveness is a quality that is valued in many of the world's religions, including not only Islam but Christianity as well.

Before anything can be forgiven, however, one first has to define and clarify the nature and extent of the guilt, wrong action, aggression, or material damage. One has to know what he is forgiving before giving his or her forgiveness. Blanket forgiveness does not serve any purpose except to encourage the wrongdoer to continue doing wrong without fear of serious consequences. Among Iranians, it is expected that if you make a mistake, even one that harms another person, that person will forgive you just for the sake of forgiveness—and perhaps even feel sorry for you for having made the mistake.

This becomes especially true in cases of mistakes that are financially costly. Once while I was driving my car, a motorcycle crashed into me from the side. I got out of my car, uninjured, and saw that the other driver was also not seriously hurt. He stood beside his wrecked motor cycle as a crowd gathered around.

People from the crowd came up to me and said, "Sir, he is a poor man. Please forgive him and let him go."

In principle, I had no problem with that. I said, "I will forgive him, but first let the police come and decide who is at fault and how much damage has been done. If they decide that it was his fault, I will forgive his liability for financial damage."

After a short time, the police arrived and made their assessment. They judged the motorcycle driver to be at fault and estimated the cost of repairing my car.

I told the other driver, "I am ready to forgive you that amount of money."

He said, "Sir, I'm not a poor man. I don't ask for your generosity and don't require the charity of your forgiving me."

The moral to this story—and also to that of the student who came late to grand rounds—is that people expect forgiveness without always clearly understanding what is to be forgiven. The student did not seem to grasp the underlying principle about the importance of personal discipline and promptness; the crowd gathering at the crash scene did not know that the motorcycle driver was financially capable of paying for the damages, and they assumed he was entitled to forgiveness of his debt.

I brought up this subject on various occasions with my students and residents. The discussion was an eye-opener for them. When I explained the point, they seemed to accept the importance of connecting the concept of responsibility to those of guilt and forgiveness, and they gave me the impression that they would apply those definitions in their personal and professional lives in the future.

I have known many people in the U.S. and Europe who are also capable of forgiveness, but they expect each other to assume responsibility for their own acts and be ready to make amends for their mistakes. A person who commits an error can ask that the slate, in his case, be wiped clean, but it does not happen automatically. That basic element of responsibility is what lies at the heart of the West's success in developing the highly advanced technological societies that we know in North America and Europe.

In time, I came to understand that, despite the strong desire among Iranians to acquire modern skills and technologies, and to develop their country into a showcase of modern progress and achievement in Asia, there are some cultural handicaps and traditional habits that make it difficult for them to live up to their intentions. I believe these handicaps have nothing to do with what I might call the "deep" cultural roots of Iranians, and certainly not with anything in the nature of the Islamic religion; rather, the handicaps spring from the agrarian lifestyle that molded the society's ethics and norms, shaping the people's interrelationships in ways that best served their traditional lives. The cultural habits grew up in the course of Iran's history over the past several centuries and have their counterparts in neighboring Muslim countries.

In other words, modernism is not native to Iran and the neighboring countries. The agrarian ethic worked well for a very long time, and when modernism was imported into the region—in the form of institutions, technology, equipment, tools, and so on—the people of the region resisted changes to their ethics and culture. They resented being told that their attitudes, habits, and norms were not compatible with modernization and industrialization.

Similar habits and cultural norms characterized European societies before the Renaissance. However, the Europeans had the luxury of undergoing the process of adaptation from an agrarian to an industrial culture over a period of several centuries, whereas the people of the Middle East had less than one century for this process. In addition, the Middle Eastern societies had to find their way into the modern era under the burden of colonialism and the imposition of a materialistic European worldview.

For me, the lesson was one that I would fully understand only after I emigrated from Iran and had the time and the distance to reflect upon my experiences. During the twenty years that I lived and worked in my homeland, the mentality of my countrymen remained, in some respects, puzzling to me. There seemed to be a cultural gap even in my own family. Obviously, I loved and trusted my family, and I was proud of my religion and my ancestry. However, I could not help but be critical of some aspects of indigenous culture and habits. There were numerous occasions when I, in another room, heard my mother and my sister talking amiably, laughing and having a good time, and then, as soon as I entered the room, the tone of their voices changed and the thread of their conversation was lost. They were conscious of my presence and controlled their conversation in front of me. They meant it as a sign of respect for me, but it made me mindful of a distance between them and me; I had a sense of something between them that did not exist when I was listening to their conversation from the adjoining room. It was not they who had changed, of course—it was I. Thirteen years abroad, thirteen years of intense exposure to different cultures, had transformed my way of thinking and my outlook on the world. I had come back to Iran hoping to bring what I knew to bear on the problems and possibilities of my own people, and I had found that I could not bridge the gulf separating us.

Eventually, I recognized the importance of culture, philosophy, and working habits in the challenge of modernization. These are some of the biggest problems Iranians, and Middle Easterners in general, face. For my students in Shiraz and Isfahan, it was not that they didn't want to learn from me; on the contrary, they were more than eager to discover the most up-to-date medical procedures and acquire skills at the highest possible level, but because of their culture, they did not grasp the need to make changes in their attitude and their way of life, and they resisted my attempts to get them to see things as I saw them.

It is now clear to me that what I witnessed as failures in the transformation of the universities and the medical profession were symptomatic of the larger problem in Iran during the 1960s and 1970s: the failure of social and economic modernization as a whole. Over the years since, I've given a lot of thought to the causes of these failures, asking myself what were the factors that prevented the well-meaning technocrats from bringing about the modernization of Iranian society? Above all, I believe the answer has to do with the masses who were the subjects of the transformation we yearned to bring about. The nation's cultural traits had taken hundreds of years to develop—the overarching religious values, the family ties, and, last but not least, the sense of honor and self-respect among Iranians, a people who were very conscious of their past glory and saw the evidence of their historical achievement in their architecture, art, literature, poetry, and philosophy. If Iran was to modernize and catch up with the industrial revolution that had begun in Europe after the Renaissance, it could not do so without the participation of the masses; and the masses could not have been expected to participate in the effort if it meant they had to forsake their deeply ingrained cultural values. This was the crucial element that the Iranian modernizers failed to understand.

Ever since the early part of the nineteenth century, Iran's leaders had opted for what they believed to be the "fast track" to modernization. They thought it would be possible to set the policy course from above and pull the masses into the future—to impose change upon a largely passive public, in other words. They reasoned that the masses would have no choice but to accept their fate. This turned out to be unsuccessful and, indeed, highly counterproductive in the long run.

Most importantly, Iran's elites failed to understand that the masses in a society count; they need to be treated with dignity and their values, respected. Iranians, including the poor from the villages and the urban working classes, have always carried a deep pride about themselves and their culture. They take strength in their emotional ties to each other and benefit from the support and guidance they receive from their extended families. They have pride, too, in their culture and their value system. But none of this means that Iranians in general have stood opposed to progress and modernization. What caused their resistance was not the goal of advancing their society in technological and material terms but, rather, the feeling of being pushed too hard, too fast, by governments that were corrupt and submissive to the Western powers; governments that distrusted, and did not appear to care about the needs, of everyday Iranian citizens.

Accordingly, a much better governmental strategy would have been the slower approach of persuasion. If Iran's leadership in the nineteenth and twentieth centuries had not taken such a paternalistic approach and had sought instead to educate and persuade the masses, they might have succeeded. The masses are not stupid; they are not blind to the benefits of progress—but it is necessary to win them over, to help them accept the necessity of change, recognize what they have to gain from modernization, and be prepared to make sacrifices in order to achieve progress. People need to understand why they are being asked to replace longstanding cultural habits with new ones. In short, the "fast track" is not the way to the future; progress and modernity can come only with time, with patience for the inevitable ups and downs, successes and temporary failures.

Instead of achieving the desired progress toward modernity, the practices of Iran's leaders backfired, resulting in a reactionary revolution based on a narrowly religious worldview and value system. I witnessed how the Islamic Revolution took shape in Iran at the end of the 1970s, and I saw and felt the power of the masses. The transformation of Iran is a long-term process that is likely to take several generations before it finds its ultimate form, but there is no question that the current direction, which is expressed in a self-consciously anti-Western, anti-secular ideology, has developed as a reaction against the failure of the pro-Western, secular, and anti-democratic realities that preceded the revolution.

Looking back at it all, I now understand that, to bring about change, to bring progress to a community, two components are needed. First, it is essential that there be a group of dedicated experts, a qualified and sincere cadre of trained professionals with the capability of analyzing what needs to be changed and addressing the issues through systematic, concrete policies. The proponents of modernization in Iran grasped this; that was why they sent so many young people of my generation, and those immediately before and after us, overseas to learn and to gain skills.

Second, however, it is equally important to have, on the receiving end, a community of people who are willing to accept change and undergo the process of adapting to new cultural habits, new ways of thinking, behaving, and going about their daily lives. This is what was lacking, and the government failed to see the problem. Our political leaders assumed they could impose change from above, helped by our cadre of professionals and technocrats, and hoped that the masses would somehow accept the new ways. Subsequent history has made it abundantly clear that this approach was inefficient and mistaken. In the end, the masses resisted, revolted, and turned radically away from everything the modernists, technocrats and progressive leaders in the society stood for. Looking back upon my 20 years of work and sincere efforts in Iran, I realize now that I might have fallen into the same wrong assumption that one could bring about modernization from above. To be fair, I must also say that all of my efforts, as well as those of many thousands of intellectuals and technocrats, have not been without positive effect. We can say that we at least kept the hope and desire for progress alive and showed the way.

Social change must come from the bottom as much as it comes from the top. The value system of a community and the work ethic of the everyday citizen must be consistent with the task of modernization. It seems obvious to me that within the so-called Third World, and certainly within the Islamic countries, modernization requires that citizens come to agreement about the common cause, have trust in each other's abilities and competency, and accept both a sense of personal responsibility and a spirit of working together for the common good.

Modernization is also based on a philosophical foundation. Human rights, the authority of reason, the fallibility of all kinds of knowledge, the separation of church and state—these foundations are lacking in our tradition. Leaders and masses alike must have the courage to be critical of their past. They must allow themselves to rethink their social and ethical values, and keep an open mind toward new ideas. All must put in practice those standards of personal, social, and business ethics of which we spoke at the beginning of this book: honesty, reliability, hard work, fairness, teamwork, goal-orientedness, and self-sacrifice. Until the masses of a society come to a deep and honest understanding of this, true modernization will not succeed.

This concept is not quite as radical as it might seem. In Iran's case, the ethics and standards of social behavior to which I am referring do not have to be imported from outside the country. They exist amply within the framework of the indigenous culture. They stem from the religious teachings of Islam in its purest form and can be found in the nation's history, going back many centuries. To revive those values would shorten the path to modernization for the Iranian people.

* * *

I do not think that my enthusiasm and optimism upon returning to Iran in 1963 marked me as naive. I was young, and there seemed to be every reason for enthusiasm and optimism as I began my professional career. Certainly my experiences over the next two decades of work in Iran taught me some valuable lessons. Modernization takes time. Progress in any society generally advances in an irregular pattern, two steps forward, one step back, one step sideways, and so on. We can easily become impatient with the pace of progress. Perhaps that was what bothered me during the first fifteen or sixteen years of my work in Iran.

Yes, there were frustrations; there were setbacks. And yet, my work provided me with a comfortable living and gave me the satisfaction of knowing that I was doing my best to treat patients and train future physicians. I would probably have stayed in Iran for the rest of my days had the political system not taken a radical turn that eventually made it impossible for my colleagues and me to achieve our highest goals.

CHAPTER SEVEN
Resentment, Resistance, Revolution

On the first of February 1979, a chartered Air France jetliner approached Tehran, carrying Ayatollah Ruhollah Khomeini, along with his family, his aides and a number of clergymen close to the ayatollah, as well as an international entourage of news reporters. The Boeing 747 had taken off from Paris amid rumors and questions: Would Iranian officials allow the plane to land? Would the Iranian Air Force shoot it down? Air France had restricted the passenger load to one-half of the Jumbo Jet's capacity in case it had to turn around and fly back to Paris without refueling. Still awaiting approval to land, the pilots descended to an altitude of a few thousand feet and circled for twenty minutes. Finally, they made one more descent, straightened out, and touched the ground. The aircraft taxied to a deplaning area near a terminal, where a stairway was waiting, and came to a stop.

Moments later, the front passenger door opened and the ayatollah, an elderly man with a black turban and a long, white beard, stepped out, ushered by a flight attendant. He appeared frail as he slowly descended the stairs. At the bottom, he stood still while a group of young revolutionary activists, lined up in front of him, sang a song of welcome. This was something unusual for Iranians; it was not our custom to welcome somebody with song. Later, I learned that singing a song as a ceremonial welcoming gesture was a custom in communist countries. It was an ironic sign that even leftists were out in force to salute this religious leader who so many believed would be the savior of our country, now returning after more than fourteen years in exile.

Khomeini got into a sport utility vehicle of an American make and rode directly to Behesht-e Zahara, the city of Tehran's huge cemetery, where the victims of the resistance movement during the previous government, as well as the recent casualties of the revolution, were buried. An enormous crowd, perhaps five million supporters, engulfed the car. The people were rapturous, full of love and devotion toward the ayatollah, and they had to be pushed away for the car to make any progress. The motorcade inched along through the streets of Tehran, the pressure of the people so strong that, at one point, Khomeini fainted. At the cemetery, he paid homage to the martyrs of the Islamic Revolution and made a speech, now famous, accusing the shah of letting our cities go to ruins and making our cemeteries "flourish with the blood and bodies of our young people." He vowed to fight against anybody who tried to return the recently deposed shah to power. He encouraged everyone to "gather around one word" and revive Islam as the guide to our revolution. Khomeini's speech was delivered in person to 250,000 emotional listeners, and carried live on radio and television to many millions across the country.

Our family watched the events on TV at home in Isfahan, along with nearly everybody else in Iran. We sat on the edge of our chairs, listening to every word and watching with interest the ayatollah's every physical movement. The children and I were excited and enthusiastic, but my wise and farsighted wife Fereshteh was less excited and remained cautious in her reactions. She even appeared to have some immediate misgivings about the deposition of the shah, because she saw him as a modernist, and the ayatollah's return, because she saw him as a conservative and traditionalist with a potentially negative influence on the private and public life of Iranians.

What did we expect? The shah and his government had been overthrown—the shah who had hoped to catapult his country into the ranks of the twentieth century's advanced societies, who had spoken of Iran as "the Japan in Western Asia," but who had failed and, in failing, had become a harsh and unpopular ruler. It was not that the people hated their shah; Iranians had lived under the rule of monarchies for thousands of years and, by and large, respected the figure of the shah as their leader. As they became more familiar with modern European systems of government, however, Iranians came to expect more social justice, and by the 1970s they had become disappointed and frustrated with the government they were experiencing. To many, the solution to their frustration was to change the system by abolishing the monarchy.

In a sense, the shah was a tragic figure. He reigned for 37 years, and he was not always hated. He came to the throne as a young man intent on being a democratic monarch and was at first loved by his people. During the first 10 years of his reign, he kept the country together in the face of communist aggression from the north and the British pressures from the south. Things changed in 1953 after his return from exile and the overthrow of Mossadegh. The shah quelled the nationalistic uprising and became dictatorial, drawing his strength from the support of America and other Western countries. Over time, he became separated from his people and was surrounded by politicians who sheltered him from the truth. He developed grandiose plans for an industrialized and prosperous Iran, but the projects on which he embarked did not improve the conditions of his people. Toward the end of his reign, the economy was in shambles, with high inflation and massive capital flight.

Now he had been dethroned by a revolution from below, a revolution that would soon culminate in the assumption of power by a small circle of clerics led by the 78-year-old Grand Ayatollah Seyyed Ruhollah Khomeini.

To understand how Iran got to this point, it is necessary to take a few steps back in history. In the early years of the sixteenth century, the Safavid dynasty developed a stable social and governmental system built upon two separate powers: the shah and his government, on the one hand, and the hierarchy of the Islamic clergy. These powers supported each other mutually in a dual authority structure. It was an effective form of rule, accepted by all elements of Iranian society. The dual system functioned throughout the reign of the Safavids and continued in place through the dynasties that succeeded them in the eighteenth and nineteenth centuries.

During most of this lengthy period, the average Iranian had no appreciable contacts with the West; only a limited elite of tradesmen and official emissaries traveled to Europe or any other place far beyond the borders. The religious leaders and the religious hierarchy, in particular, did not see any need to inform themselves about the great scientific and technological advances sweeping across the Western world. They were content with their knowledge of medicine, astronomy, mathematics, philosophy, and geography as it had been introduced into Islamic teachings during the early centuries of Islam. Nor were the secular rulers interested in "rocking the boat" by introducing new ideas to their country, for they feared the reactions of their subjects and the influential clergymen. Up to the mid-nineteenth century, most Iranians remained unaware of the religious upheavals, political revolutions, and technological innovations that had transformed Europe ever since the Renaissance.

During the eighteenth century, Iran had nevertheless entered into an increasing number of trade agreements with Western companies, granting them lucrative and mostly unfair patents. Gradually, the political rivalries among the European powers spilled over to the Middle East, and the British, French, and Russian governments began to meddle in Iranian politics with the aim of gaining the advantage in trade and strategic influence. In their growing contacts with the Iranian governmental and commercial interests, the Europeans mostly ignored or bypassed the religious leadership, who were in fact the learned class and the opinion leaders among the Iranian masses.

In time, more and more Iranian intellectuals and high government officials began traveling to Europe for business, trade, and studies, and witnessed the great social and industrial progress there. One thing they noticed was the growing trend toward separation of religion and government. This was new to the Iranians, and those who were exposed to the European way of thinking came to believe that the social progress in the West was, directly or indirectly, the result of limiting the power and influence of religious leaders. In particular, the Iranian political emissaries in Egypt (Cairo), Turkey (Istanbul), and Russia (Baku) during the eighteenth and nineteenth centuries came under the influence of their counterparts in the European embassies. Converts to Western thinking, individuals such as these later on returned to Iran with their new ideas and became the leaders of the modernist movement in Iran.

When modernity was brought to the Middle East, it met governing structures that were radically different from those in Europe: absolutist, hierarchical governments that were generally imposed upon the people by a military leader or tribal chief who had conquered the previous ruler and become all-powerful. These rulers gathered their cronies around themselves to administer the affairs of government. Most of the time, the clergy adapted themselves to the political ruling class in order to protect Islamic religious values, protect themselves, and maintain their religious influence over the masses of faithful Muslims. When they objected to corruption in the court or transgressions of government functionaries against the people, the government mostly gave them lip service. The religious elites were powerless vis-à-vis the all-powerful sultans and government leaders. Over time, they became content with their position as religious authorities and did not seriously challenge the right of the shahs and sultans to exercise supreme political power. Thus, the message of modernity came to the Middle East minus its attachment to the Enlightenment values that produced popular, democratic rule in Europe.

Eventually, however, a movement toward social and political modernization in Iran developed in the latter decades of the nineteenth century, during the reign of the Ghajar Dynasty. The movement was led by a small but growing class of intellectuals and tradesmen, influenced by the West, who wanted to limit the absolute power of the shah and bring about reforms in the government. They attracted the cooperation of some religious leaders, who were concerned about the poor economy, the social and economic injustices inherent in the system, the overall backwardness of the society, and the unfair economic and political influence exercised by foreign powers. Working together, these forces eventually prevailed upon the monarchy to introduce a parliamentary government. In 1906, Mozafaredin-Shah Ghajar signed a decree establishing a constitutional monarchy. Soon thereafter, a parliament comprising elected representatives of the people convened.

At the beginning of this new, constitutional era, there was a balance of power in the parliament between modernists and religious conservatives. Over time, however, the modernist intellectuals managed to limit the religious conservatives' numbers in both parliament and government positions. Their influence declined, and eventually Reza Shah, who established his rule as the head of the new Pahlavi Dynasty in 1925, gained total control of the government.

Reza Shah came to the throne by way of a parliamentary coup. As prime minister, he had pretended to be supportive of religion and cooperated with some of the remaining religious forces in the government. After he became shah, however, he drifted away from those forces and fell under the influence of a few secular, modernist intellectuals. His government now brought about a wholesale shift in social and cultural policies, attempting to change the face of Iranian society along European lines. A rapid series of parliamentary acts took the institutions of justice, endowments, and education away from the religious leaders and transferred them over to the government, to be run mostly by organizations and systems modeled after European institutions and headed by European-educated elites.

Iran's modernization efforts had begun to show results: large-scale construction projects, the introduction of a new educational system, the building of roads, the development of a modern military force, and the establishment of a unified centralized government structure. Both the intellectuals and the man in the street saw the positive value of these accomplishments. However, as the secular intellectuals' influence on people's affairs grew, the Iranian masses saw that importing modernity brought with it some of the negative aspects of Europe, such as the licentious lifestyles of the court, sexual promiscuity, drinking, loose family ties, and other vices. The religious classes came to associate these undesirable phenomena with the Western way of life. In the eyes of traditional Iranians, who constituted the vast majority in cities and villages alike, the positive aspects of modernization were inseparable from the negative qualities and vices that defined Westernization as immoral. Religious leaders and their followers thus tended to condemn modernization as a treacherous concept that brought harm and degradation to a society. The average man in the street was confused. He liked the effect of modernization in his daily life, but he was seriously annoyed by the new customs and cultural by-products of the Western civilization that, he believed, were contrary to his religion and harmful to his family and society. He also noticed the increasing corruption among political leaders as the government implemented its modernization projects.

The schools presented a particular stress point in the confrontation between modern and traditional forces. The traditional system of education in Iran centered on religious schools. At the base were the *maktabs*, small local schools that taught basic writing and reading skills to children before they reached the age of maturity and took jobs. In addition, there was a hierarchical school system for the education of religious leadership, starting with schools in small, medium-size, and large cities and ending in large seminaries in cities such as Qum and Mashhad. For centuries, this system had provided educational facilities for talented boys, who entered the system at an early age and continued to study within the confines of the religious school for their entire life. All of the religious authorities, poets, philosophers, scientists, and cultural icons of Iran's classical era were educated in these traditional religious schools.

In the late nineteenth century, a handful of educational reformers started a modern, secular system of education in Iran. Vehemently opposed by most Islamic religious leaders, the new schools had a difficult time at first, but eventually the modernizing governments of the early twentieth century adopted the cause of public education. Also of importance were the schools that were set up and run by Christian missionaries from Europe and the U.S. Those attracted mostly children of the well-to-do families and acted as a vehicle in promoting modern education in Iran; the Alborz School, where I completed my secondary education, was one such school.

The Pahlavi Dynasty intensified the trend toward modern, public schools modeled after European standards, seeing the new schools as the breeding ground for the secular society envisioned by Reza Shah and, later, his successor Mohammad Reza Shah. The system of Islamic schools continued to function in parallel with the public schools, mirroring the bifurcated reality of the entire Iranian society.

The division between modern (which was equated with secular) and traditional (religious/Islamic) persisted in Iran throughout the rule of Mohammad Reza Shah. As time went on, it became apparent that there was no middle ground on which the political forces could meet. Some modernist politicians went so far as to insist that Iranian society would never overcome its difficulties until every Iranian accepted the totality of European civilization "from head to toe," as one of them put it. "Importing European civilization to Iran without having the local culture modulating it" was another slogan. It is important to mention that, toward the end of the shah's reign, a few sincere modernists with religious backgrounds tried to set up schools in cooperation with well-respected Islamic leaders. These schools were called *Maktabe Islam*, and in them both the government curriculum and religious subjects were taught. The *Maktabe Islam* flourished in the beginning but were closed by the government after a few years.

Obviously, the shah himself believed in the philosophy of modernization for Iran. I recall again the moment when I, as an eighteen-year-old, met the shah in his Marble Palace before departing to Europe for my studies and listened to his words of advice as my cohorts and I prepared to be trained abroad for the future development of our country. He did not tell us to honor the richness of our past and try to build our future on the foundation of those precious elements. He did not tell us that those elements are the heritage of every Iranian, rich or poor, city dwellers and farmers, modernists and traditionalists. He did not tell us that we have a living tree of culture that has survived centuries of good and bad events, and has safeguarded the identity of Iranians with honor. I wish he had told us to preserve and nurture that tree, and bring only a graft from Europe to strengthen and supplement the tree's functions. Instead, he implied that we should seek to understand the forces behind the advancement of European societies and strive to implement them in Iran after our return. Perhaps the greatest mistake of the shah was his implicit denial of the fact that our country and its people were the heirs to a great and worthy tradition, and his refusal to believe that we could incorporate technical and scientific advances into our own cultural milieu.

Ultimately, it became clear that the majority of Iran's population would have a hard time buying in to this notion and preferred to follow the teachings of their religious leaders. The tension between the secular/modernizing and religious/traditional forces underlay the political strains leading up to the Islamic Revolution and the assumption of leadership by Ayatollah Khomeini.

The mounting revolutionary sentiments during the 1970s were fed by the regime's wholesale attempt to import Western worldviews and values to Iran. It was not the first time the shah's efforts had backfired; the election of Mossadegh had also resulted from the public's disaffection with some of the monarchy's policies. At that time, it was the British who were the primary focus of national resentment, but after the overthrow of Mossadegh in 1953, the United States eclipsed Britain as the main outside influence. American-trained technocrats dominated the government agencies, and the heavy presence of American advisers was felt in the military, in banking and many areas of industry, and in the public media. There were in Iran more than 40,000 American military advisers, who were paid exorbitant salaries out of the Iranian treasury.

On television, Iranians watched soap operas that were produced for the American audience, and the 1970s-era "Dallas" series was very popular. Tourists dressed in Western fashions; women with short skirts and bare shoulders, and men with bare chests, wandered through the streets and bazaars. Many Iranians were offended by the tourists' clothing, and a merchant in the Isfahan bazaar once told me that the presence of those young women in their skimpy dress was stressful for his young employees. The public face of Iranian society became more and more materialistic and pleasure seeking, and many thinking people became disturbed by the growing reality that their countrymen were being encouraged to become consumers of goods produced in foreign countries.

One day, as I drove out to the north of Iran in an area close to the border of the old Soviet Union, I saw a lot of electronic gadgets on a mountaintop. I asked a local person what was up there. He said he didn't know, but Americans were always coming and going. When I eventually learned that it was a listening station aimed toward the USSR, I was insulted by the ugly fact that the Americans could have something like that on our property without the people even knowing about it.

What had happened, of course, is that our country had become a strategic element in the Cold War. Just as the British had valued Iran during World War II as a buffer to German interests in the Middle East—and especially as a source of oil—the United States now valued us as a buffer against the power of the Soviet Union, just across our border to the north, and a source of oil as well. If the U.S. wished to see our country develop economically, it did so for reasons that had more to do with American strategic and economic interests than with the well-being of our people. And the shah was happy to play along with those larger global interests. Our military alliance with the West provided the U.S with a market for the sale of expensive weaponry and a convenient foothold in the region for purposes of intelligence gathering, and Iran's industrialization program was oriented to producing profits for Western companies. For the most part, our industries existed for putting together products at the end stages of production and selling them mostly in the domestic market. In the more sophisticated areas of technology and innovation, Iran lagged behind; in the medical field, for example, Iran was a consumer of finished pharmaceuticals and technical gadgets, not a producer of such goods.

As I worked with American advisers and professors, I became disillusioned even with the nature of the relationship among scientific colleagues. I understood the Americans' methods and worked smoothly within their organizational and technological frame of thought. I retained the admiration I had developed earlier for their systems. On another level, however, I came to realize that the Americans in Iran did not consider us their equals but, rather, looked down upon us as if we were children learning at their feet. I never had the feeling that our American advisers understood or respected our dignity. As an example, during my time in Shiraz and Isfahan I was involved in the research and promotion of birth-control methods aimed at curbing the population explosion in Iran. Most of the funding came from a U.S. State Department AID program. In order to receive the research grants, I had to partner with an American university, who would receive the grant on our behalf and control its dispensation. It was insulting to us that our own institutions were not trusted to administer the funds. As a further insult, my Iranian colleagues and I received a much lower per diem allowance than our European and American counterparts when we attended scientific meetings on birth-control methods, despite the fact that we were doing virtually the same work.

Many of the Western-trained Iranians who served as university professors and government technocrats assumed they had all the answers to the problems of our society. Like the shah's government, they were more than ready to push through new ideas and programs based on Western models and values, paying little attention to the sensitivities of the larger public. In the middle were those of us who tried to mediate as we did our work, but we could not impress the bureaucracy with our ideas or focus their attention on the real needs of the masses. And we, educated intellectuals in charge of the government programs, were not united among ourselves because of the different environments and schools of thought to which we had been exposed during our educations abroad in the U.S. and Europe.

As the government pursued its efforts to force the society into a secular, quasi-European mold, public resentment grew and festered under the surface. I experienced this growing conflict in my work with students, for many of them identified me with the Westernized intellectuals—even though I was known to be a practicing Muslim.

And yet, I found myself still wedded to the influences of my training in Germany and the U.S. These were good influences that had given me valuable skills and disciplined habits that were vital to my career and my work as an agent of change. But the attitudes I had gained in the West represented a constant source of conflict for me as I tried to come to grips with those deep-rooted Iranian cultural traits that are strongly resistant to change. The stress of this conflict gradually wore me down until I eventually lost my hopes and expectations that European- and American-trained intellectuals could bring about major and enduring positive changes in Iran as long as the shah and his government were still in power and their aim was to change the face of Iran according to the model of Western societies.

I was not a member of the political opposition that evolved during the 1970s, but I understood where the sentiment came from. In fact, the movement that culminated in the revolution of 1978–1979 had its roots back in the 1950s, when there were contacts between the progressive religious leaders and certain intellectuals who opposed the government's foreign dependency. These forces cooperated actively during the Mossadegh revolution, and they would also form an alliance amid the revolutionary ferment of the late 1970s. In the meantime, the opposition forces were constantly beaten back by the regime, but with time, their voices grew louder and their influence on the political scene slowly increased.

In 1978, the ferment bubbled over. People had had it with the monarchy—and they were especially angry and fed up with SAVAK, which we all knew was responsible for many unjust deaths and incarcerations. Demonstrations, especially among university students, went on for six months. The violence escalated, and many people were swept up in a revolutionary fervor that, more and more, began to express the ideology of an Islamic political movement. It was by no means clear where these events were leading us. We were like drowning people looking for something, or someone, to save us.

Into this situation stepped Ayatollah Khomeini. Despite the fact that he had been out of the country for a decade and a half, Khomeini's name was widely familiar and increasingly respected. He had been imprisoned in 1963 and sent into exile in 1964 because of his fearless statements denouncing the shah's injustices, dependency upon America, and close relationship with Israel. Khomeini had spent most of his exile next door in Iraq, but recent diplomatic maneuvering had forced him out of the Middle East and into sanctuary in France. The average man in the street, the nationalists, the socialists, and in particular the religious authorities in Iran hoped he would return if and when the shah was forced off the throne.

Many began to view Khomeini with great hope. We longed for the guidance of a righteous man, uncontaminated by the evils of the political system and detached from the foreigners on whom we blamed many of our problems. We thought that Ayatollah Khomeini might be such a man, a spiritual leader with an unblemished past, who would bring his wisdom and moral authority to the task of establishing a new kind of government to set Iran on a course of independence and constructive progress. It seems naïve in retrospect, but there was a widespread belief that if the shah left and Khomeini came back, whether as a political leader or just a moral force in the land, everything would be all right; injustice would disappear, cronyism and favoritism would end. Religious people, we assumed, were not corrupt, and the presence of a holy man at the top would ensure righteous governance. This is what the masses believed—and I, too, at that early stage of the revolution, harbored such hopes.

And still, I remained skeptical. Some of my colleagues and friends had embraced the Islamic Revolution, but during my two decades' work with students and patients, I had built up a picture of the Iranian psyche as one that would not easily change its collective orientation to constructive change. I did not go to the political meetings and did not participate in the political processions.

Then one day, as I was returning from the university campus to my home in Isfahan, I encountered a huge political procession. People were carrying banners against the shah's government and in favor of Imam Khomeini, who was still in Paris. The demonstrators were peaceful, and their lines stretched for at least four miles. I saw a well-dressed young teacher in the procession who was reading aloud pages of the Qur'an. An entire section of the procession around him was listening to his reading, solemnly and approvingly. Suddenly it dawned on me that the revolution based on Islamic values and Qur'anic teachings was real; these young revolutionaries thoroughly intended to follow the Qur'an and employ what they had been taught about Islam as guiding principles in the revolution. This vivid and impressive sight lit a spark within my soul and created hope in my heart that the Islamic Revolution would open the road to progress and success in Iran. I became a supporter of the revolution.

At this time, it was still unclear how the situation would develop. There were forces on the Left, socialists and communists and others, who were working with Khomeini, hoping that his return would provide the impetus to push the shah off the throne—and then they, the leftists, would step in and take the reins of power. They had guns and training. They began attacking the police and the garrisons, and they succeeded in paralyzing the government. Ultimately, the military forces who had long aligned themselves with the shah proved unable, or unwilling, to put down the surging power of the masses. In January of 1979, the shah was forced to flee and became an exile himself.

And then Ayatollah Khomeini arrived to a tumultuous welcome. People were overjoyed. It was the end of the shah and the dawn of a new day in Iran. It felt like a time of national unity.

Khomeini stood at the center of the evolving political order, but there was no clear power structure. The rapidity of the events meant there was no time for intellectuals and religious leaders to develop a theoretical underpinning for the revolution; nor did they have time to think through the possible future difficulties and plan for them. Once the revolution succeeded, various individuals and groups drifted around the ayatollah. The majority of them, in the foreground, were intellectuals who were mostly oriented to the left wing of the political spectrum, and as the question of institutional leadership sorted itself out in those early days and weeks, socialists and communists were among those who stepped into positions of authority. However, there were also religious leaders and clergymen, in the background, who had a much longer history of cooperation with Khomeini and were unquestionably more loyal to him than the revolutionary intellectuals.

People like me felt a surge of renewed hope. We looked back upon the first revolution, the Mossadegh revolution, as a failed attempt to break our economic and political dependence on Europe and reestablish our national identity; we now saw this second revolution, based on our own religious values and led by Imam Khomeini, as a struggle to restore and preserve our cultural identity and religious values. Those of us in the intellectual ranks saw no contradiction between these goals and the modernization of our society. We would continue to pursue the application of science and technology to our developmental tasks. Far from feeling threatened by the rise of Islamic forces within the state's power structure, we believed that a government guided by men of high religious principles would reinvigorate our efforts and empower us to overcome the obstacles we had faced from the shah's bureaucratic organizations. We even hoped to find a way through the layers of resistance separating our goals from the attitudes of the Iranian masses. Thus it felt like a natural progression when I came to put my hopes on this new, revolutionary government guided by Islamic principles, a government that I thought gave us a real chance to move forward, at last.

As I recall that time now, my memory takes me back to the atmosphere of hope and optimism that prevailed during those early weeks and months of the Islamic Revolution. As Ayatollah Khomeini gathered the support of his allies from numerous political backgrounds in those early days of revolution, the economy broke down. There was no gasoline available for our cars, no kerosene for our heating stoves. Food was scarce, and there were long periods without electrical power. The police and military forces were not protecting people. This period of scarcity and insecurity lasted for two or three months. During this time, however, committees sprang up in mosques, and the government worked smoothly with these committees to distribute food, gas, and kerosene to the people.

Still, the supplies were very limited. Isfahan, like many other cities, was completely dark during the night, and people were stuck in their homes because of a curfew imposed to maintain order. The amazing thing, as every Iranian remembers, was that during those long hours of dark nights and the lack of protection, not a single incident of aggression was reported; there were no fights in the streets, and no homes were burglarized. The people were united in their hopes for the future and their willingness to work together so that all could make it through the hardships of the present. Every Iranian who talks about that time will testify that Iranians are basically good; we showed that goodness during the revolution, in spite of the shortages, and we took care of each other.

A new spirit of community responsibility began to emerge. Popular enthusiasm for the revolution spread, and many who had held back during the tumultuous months of 1978 and the earliest days of 1979 joined the bandwagon. Those who had money to contribute did so through a new institution that rose up to pay the bills and advance the cause of the Islamic Revolution. Housed within the National Bank of Iran, it was called the Account of the Imam. A person could go to any branch of the nationwide bank and contribute to the Account of the Imam. Millions did so—university professors, shopkeepers, the man in the street, women who willingly gave up precious jewelry for the support of the revolution—and they did so without getting a receipt, purely on their faith and hope for a future guided by new leaders centered around one man presumed to be righteous. Eventually, a great many of these early supporters would be disappointed, but for the moment, it was a heady time.

Subsequent events would turn the euphoria into disillusionment. Our neighbor, Iraq, would attack us, and our country would be engulfed in a long and senseless war, eight years of destruction and misery. Our Islamic Revolution would turn sour as radical forces seized control and life became particularly difficult for intellectuals, even those of us who were faithful Muslims.

For that moment of euphoria, though, I, like millions upon millions of my countrymen, was swept up in the excitement. And again, when I close my eyes and try to picture that brief time of hope, I am able to see the beautiful city of Isfahan as it was immediately after the revolution. The gasoline shortage had temporarily solved the city's traffic problems, and the air was clean. The trees were wearing the fresh, green colors of springtime, and flowers were blooming everywhere. Our house was near the river, where there were parks that had been developed during the time of the shah, a time of which we now spoke in the past tense. Every morning, people came out and strolled along the riverside. I remember vividly the blue skies, the flowers, the clean air, and the vision we had of Iran becoming a land of democracy, justice, and prosperity. The blue domes of the mosques were shinier than ever before, the streets were cleaner, and smiling faces expressed joy and optimism. Memories of those few moments have remained with me ever since.

CHAPTER EIGHT
Leaving Iran Again

Immediately after Ayatollah Khomeini's return to Tehran, he settled into a government school and made it the headquarters of his activities. He was heavily guarded by his newly organized militia, but nevertheless his first act was to give audiences to people who wanted to see the man they believed would lift Iran from the morass of its recent past. Thousands stood in line to catch a glimpse of him and kiss his hand. Elsewhere, all eyes and ears were fixed on radio and television as Iranians listened first thing every morning, and last thing at night, for news of what was happening in their country.

Revolutions almost inevitably pass through a time of uncertainty after the overthrow of the old regime, and Iran in 1979 was no exception. At the beginning, the political situation was dynamic and confusing. All forces were jockeying for power—the religious leadership, the communists, the National Front, forces still loyal to the deposed shah, and many more groups, some of them well organized and some not. Ayatollah Khomeini appointed a Provisional Revolutionary Government, but it was not immediately clear what the new political system would look like. Many people who enthusiastically welcomed Khomeini, especially religious intellectuals, hoped for a national progressive government with the moral support of respected religious leaders. They did not believe it possible that what would emerge would be a theocracy.

At first, Khomeini thrust the reins of the government into the hands of religious technocrats, maintaining that the clergy were not interested in governing per se, but would act as a spiritual and moral power in the background. He appointed an interim government, led by Engineer Mehdi Bazargan as prime minister. Bazargan was a popular leader who had been a professor at the Technical School of the University of Tehran. He was a liberal who helped build the National Front that had operated closely with the Mossadegh movement in the early 1950s. After the fall of Mossadegh, Bazargan championed the cause of freedom in Iran. He wrote articles and helped to keep alive the hopes of intellectuals for achieving their goal. His opposition to the shah, however, had cost him his position at the university and some time in jail.

It is hard to say exactly what Khomeini himself had in mind at the beginning, but it did not take long for him to consolidate power around himself and his closest clerical associates. If he had indeed intended to keep the religious forces in the background of the new government, he appeared to change his mind amid the political maneuvering of those early months. He said that three times Iran's religious leadership had supported and participated in revolutions against oppressive governments, and each time the revolution was hijacked by pro-Western, secular groups after its initial success; this time, he vowed that it would be different.

And he had the majority of the population behind him. On April 1, 1979, a national referendum was held on the single question of whether or not Iran should become an Islamic Republic. Iranians voted overwhelmingly in favor. There was an attempt by some intellectuals to exclude the word "Islamic" and call it the "National" or "Democratic" Republic of Iran, but Khomeini vehemently opposed that, saying "Islamic Republic—not a word more, and not a word less." He got his way.

A few months later, a National Assembly was elected to write a new constitution. It took some time for the new constitution to come together, but one concept that was included without much discussion was that of *Velayat Faghih* (literally, the "guardianship of the *Faghih*," the clerical authority in Islamic jurisprudence). According to that provision, the grand ayatollah would be the ultimate authority and decision-maker in the government of the Islamic Republic. In the meantime, technocrats who were intelligent and well intentioned but had little experience at governing led the provisional government. They faced a multitude of difficulties—various opposition groups, serious disruptions in the economy and public services, and the threat of economic isolation by the West.

The likelihood of economic isolation increased dramatically in the fall of 1979 after a group of radical students, who called themselves the Followers of the Imam's Line, occupied the U.S. Embassy and took 65 Americans hostage. Thirteen were released shortly afterward, but the remaining 52 remained captive for more than one year. Public opinion in the United States and many other countries turned bitterly against the Islamic Republic from that time on. Americans were shocked when the Iranian government refused to step in to end the occupation and free the hostages, and they were incredulous at the mass demonstrations expressing hatred toward the U.S. In fact, the provisional government of Bazargan opposed the hostage taking, but it was powerless against the revolutionary extremists. As for Khomeini and his associates, they were not involved in the planning or execution of the occupation, but neither were they willing to buck the rising tide of anti-Americanism among the most radical elements, and so they adopted an attitude of toleration toward the hostage takers. The U.S. broke off diplomatic relations and entered into an open hostility with the government of Iran. Khomeini did not hide his anger in many public speeches. Iranians were in fact much more divided than it appeared; many, including my family, did not hate the U.S. or approve of the hostage taking. Indeed, when some of the hostages were relocated from Tehran to a house near ours in Isfahan, Fereshteh and I considered making some popcorn and taking it to them to show that we bore them no ill will.

The hostage crisis was a much bigger event in America than in Iran. This is not to say that Iranians ignored it or were uninterested. Many people gathered in front of the American Embassy and showed their support for the hostage takers by shouting slogans. They may have supported the young revolutionaries because they felt the Americans needed to be taught a lesson about the arrogant attitudes they and other Westerners had shown toward Iranians during the years of the shah's rule. But more importantly from the Iranian perspective, the hostage taking occurred during a time of great political instability, a reality that commanded far more public concern. To be sure, the government was not above exploiting the hostage situation for both domestic and international purposes at this time when the country was rent by internal divisions and threatened, or so many believed, by outside forces (first and foremost the U.S.). America had secured for itself a lot of political and economic interests in Iran during the reign of the shah and wished to see the new government, who opposed those interests, fail.

Nearly all of the Western countries became frustrated with the revolutionary regime. They were losing economic and political influence in Iran, and they could do nothing about it because most of their political contacts in Iran had either been deposed from their positions or left the country altogether. In addition, spokesmen of the Iranian government were constantly vilifying the Western powers. In response, Western governments in general—and America in particular—put enormous economic and political pressure on Iran and gave free reign to their mass media to spread negative propaganda about Iran. Educated Iranians, who tended to favor the good relations we had enjoyed with the West in the past, became fearful of the future.

As internal tensions developed, one of the first groups to assert itself against the Islamic Republic was the *Mujaheddin-e-Khalq* (People's Mujaheddin), made up of Islamic socialists who had helped Khomeini during the early days of the revolution by attacking the stations of police loyal to the shah and confiscating their weapons. The Mujaheddin were true fighters for an Islamic Revolution, but soon they came into conflict with the clergy around Khomeini. The tension developed into open hostilities, and the Mujaheddin began engaging in acts of sabotage, for example by bombing the headquarters of an Islamic party and assassinating some of the ayatollah's leading associates, including, at one point in late 1981, the country's prime minister and president. It took Khomeini's militia years to defeat the Mujaheddin, but eventually they were suppressed.

Another major difficulty for the new government was the competition for power between the organized religious leadership and the new government of technocrats. This competition moved gradually to the surface, and eventually, the religious leadership openly opposed the government of technocrats.

Beginning with the spring and summer of 1979, then, the revolution confronted a serious crisis, and the moderate Provisional Revolutionary Government appeared on the verge of disintegration. Seeing the danger,

Khomeini and his circle of clergy enlisted dedicated cadres of young revolutionaries to help them take control of the power centers and spread their rule throughout society. In subsequent months, the clergy and young revolutionaries overran all government institutions, occupying key political and administrative positions. The universities were closed down and the borders of the country sealed. The government of Mehdi Bazargan found itself working alongside a parallel government that overruled his on nearly all important questions. Bazargan once described himself as holding a knife handle without a blade.

The National Assembly wrangled over the constitution, but in a few months' time delegates came to agreement on a document that included numerous principles of theocracy. In another overwhelmingly favorable referendum vote, Iranian citizens approved the new constitution at the beginning of December 1979. The next month, Abol-Hassan Banisadr, one of the men who had accompanied Khomeini during his brief stay in Paris and his return to Tehran, was elected to a four-year term as the first President of the Islamic Republic. Banisadr, a capable layman of moderate political leanings, did not fill out his term of office; he was impeached and removed from the presidency in 1981 by the *Majlis*, with the approval of Ayatollah Khomeini.

The tension between intellectuals and clergy continued to play out in the open. The clergy held a majority in the *Majlis* and continued to assume more and more power, both in parliament and in the executive branch. One institution that worked to their advantage was the position of the Friday Imam, the clergyman who directs the Friday prayers in every city. The Friday Imams were very respected within their communities, and closely connected to each other. The leader of their overall network was Hossein Ali Montazeri, a confidante of Khomeini, and in the course of the revolution, their position became more and more political. They received financial support from the government, and, in return, they watched out for the interests of the Islamic Revolution in their communities. Montazeri eventually had a falling-out with Khomeini, but in those crucial, early months and years his authority among the Friday Imams helped greatly in solidifying the rule of the high clergy throughout the country.

Still, the system lacked stability. There were opposition groups and dissidents in many places. In three provinces close to the borders—oil-rich Khuzestan in the south, Kurdistan in the west, and Baluchistan near the southeastern border with Pakistan—local clergy separated themselves from the influence of Khomeini and Montazeri, and talked about secession.

The central government made it clear that it was not above using violence to stabilize its rule. One of the first things to happen in 1979 was the arrest of the shah's functionaries—generals, SAVAK agents, and leaders in the ministries, including the prime minister. In the beginning, these arrests seemed benign, but soon it became known that those who were arrested were summarily shot on the roof of Khomeini's headquarters. It shocked and disappointed many intellectuals to think that people could be executed without proper court procedures. Khomeini justified the action by saying that those people did not deserve a court proceeding; they were guilty by virtue of their past, and they had only to be identified and eradicated. Later, a large number of young Mujaheddin who took part in an uprising were imprisoned, and when they refused to repent and pledge their allegiance to the Islamic Republic, they, too, were executed.

Meanwhile, the majority of us lived our daily lives as best we could. Aside from the opposition groups, who were scattered, there was no open hostility in the streets, and crime rates remained very low. In general, people went around with a glimmer of hope in their eyes. Life was not easy, but there was optimism that, eventually, we would pass through this time of troubles and emerge into a bright future. Ayatollah Khomeini would save the revolution—and save us.

In September of 1980, however, we came under attack by Iraq, our neighbor to the west, ostensibly over a longtime territorial question involving control of the Shatt-al-Arab waterway dividing our two lands. Under the surface, however, there might have been another cause of the war. Soon after the establishment of the Islamic government in Iran, there was open talk of spreading the Islamic Revolution to neighboring countries, with the dream of a federation of independent, revolutionary Islamic countries. Fear of this happening obviously put Iraqi strongman Saddam Hussein in a defensive position and may have pushed him to decide for a pre-emptive strike on Iran. To what degree the Western countries encouraged him to attack Iran is unknown.

In any case, a great many Iranians fled the advance of Iraqi troops from the border area. A woman whom I met, from the city of Khorramshahr, told me she and her family saw the western horizon red with fire, as if coming from the heavens. Thousands of refugees crowded into Shiraz and Isfahan, and had to be housed in school buildings. Spontaneous local committees formed; women brought food, clothing, and other necessities. Once again, amid the hardship, there was the feeling that people were taking care of each other.

The misery was only beginning, however. Iran's economy, already damaged by the disruptions of the revolution, grew even worse. Prices inflated rapidly, and food and gasoline were rationed. Foreign currencies became scarce. The clergy and government leaders appealed to our religious values and our national spirit. For the most part, Iranians gave up their political infighting and closed ranks to defend the country. Iran's military was still organizationally solid, and our soldiers fought a spirited defense against the Iraqis.

A few months into the conflict, the Iraqis flew air raids over Tehran,

Shiraz, Isfahan, and other Iranian cities. Electricity was shut off every night during the raids, which could come at any hour. We would sit in our home, waiting, and as soon as we heard the sirens, we hurried down into the basement, under the staircase, and waited anxiously until the air raid was over. We heard loud explosions in our vicinity as if bombs were falling next door. We looked at each other with fear and anxiety, and crawled slowly out of our hiding place to get information about the exact sites of missile explosions. The air raids were the most distressing and unnerving thing that happened during those years.

In the first days of the war, radio and television constantly played military music and patriotic lectures. Everybody was encouraged to join the fight against the Iraqi aggression and defend our national honor. And at this point, the ayatollahs revived the concept of martyr (*shahid*) to help recruit and embolden young soldiers.

The concepts of *Shahadah* and *Shahid* go back to the early days of Islam, when Muslims went to war against idol-worshipers. Muslims who died in the wars were considered *Shahid* in the Qur'an, and they were promised that they would enter paradise and remain alive after death, being fed in the presence of God (Qur'an, Chapter 3:169). The most prominent example of this self-sacrifice was the martyrdom of Imam Hussein, the grandson of the Prophet Mohammad *pbuh*. In 682 A.D., Imam Hussein was massacred in Karbala, along with his family and friends. Throughout the centuries, Shi'ite Muslims had always commemorated those early martyrs of our religion, and now, during the Iran-Iraq war, the concept was brought out and trumpeted by Khomeini and his associates. They told us that whoever fights against our enemy and gets killed is a martyr who will join with Imam Hussein on the Day of Judgment and go directly to paradise without having to account for his actions during his life—in other words, a clean bill for going directly to heaven. People spoke of *shahid* in schools, in the mosques, and at other gatherings, and it quickly became a big entice-ment for young men, especially those who were religious.

Thus, there were two compelling arguments for young men to join the war effort: If we defeat Iraq, we defend our honor and national identity; if we are killed, we go directly to paradise. The constant propaganda coming over the airwaves appealed to a great many young people, including thousands of high-school boys who went to war and were killed because of their inexperience and over-enthusiasm.

Personally, I agonized at the numbers of young people who were emotionally charged with religious slogans and promises of rewards in heaven. As the war continued, the line of caskets that passed through the streets every day filled me with horror. My son Ali was within a few years of military age, and I could not help feeling sick with sorrow at the thought that he might one day pass through our streets in one of those boxes.

And then, amid the fighting, the news broke that the imprisoned *Mujaheddin-e-Khalq* partisans, many of them only teenagers, had been executed en masse. I choked with grief at the news, and the feeling of disgust and horror was widespread. By this time, however, no one dared speak out against the regime. Everybody was saying, "It's wartime, and we have to stay united if we are to defend our country."

After almost two years, the initial Iraqi invasion stalled. In a count-er-offensive, our forces drove the enemy out of the western territories they had occupied and struck across the border into Iraq, driven by the belief that God was on Iran's side. But then the Iraqi lines hardened, thanks to new war machinery, ammunition, and intelligence received regularly from abroad and used against Iranian forces. As a result, our forces bogged down, and the war dragged on with no end in sight. The hardship and misery grew worse, and our government became more and more authoritarian.

Every family suffered because of the war. In our case, the war affected us in a particular way. In addition to the hardship and our concern for the future of Ali, the fact that the borders were closed tore our family apart because our daughter Manya had gone to Germany to study German. After the war started, she could not get home and we could not go to visit her.

The war, the deteriorating economy, and the government's harsh controls affected every aspect of our lives. During the early months of the revolution, the young revolutionary guards—the foot soldiers of the Khomeini order—had been dispatched to factories, government offices at all levels, schools and universities, and other social organizations to make sure that all went according to the interests of the Islamic Revolution. As the influence of the clergy and revolutionary guards increased, that of the technocrats and intellectuals declined. Among the intellectuals and professionals across the country, disappointment replaced our former optimism about getting Iran on the right track toward progress and modernization. Blind loyalty and absolute support for the government became the primary criteria for those who would hold positions of authority. Those who did not and could not blindly support the government and its actions were increasingly isolated. They were looked upon with mistrust and called "*Taghuti*," a word taken from the Qur'an meaning those who have strayed and are following Satan. Well-to-do families had to hide their wealth, their jewels, and their expensive carpets because it was assumed they were supporters of the shah.

The war dragged on for eight years of suffering, grief, economic hardship, and increasingly harsh political controls. The defense of our country against Iraq became the defense of the Islamic Revolution, and the government became more and more intolerant of its political opponents.

The universities underwent a change of leadership that brought them under the control of the young revolutionaries. The revolutionaries installed their own hand-picked heads of departments, often people in their twenties and thirties, recent graduates who were devoted to the religious leadership and had no administrative experience. At faculty meetings, they turned the agenda away from issues of teaching, research, and medical practice, and focused instead on preserving and strengthening the revolution. The professors were powerless and treated with disrespect, sometimes even in public.

I recall one meeting at which we were discussing how to make best use of our hospital beds. Several of the young revolutionaries, who were representatives of the Ministry of Higher Education, demanded that we set aside a certain number of beds in the Children's Ward for political emergency—for Revolutionary Guards, and possibly for injured soldiers. It was a complicated issue, because there was a shortage of beds. A ranking member of the Pediatrics Department argued that if we reserve beds for Revolutionary Guards, we would have to deny them to children brought to the hospital for emergencies.

"That does not matter," said one of the officials. "Our primary concern is to save the revolution at all costs."

His comment shocked us, but none of us felt free to argue.

A similar situation took hold in the classroom. The most radical students were quick to pounce on a professor if he said something that the student felt reflected negatively on the Islamic Revolution. Some would stand up and shout, "You don't have the right to say such a thing!" They managed to intimidate the older professors and other university authorities to the extent that the authorities always backed the students.

I became an unwilling bystander, watching the young revolutionaries take over my university as the clergy concentrated the government's power into their own hands. These new elites drew the support of the masses by appealing to their emotions; they argued that all of the revolutionary policies flowed from religious purposes and those who opposed the policies were opposing Islam. In the minds of the new elites, anyone who opposed the revolutionary policies must have been a beneficiary of the privileges given out by the former shah and was, therefore, an enemy of the new government. The new rulers' religious purposes, however, were focused on enforcing the traditional dress codes, participation in the Friday prayers, religious mass gatherings, and behavioral patterns representing the most conservative tendencies in our culture.

Simultaneously, the Islamic Revolution became vehemently resistant to everything associated with the West. The production, sale, and use of alcoholic beverages were forbidden, and violators were prosecuted. Those who were accustomed to drinking bought alcohol on the black market and consumed it in the privacy of their homes; in public, they pretended to be practicing Muslims. A joke went around: "During the shah's time we prayed at home and drank in public; under the Islamic government we pray in public and drink at home."

As for those intellectuals who had supported the revolution at the beginning, they gradually lost influence and were pushed out of governmental positions in favor of the young revolutionaries and the radical clergy. Mehdi Bazargan, the first of the new government's prime ministers, lasted no longer than November 1979, and, as we have seen, the first President, Abol-Hassan Banisadr, lasted less than a year and a half.

Those of us who had long hoped for the opportunity to free ourselves from the corruption of the shah's regime and its restraints upon our work soon found ourselves in an equally bad situation. The new regime, which had come into being amid euphoria about its prospects, turned against all we considered vital to our country's development. Modernization, especially if it was associated with

Westernization, was anathema to the new order, and anybody who had brought Western ideas into Iran—including me—was suspected of opposing the values of the Islamic Revolution.

My own students turned against me, and I watched as twenty years of my work evaporated in front of my eyes. I recalled the countless hours I had spent in honest and sincere efforts to influence my students' cultural attitudes, to instill in them the discipline and work ethic I had learned and practiced. I tried so hard to train them in logical, scientific thinking, and how to apply modern science and technology to the problems of Iranian medicine. Moreover, it seemed that the efforts of my colleagues, throughout my university and all across the country, had come to little, and that the work of an entire generation of intellectuals and technocrats was being rejected.

Our family's life, too, became complicated. My second daughter, Shahrzad, an honors student in high school, was refused admission to the University on the grounds that we were too Americanized: I did not go to Friday prayer sessions, and my wife Fereshteh had not worn a headscarf in public during the time before the revolution. Everybody knew that I had been a faithful Muslim all my life, but, as a sympathetic student told me, "Your Islam is not good enough for them because it is not a revolutionary Islam." Thus, Shahrzad was barred from the institution that I had helped develop, the institution to which I had given many of my best years.

It was not only Shahrzad's future that was at risk. We were worried that Ali would eventually be drafted and sent to war. Obviously, our feelings about the revolution and the current state of affairs did not make us eager to sacrifice our son.

And so, with one daughter already in Germany, we decided to send both Shahrzad and Ali there, too. We managed to secure passports for all of us and, with the help of a German lady who was one of my patients in Isfahan, we got visas for Germany, and we took the two children there to study. I also offered to take two of Manya's teenage cousins out of Iran, and their parents were overjoyed. We all eventually landed in Lüneburg, in northern Germany, where they all entered the local Berlitz School to learn German before applying for the University. Fereshteh and I returned to Iran with heavy hearts, not knowing what would happen to our children in a strange country, especially given the unfavorable diplomatic relations between Iran and Germany.

I now began to look for a way to take myself, along with Fereshteh, out of the country. I saw no future for me amid the worsening circumstances, and no hope for the grand design my colleagues and I once had for the transformation of our society to modernity. Four years of the new regime left me feeling professionally paralyzed and emotionally drained. As much as I tried, I could see nothing that could raise my hopes for improvements in my private and professional life in Iran. I desperately wished to take a new road.

Luck came my way on a gray, fall day. A telegram from the World Health Organization (WHO) in Geneva invited me to accept a position in Bangladesh as a WHO medical officer supervising a sterilization program. A previous colleague from Shiraz had recommended me for the position. The telegram became the point of departure for a new phase of my life. I had never been to Bangladesh and had no idea what to expect there, but the opportunity was welcome news in that moment of frustration and hopelessness.

I accepted the WHO assignment as a temporary job, hoping to return to Iran in better times. However, something inside me was telling me that my life was in for a major, long-term change. This thought was unsettling, and for some time I would wake up from my sleep in the middle of the night weeping. I did not know what was happening to me. Had I made the right decision? Where was my life headed?

One afternoon, I was sitting alone in our living room, in the grip of uncertainty. I could not escape the thought that Bangladesh might lead to some other place, a possible future life distant from my family and my ancestral home. There was a dish full of oranges on the table before me. I picked up an orange and observed it, thinking it represented the earth. Acknowledging that the whole of the earth belonged to God, I asked myself if it would make any difference to God, and for His plan for me, if I lived on one side of the globe or the other. The answer came to me quickly, as if it were obvious: It made no difference.

Instantly, I felt a tremendous sense of relief. A load had been lifted from my shoulders. I immediately decided that I was doing the right thing to go to Bangladesh, even if it meant eventually immigrating to a far-away place.

The difficulty that remained for me was how to tell my mother, a widow since 1967, about the decision to leave Isfahan. She had moved from Tehran to Isfahan after the death of my father and lived in a separate dwelling near us. I gave her financial support and visited her every Wednesday. We had grown very close during those years, and I knew that the news of my departure would be a blow to her. After a few days of hesitation, I finally gathered my courage and told her about my plan. She looked surprised but kept calm.

She turned to me and said, "Mahmood, why do you have to go away from Iran?"

I responded, "Mother, if I stay in Iran I will have a heart attack and I will die."

She said to me in a weak voice, "My son, go ... go." And then she became quiet and sat down in the chair.

I will never forget the look on my mother's face as long as I am alive. A few years later, in 1986, she died. By that time I had moved still farther away, to the west coast of the United States. I was in the process of opening my practice in Tacoma and could not go to Iran to be with her in her last moments. I still carry a sense of guilt for failing her.

Sometime after I told my mother, we closed out my practice and rented out our house in Isfahan. In December 1983, Fereshteh and I left Iran for Bangladesh, traveling across India. Upon our arrival, I learned that I was to be stationed in Comila, a city only about 100 miles to the east of the capital Dhaka, but a four-hour trip by automobile and ferry.

It was difficult to find satisfactory housing in Comila, but Fereshteh and I were allowed to rent an apartment in a compound built and supported by grants from the USA to house faculty members of an agricultural school. Fereshteh did a marvelous job of furnishing our apartment and making it comfortable. Unlike most Bangladeshi dwellings, our apartment had running water and a good kitchen. Like most foreigners, we had the services of a cook and a chauffeur. Fereshteh enjoyed shopping at the local markets for fresh produce, and in general, we ate well and in the style corresponding to our tastes back in Iran.

My work was part of a family planning program supported by the U.S. Department of State's Agency for International Development (AID). I was on one of several small teams that traveled to our assigned areas of the country, examining hospital facilities to certify that they were in compliance with the standards of a sterilization program. This compliance issue was important because a delegation of visiting American Congressmen had reported that only poor women in Bangladesh were being sterilized and they were recruited through monetary incentives. They also reported shortcomings in sanitation and surgical standards. WHO had come to the rescue of the program by sending our teams of supervisors. It was our job to make sure that sterilization was being performed on women without coercion and in safe conditions.

Our work took us to remote cities and villages, and the roads were frequently unpaved. Our United Nations Jeep bounced and careened on the worst roads, and once, as a result of the shaking, I dislodged a kidney stone and had to fly to Thailand for medical care.

There were two major benefits that came with my position: a monthly salary of about $3500, which seemed like a lot of money, and eligibility for a United Nations passport, which gave me quasi-diplomatic status for traveling. I made good use of both, going back to Iran to visit my relatives and to Europe to see our children. Our kids, in turn, were able to visit us in Bangladesh several times. I was also able to save some money for the future.

Fereshteh often came with me on my rounds within Bangladesh, and we enjoyed traveling around together. We also found time to cross the borders and visit India, Thailand, and Nepal. When our children came from Germany to visit, we showed them the sights around our region. Once our daughter was startled to find a snake that had crawled up the outside water pipe and made its way into our bathroom. We lived; it appeared, very close to nature in our compound.

My work was pleasant and mostly free of tension, but I was shocked by the degree of poverty and underdevelopment we found. People lived in shacks built of wooden poles covered with jute. Sanitation standards were appalling; any outside place—the corner of a building, an open field—could serve as a toilet, and city streets smelled unpleasantly of urine. The average family's income was less than $20 per month. Still, we found the local people to be peaceful, hard-working, and, as far as we could see, harboring no resentment toward us foreigners who lived in relative affluence.

One life-changing experience I had in Bangladesh was meeting another Iranian family, Ali-Joon Ispahani and his wife Ameneh. Ali-Joon was a tea merchant from a family line that had left Iran in the

1850s to follow the trade into India and East Pakistan, the former name of what had become Bangladesh in 1971. Despite the fact that their ancestors had lived on the Indian subcontinent for generations, they had kept their Iranian identity and Iranian passports. The Ispahanis were a wealthy and influential family, and Ali-Joon, who had graduated from Cambridge, had a cosmopolitan, Western outlook.

We became friends, and they invited us to their home whenever we were in Dhaka. What struck me especially about them was that they were devout Muslims. While we visited, Ali-Joon would excuse himself to practice his evening prayers. Still, he retained his ties with the West, carried on his business, and felt no contradiction in his life as a result. I pointed out to him that in Iran, people with a Western education and a modern outlook generally do not pray and, in fact, brag about having shed their religion and taken on a secular outlook.

He said, "My forefathers left Iran when the Iranians enjoyed a traditional, religious way of life. During our more than 100 years in India, the family kept up its identity, both religious and national, with pride. We were spared the forced secularization that took place in Iran after 1926 by the Pahlavi Dynasty."

The Ispahanis' way of thinking inspired me. At a time when I felt confused about the value of Islam and the seeming contradiction between religious and modern attitudes, Ali-Joon and Ameneh demonstrated that one could be both a devout Muslim and "modern." Clearly, leading an Islamic way of life had not interfered with the Ispahanis' success at living in the contemporary world.

My two-year assignment in Bangladesh passed quickly. Back in Iran, the Islamic government was in full control, and the war against Iraq was still going on. It seemed that nothing had changed since the time Fereshteh and I had moved from Isfahan.

By this time, I had begun to understand why my efforts in Iran did not produce the results I had hoped for. Iranians hid behind a curtain of local Islamic culture; they were not willing to pay the price of modernization by changing their behavior, developing personal discipline, and practicing the ethics that are part and parcel of successful modern societies. They seemed to be content with the interpretations of Islam handed down to them by leading clergymen, an interpretation that ignored progress, science, technology, and rational thinking. It was clear that I could not change this reality, and there seemed to be no good reason for me to return to Iran.

Working for the WHO was not my goal in life, but I nevertheless applied for positions in North Africa and Europe, where Fereshteh and I could be closer to our children. However, I was not offered a new assignment.

This is when it dawned on me that, when I left Iran two years earlier, I really was beginning a process of immigration. The option I had reserved for myself years before, the option of returning to America, was the most viable path. It saddened me deeply that I was about to take permanent leave of the land in which my ancestors had lived for thousands of years, a country that had given birth to major world civilizations. Yet the change was exciting and challenging. I was about to start a new life at the age of 54.

I still recall my discussion with an old lady who was running the dormitory in Munich where Manya was living. She saw a worried look on my face, and I shared with her my concern about immigration after the peak of my professional life, as well as the responsibility of supporting my family and three teen-age kids.

She turned to me with a reassuring look in her eye and said, "Sir, I do not have any concern for the success of a man who has the courage to cross the ocean at the age of 54."

I felt good about her words.

Still, it made me unhappy to think that I would be moving from an Islamic country to one that was not. Emigrating also meant leaving my mother, my siblings, and other family members behind, with opportunities to visit only on occasion. It was a heart-rending prospect for all of us, and during my last time in Isfahan prior to emigration, my mother and I talked about it again. Once again, she accepted my decision with sadness.

I realized that not only was I leaving my family; I was leaving Isfahan, the beautiful city of my birth. I was leaving the stadium where I played soccer and watched our school matches. I was leaving the old bridges and historical buildings. I would miss the little mosque that I had passed every day, where Avicena, the great physician, philosopher, and interpreter of Aristotle, had taught his students in the eleventh century. All of this, and more, would now be in my past.

And still, I had to do it. I recalled that moment in our home back in Isfahan, with the orange, and knew that the time had come.

* * *

I have always had a high regard for the leaders of my religion in general, believing they are good, unselfish men who carry out God's will, interpret His teachings, and help the poor. Those positive feelings were what made me hopeful about Khomeini's leadership in the beginning. When the revolution was taken over by young fanatics, however, I began to develop doubts about the sincerity of some of the religious leaders; what I saw in their everyday actions was discouraging, and eventually, I had to conclude that they were unable to achieve what they promised. In their defense, I must say that the ayatollahs were up against some tremendous obstacles—chaotic political conditions at home, a war imposed upon them by Iraq (who was supported by Western powers), economic devastation, and the threat of hostile actions by numerous nations abroad. It is not hard to understand what drove the religious leaders to extreme political measures which they often had to justify. They also had limited exposure to ideas about human rights, democracy, and separation of church (mosque) and state.

To this day, I believe it is crucial to separate the religious from the political in Islam. Radical, militant interpretations of Islam are a political expression, not a religious mandate. Ayatollah Khomeini's first instinct, that the religious leaders should not take control of the government but should instead remain in the background as a moral force, was the correct approach. Unfortunately, he was not able to hold to that first impulse. Faced with protracted turmoil within Iran and the threat of hostile outside forces, he succumbed to the momentum of radicalism generated by his most ardent followers and led his country into a theocracy that turned its back on the positive features of the modern world. Sadly, through its interpretations of Islam, the Islamic Republic may have distorted the face of the great religion on which it was based.

The troubles Iran has faced—and the troubles that have long plagued the Middle East more widely—are not entirely the fault of the local populations. The many years of Western colonialism, the imposition of foreign attitudes, the arrogance of those who came into the region and saw it as a culture of only camels and swords, and the political and economic deals concluded between the Westerners and the local leaders—all of these factors have woven themselves into today's Middle Eastern mentality. In Iran, as in Iraq and Syria and other countries of the region, the United States came to be seen in a negative light—not the American people, and not the United States as a nation and a symbol of democracy, but the United States as an intruder, led by corporate culture with its own economic interests at heart and its regrettable disregard for the validity of the local cultures.

I myself had lived in both Germany and the United States. I had received the ideas, skills, and assumptions of the Western world. I had taken those qualities with me and attempted to apply them, however I could, to my work in my homeland. My efforts to implement modernization as I learned it failed, along with the effort of hundreds more who had studied abroad and absorbed the methods and values of the foreigners. This was what led me to believe that there was no future in the current system for me: the thought that we had failed, and the circumstances that followed in the wake of our great political eruption, the Islamic Revolution, meant a total rejection of what we had stood for.

It took me a number of years, still, to understand all that happened during this time. It was only in America as an immigrant, only when I had removed myself from Iran permanently, that I realized how it was that Muslims had lost their original, basic values and came to find themselves in a weakened position in their long confrontation with the West. I shall reflect on those thoughts in the final chapters of this book.

* * *

After I immigrated to the United States, several years passed before I visited Iran for the first time. When I got back to the States, an American friend asked me how I felt about returning to Iran.

I said, "I felt like a boy who comes home from a long trip to lands far, far away, and when he returns he finds that his father has died, his mother has married a new man, and she is living with him in a totally unfamiliar house."

It was indeed how I felt. The place where I had once been at home was now a strange land. Its people's outlook on life was different from mine, and I could not connect with it any more.

CHAPTER NINE

In America Again:
A Doctor ... and a Muslim

Whoso emigrates in the way of God
will find in the earth many refuges and plenty ...
– The Holy Qur'an (4:100)

Our life is a journey, and our goal is to move out of our own small world, our own chamber, and into the vast realm of God. This is one of the great mysteries to which the Qur'an refers. It is embedded in the Creation story that whoever leaves his home for a good cause and ventures into the world seeking the bounties of God will find God's gifts amidst the vastness of the earth's resources—as did the prophet Abraham and his nephew Lut (29:26). The sentiment of the verse quoted above echoes that of another (4:97) that speaks of souls who are asked on Judgment Day why they did not leave a place where evil was being done: "Was not God's earth spacious enough for you to move yourselves away?" God does not want His people to stay put in situations where they will waste their talents and their lives.

Life is a journey in the garden of Creation. We are challenged to gain wisdom, to learn about our Creator and ourselves, and to seek out His intention for us, wherever our paths may take us.

By 1986, my life had passed through three phases. There was my childhood, when I lived, grew up, and completed my basic education within one culture. It was a Muslim community, where the bonds of family were strong and the weight of my heritage intense. Then there were the years of an equal intensity when I received my higher education in Germany and the United States, where I became fully familiar with, and accepted, the Western rational approach to life and nature. I accepted, as if by osmosis, the Western system of social values but resisted the temptation to compromise my faith or depart from the religious practices with which I had grown up. I returned to Iran and spent twenty years attempting to bring the fruits of what I had learned back to my home country—to give all I had learned about Western science and medicine, as well as Western social norms, to my countrymen for their benefit.

In the West I had received not only an education and professional skills, but also Westernization itself: a way of thinking, a system of working habits, a discipline. I returned to Iran eager to implement these gifts of the West. I tried to find a compromise, a way of marrying the Western rational approach to life and the Islamic spiritual approach. This had been difficult during the time of the shah, and in the aftermath of the Islamic Revolution it became even more so. The leaders of the Islamic Revolution insisted that we Western-educated technocrats had it all wrong, that we had to start anew from square one and play by their rules. It didn't make sense to me, this leaping from one extreme— that Westernization is all good and tradition is all bad, to the idea that Westernization is all bad and therefore it could not coexist with Islamic values and lifestyles. Little by little, I came to the sobering conclusion that I had failed. The magnitude of my failure felt enormous, and when I decided to leave Iran permanently, I did so out of a sense that the task I had assigned myself as a young man was next to impossible. I needed to start over again somewhere else.

Living outside one's native land is different when it becomes permanent. In Göttingen and Freiburg, St. Louis and Chicago, I had known that my sojourn would end and I would return home with a well-defined mission. When Fereshteh and I made the decision, while living temporarily in Bangladesh, to move back to the United States, we knew we would not return again to Iran except as visitors. From now on, our home would be somewhere else.

The years since our immigration to the U.S. have been a time of much reflection on my part, and a gradual consciousness of what went wrong in Iran—but such reflection and consciousness did not come about immediately. At the beginning, I had no time to sit quietly and ponder the deeper meaning of where we had been; nor did I have time to feel caught between the world we had left and the world I was returning to. In fact, once we started making plans to leave Bangladesh and head for America, events moved rapidly. This did not mean that everything was clear and simple. Indeed, we were stepping into a future colored by uncertainty. We had to settle in America, and I had to find a job in a foreign land. What would our new life bring? How would we find our ultimate purpose? If we were emigrating in the way of God, what did He have in store for us halfway around the globe?

As our first step, we decided to apply for a permanent U.S. visa, the so-called green card. Our older daughter Manya, born in Chicago, had turned 21 and, as an adult with American citizenship, she was able to sponsor the rest of us in our applications. At this time all of our children were living in Munich, and so applying from Germany seemed like a sensible approach. Fereshteh and I flew from Dhaka to Munich and joined the children there. We all then traveled to Frankfurt and went very early in the morning to the American Consulate General to be first in line. Our immigration file had been sent ahead of us, and we were all excited, but also worried. What if we were refused the permanent visa? What if we hadn't sent all the papers that were required?

We arrived at the consulate gate only to find it closed. We waited for a while until somebody told us that the consulate was closed because it was the Columbus Day holiday. Of course we were disappointed, but we returned again early the next morning.

The consular and immigration officers were pleasant and helpful. When the interviewing consul examined our papers and discovered discrepancies in birth dates, he turned to Manya and asked her, with a twinkle in his eye, "Are you sure he is your father?" We managed to resolve the discrepancy and received the papers we needed to travel to the U.S. and complete the process.

In January 1985, Fereshteh and I arrived in Seattle via New York, where we handed our papers to the immigration officer. Again we experienced a moment of uncertainty as we waited for his response.

"Welcome to America," he said, and he stamped our passports. "You are now immigrants and legal permanent residents of the United States. You can travel in and out of the country with this temporary visa in your passports until your green cards arrive in the mail."

It is hard to express how relieved we were—and how truly welcome we felt by encountering such cordial and, indeed, friendly attitudes. America at that time had not yet developed its fixation with illegal aliens and the fear of terrorism that make immigration, and even visiting as a tourist, so difficult today. I still have good memories of how welcoming the officials were to new immigrants in the mid-1980s.

One year later, in January 1986, I left Bangladesh and re-entered the U.S. to seek work and establish myself as a new immigrant. Because I had kept my license to practice medicine in the State of Washington valid, I came directly to Seattle in hopes of finding a job. Fereshteh came with me, and we rented an apartment, but soon she went back to Iran to gather and secure our belongings and rent our home. I expected that my qualifications would make it easy to find a position in Seattle, just as it had been in Iran twenty years earlier. It turned out not to be easy at all. I combed through the announcements sections of medical journals, talked to Iranian colleagues who had come to Seattle before me, and had several interviews. Everywhere I was received politely, but I did not receive a firm offer. I was discouraged, humbled, and frustrated. Finally, I thought to contact Dr. Morton A. Stenchever, the chairman of the Department of Obstetrics and Gynecology at the University of Washington, expecting that he would help me on the grounds of academic collegiality.

I had always had it in mind that the natural place for me would be an academic position, but I hadn't gone to the university earlier because that is not where my existing contacts led me. Now I took the initiative and wrote a letter to Dr. Stenchever. He wrote back a kind letter and advised me to make an appointment with his office to meet him. I was hoping to find a position on the staff of Dr. Stenchever's department.

Dr. Stenchever greeted me with a kind smile, and as I sat down, he asked me if I had brought enough money with me from Iran to live in the U.S.

"No," I said firmly.

He said, "Then you'd better go into private practice." He explained that, at my age, I could still work actively for ten years and be able to save enough for my retirement.

"I have been an academician and a teacher all of my life," I said, "and I expect to be successful if I am given a chance."

He said, "If you insist, I could find some job for you here or in another department, but you will be more successful if you go into private practice."

Our conversation went on like this, back and forth for several rounds, and each time Dr. Stenchever firmly discouraged me from pursuing an academic career. Finally he turned to me and said, "Dr. Sarram, if you hope to support your family, send your children through professional schools, and save enough money to fund your retirement, an academic position is not the right choice for you."

I thanked him and left his office in a sweat, feeling humbled and in despair. It seemed that my twenty years of academic work in Iran did not count to my credit. I had left my professional life in Iran and must now start from the ground up.

Despite this unhappy beginning, I was determined to find a satisfying way to practice medicine and provide for my family. I continued searching and came across an advertisement for the sale of a private practice in Tacoma. I drove the 30 miles to Tacoma to check out the opportunity but found some legal issues pending on the practice. I decided not to buy that practice, but then I happened to meet Dr. Thomas Brown at Lakewood Hospital, in a Tacoma suburb, who encouraged me to open my own practice and settle in Lakewood, where there was an acute shortage of obstetricians. Dr. Brown urgently needed another obstetrician to share hospital calls for emergency room patients. It sounded like a good break for me, and I agreed to come on board.

The next step was setting up an office. Dr. Brown described all the steps that I had to take: signing up with a professional medical liability insurance company; getting my 401(k) pension fund started; meeting with the man who became my personal attorney, James A. Krueger, of Vandeberg, Johnson & Gandara; and signing up with Medicaid,

Medicare, and all major health insurance companies (critically importantly for working within the American healthcare system). Dr. Brown's generous help was a godsend.

But there were still some hurdles to overcome. I had no equipment for a medical practice and needed cash to buy it. Acquaintances and Rotarians came to my aid. I had joined Rotary International in Iran earlier and transferred my membership now to the Rotary Club of Lakewood. Ash White, a fellow Rotarian and a banker with Puget Sound Bank, secured a loan for me to set up my practice and personally helped me write a business plan. Others helped me find a suitable office space in a multi-specialty office building, work out a lease-improvement agreement with the landlord, and receive hospital privileges from various Tacoma hospitals.

In due time, I took my specialty board exam and passed it. The oral examiner for the board, who was younger than I, got to know me and my background in the course of the examination. He gave me a good grade, possibly out of respect for my previous work in Iran. One by one, I got the approval of all major health insurance companies as a healthcare provider. Soon I was treating patients, operating in operating rooms, and delivering babies in hospitals.

It had been a long process, but thanks to the shortage of ob/gyn specialists and referrals by satisfied patients, my practice now picked up rapidly. In retrospect, I see all of the events leading to my eventual success—finding the people in Lakewood who helped, making my way through the business arrangements, and passing the exam under stress—coming as the result of divine help. Others might call it simple luck, but I am convinced that God was with me as I struggled to find the way to realize His purpose for me.

Fereshteh had stayed in Iran while I went through my job-hunting ordeal. It was at this time, while I was alone and commuting between

Seattle and Tacoma, that I learned of my mother's death. She was living in our house in Isfahan and had been severely ill for some time, so the news was not unexpected, but it was nonetheless a blow to me and I immediately regretted that I was not at her bedside in her last hours. I was operating in survival mode, though, and the urgency of my need to find a job and build a new life kept me going in spite of my sadness. Fereshteh remained in Iran until my mother was buried and the traditional ceremonies were completed. By the time she arrived back in Seattle, I had established my practice in the Tacoma area.

We rented a house there and moved from Seattle so that I did not have to continue the tiring daily commute. Fereshteh became my office manager; she had worked with me in the same capacity in Isfahan and had no difficulty mastering the routine. With marvelous foresight, she negotiated with a high-tech computer company to computerize our office, investing $16,000 in a server, specialized software, and two terminals. Ours was only the second medical office in Tacoma where all the transactions, billings, and referrals were computerized. Two years after our arrival, we built a new home in a beautiful gated community near a small lake.

Our children came over from Germany one by one. Ali arrived in time to start his final year of high school. He had no difficulty finding friends and progressed well in his studies. He finished high school and entered the University of Washington where, eventually, he became trained in medicine. In the meantime, Shahrzad completed her second year of dental school in Würzburg, and she followed Ali in rejoining us. She took English as a Second Language classes at Pacific Lutheran College and eventually transferred to the Dental School at the University of Washington. Manya was the last to come to the States. She had finished pharmacy studies in Germany and passed the required certification process that enabled her to work in various Tacoma hospitals before entering the Doctor of Pharmacy program at the University of Washington. Thus in a short span of time, all of our children moved to America and started their studies at the University of Washington.

The technical aspects of my work in the office, operating rooms, and birth centers were mostly familiar to me, but there were numerous administrative and regulatory conditions that were unfamiliar in the beginning. First of all, I was now working not in a single hospital but within a larger system that had developed over many years. The medical and nursing staff knew the system and operated according to established routines. I had to learn those routines, just as I had had to learn the routines in St. Louis, Chicago, Shiraz, and Isfahan. New to me, for example, were the structures of controls over our practice, the systems and organizations that monitored all aspects of healthcare. There were government and professional agencies such as the Joint Commission on Accreditation of Healthcare Organizations, as well as local government agencies that supervised and implemented standards of quality in medical care. There were mechanisms employed by the nursing staff to monitor the services of the doctors: reports sent to the hospital administration and quality care reviews by chart review committees. In addition, insurance companies had their own system of monitoring doctors. Last but not least, doctors were conscious that they could be sued by patients and trial lawyers and convicted for negligence and substandard care.

All of the structures, procedures, and controls made it difficult to develop personal relationships with patients, but I did my best. Every time I helped a woman deliver a baby, I would tenderly take the baby in my arms, gaze at it in wonder, and then carry the baby toward the mother and put him or her in the mother's arms. Then I would stand at the mother's bedside and enjoy the process of bonding between her and the newborn baby.

I really enjoyed my work. It pleased me to serve not only affluent and well-insured patients but also those on the welfare rolls. I connected well with my patients and felt warmed by the looks of gratitude in their faces. Patients trusted me; they respected my work and easily followed my instructions—in contrast to my previous experiences with Iranian patients. From the beginning, I realized I was working with people who accepted me as I was, a foreigner who spoke with an accent and exhibited some different cultural habits and expressions. To my surprise, I soon felt at home again, in harmony with the people and their social behavior.

And I relished the opportunities to improve my skills. I attended professional conferences and learned new procedures and technologies then coming onto the medical field, such as laser and laparoscopic surgery techniques. I felt once again, as I had years earlier, that I was on the cutting edge of medical science and knew that I was practicing the best, most up-to-date medicine possible.

I also enjoyed collegial and supportive relations with my colleagues. Doctors, including even a newcomer like me, were captains of their hospital teams; nurses and others on the staff were accustomed to following my instructions for patient care. We were all part of a united front vis à vis the hospital administration and insurance companies. And we all got along with each other to a greater degree than had been my experience, for example, at the Chicago Lying-In Hospital. But first and foremost, we were all conscious that, in every case, the patient was the focus of our attention and everybody was dedicated to serving the patient.

Within a few years after I joined the medical staff of St. Joseph's Hospital in Tacoma and the Lakewood General Hospital, my colleagues honored me by choosing me to chair the Department of Obstetrics and Gynecology in both hospitals.

Our family has lived a modest American success story: an immigrant arrives, finds his place in the community, works hard, prospers, and helps create opportunities for his children. America is built out of immigrant stories and continues to be shaped by new arrivals from every part of the world. Each person and every family have a unique story, and yet they are similar, so many of them over the past several centuries.

America has been good to me, and I am still grateful to each and every one of my fellow Americans who supported and helped me during those early years in Washington State. Fereshteh, too, is grateful, and to express her thankfulness especially for our children's education, she has mentioned the University of Washington in her will.

But back to those early years in Lakewood and Tacoma. By all measures, I should have been happy and content with my life in the new country. I had a good job and a lovely home. My children were on their way to successful professional careers. Strangely, however, I did not feel content. Something was missing in my life and in the lives of my children. With a certain nostalgia—but more than nostalgia, a yearning for something essential—I recalled the Islamic religious teachings and Iranian culture. Driven by a spiritual need, I started visiting churches and engaged in discussions with my fellow Americans about spirituality and the purpose of life. I had a sense that I had something to add to the conversation, and in the process, I rediscovered the values in my religious and cultural background. That rich heritage had been a source of pride and strength to me during my life in Iran and my studies abroad, and now I needed it as much as ever.

But it was not just my personal need that drove me. I realized that by leaving Iran, my family had been uprooted from their traditions and their religious way of life. Now that I had taken care of the immediate needs of myself and my family, I felt a passionate urge to do something for my children and others, something that would make our cultural and religious heritage accessible to future generations and preserve their identity as Muslims in America. I was quite aware of how rapidly our people could forget the great spiritual and intellectual achievements of our Islamic past amid the pressures of life in a new environment. It troubled me to observe so many Iranian immigrants who came from secular backgrounds and were all too ready to cast aside their religious and cultural identity out of anger toward the revolutionary Islamic government in our former homeland. The urge to right this wrong and do something constructive for the future became almost uncontrollable. That was when I began thinking about how to build Islamic institutions and organize a community structure in the Puget Sound area.

Fereshteh agreed to help, and we began by approaching our natural constituency, the Iranian families in the Tacoma/Lakewood area. Fereshteh assembled a telephone directory among this group and started networking with them. We invited people to parties in our home to celebrate national and religious holidays. With the help of others, we established a weekend school that provided religious education for the children. Fereshteh and I held the traditional Thursday Komeil prayer (*Shabe Joma*) in our home. And at first the idea of building a community among local Iranians drew a positive response. A few of us talked about the children and their need to learn about their identity and culture. We discussed how to keep the Farsi language alive as the younger generations grew up in an English-speaking culture.

Interest in these ideas continued as long as we and a few others made the arrangements and paid the expenses, but there was no appreciable groundswell from the Iranian population at large, no widespread grass-roots participation. Nobody outside of our immediate, small circle stepped forward to take the initiative for organizing new gatherings or developing ideas about how to grow into a mutually supportive community dedicated to preserving our heritage.

In fact, we soon ran into some confusion and disagreement over what we meant by "community." In Iran, community is taken for granted; the community structure is invisible, but it is ever-present and responds to everybody's needs. It is there in the extended family structures, where all find their most important set of relationships, taking special care of children and older people, celebrating births and deaths and religious holidays, and operating on the basis of unwritten rules, strictly observed obligations, and role models. Community in Iran also forms around religious institutions—mosques, cemeteries, charitable organizations, and religious educational circles such as the circle around Sheikh Rajabali-Khayyat in which I participated as a young boy—and has its rules in the judgments and *fatwas* of religious authorities.

Another widespread manifestation of community among Iranians is the *doreh*, gatherings in the form of evening and weekend parties with friends and acquaintances outside the family. These are particularly popular among government officials and wealthy urbanites, involving meals, backgammon or card games, friendly conversation, and other amusements that take place in the homes of participants. In the course of our initial meetings in Lakewood, it became clear that the majority of our people were nostalgic about the *doreh* and envisaged an organization to serve that purpose.

My idea was different. I was hoping to establish a community organization, similar to a church or synagogue that would respond to the social needs and religious education of Iranians and their families. A few of us assumed leadership and, despite the continuing lack of consensus on our main purpose, we started to hold weekly meetings in Lakewood to focus on planning. We divided the organizational tasks among various members of our group and set to work.

Our differences, however, proved to be insurmountable. At its basis, the disagreement was about not only the purpose of the community but also, critically, the core values upon which we should build our community. The majority of our people were from a secular background. They, for the most part, agreed that it was desirable to preserve our Iranian identity for our children and ourselves but argued adamantly that teaching them about Islam should be only a marginal concern. Iranians include various religious minorities, they said, and it would be wrong to exclude those minorities by basing our community on Islamic teachings.

On the opposite side of that question, there were a few people who disputed the value of trying to preserve our national identity. They contended that, over time, immigrants tend to identify less and less with their former national cultures, and by the time of the second or third generation, everybody becomes Americanized. This group believed that our religious identity, on the other hand, went beyond national boundaries and was far more likely to persist; that, as our children and grandchildren's identity as Iranians faded, their identity as Muslims and heirs to the long Islamic culture would survive, to be handed down to future generations as a guide to family life, happiness, and success in American society.

I belonged to a minority within the minority who cherished the Islamic identity, wanted to build the community around it, and also felt it desirable to maintain our sense of being Iranians. Our small group argued that if we could manage to hold onto our religion in America, our national identity would also be preserved.

The discord among us persisted and enthusiasm waned, especially when it came to footing the bill and contributing time toward realizing plans and initiatives that might foster community. People began drifting away from the weekly meetings and did not show up for their duties. After a year or two, the meetings stopped altogether. Among the Lakewood Iranians, people formed regular friendship circles and met in their homes, happy to substitute these *doreh*-type gatherings for true community-building.

My dream was evaporating. It was time to either give it up or rethink the idea.

CHAPTER TEN
The Struggle to Build Community

Religious teachings and childhood upbringing are the most powerful and effective forces for shaping the value system and behavioral norms of most societies. Even atheists and secular humanists cannot escape the fact that their values and ethics are rooted in the religious teachings of their culture. The humanist movement in Europe that began during the Renaissance and influenced all of the West's subsequent history was based in Christianity and Judaism. Emigrants to the New World brought their traditions with them, and there can be no doubt that current-day values, legal codes, and standards of social behavior across both Europe and the Americas owe much to the Judeo-Christian tradition.

This is also the case with Muslims of today. We have formed our own diaspora of emigration from our countries of origin, but whether we have landed in Europe, America, or Asia, we bring with us our traditions, our values, and the religious teachings that guided our ancestors.

Historically, Muslims have not immigrated to the United States because they prefer American culture to that of their homelands. They generally do not consider the Western way of life superior to their own, and they do not come here to replace their system of values. The majority of Muslims have migrated to the U.S. over the past half-century for economic or political reasons; they came in search of a better life, or to escape tyranny, injustice, instability, revolution, and often violence. Their first priorities in the new country were economic survival and, eventually, prosperity for their families, and they wanted to meet a few friends from the old country with whom they could socialize. They were not prepared for the social and environmental forces to which they and their children were constantly exposed in America and when they became aware of them, they often did not know how to assert themselves and counter the undesirable effects of these forces. They had to cope with and manage the unfamiliar environmental pressures individually by trial and error because they did not have in place the organizational structures to bring to their attention the values and strength of their own culture and give them comfort and support for maintaining their own ways of life and value system within American society. They had few resources to teach them how to deal with their new realities.

These were the thoughts that gradually gave rise to my dream of finding a way to help Muslim immigrants preserve their religious and cultural identity in America—and centering that identity around Islam, the spiritual force that binds us all together, Shi'ite and Sunni, Arab and Iranian and Kosovar and Pakistani. My first efforts among the Iranian community of the Tacoma/Lakewood area had proved disappointing, but my devotion to Islam and my love of Iranian culture, poetry, art, and literature drove me to continue the struggle.

I studied the history of other minority immigrants—the Chinese, the Greeks, the Japanese, the Lithuanians, the Irish, Jews, and Scandinavians—and learned that each of these groups spared no effort to build their own communities in the context of the surrounding

American society, making financial sacrifices and devoting much time and effort to the cause. It became for me an obsession to convince other Iranians and other Muslims to work together toward building our communities.

I visited a number of mosques in the Puget Sound region—in Seattle, Tacoma, Lacey, and Portland —most of them built by financial support from overseas religious organizations, particularly in Saudi Arabia and the Gulf States. They catered primarily to Sunni Muslims and tended to perpetuate the Arab culture. I tried to interest the people in community-building activities that might bring Sunni and Shi'a together and give them a unified identity within the American society, but they did not show any enthusiasm for my ideas. And when I spoke of adapting our basic Islamic religious teachings to the needs of the time or of the need to assimilate into American society, they became suspicious, mute, and noncommittal. Most of their imams were trained outside of the U.S. and, naturally, led their communities in the way they were taught to lead. Both clergy and laity seemed content to remain isolated from the American mainstream and were driven by the desire to return to their home country whenever the situation there would improve; they did not see America as their home over the long term.

I did not agree with these approaches to Islam in America. I considered the USA my newly adopted country and believed that my fellow Muslim immigrants should also accept it as such. When I took the oath to become a naturalized citizen, I meant every word and sentiment: from that moment on, I transferred my loyalties to my new country and vowed to remain loyal as long as it is compatible with my conscience and my basic Islamic beliefs. I tried to convey to my Muslim peers that changing our loyalty did not mean the unconditional and uncritical acceptance of American culture and the totality of the

American way of life. I told them that we are not obligated to accept American ways whenever they contradict the Islamic values and moral codes of behavior. For me, the Islamic teachings and the cultural achievements of Muslims are too valuable to be cast aside; they are indispensable assets in our effort to achieve progress within the American environment. I knew that I could be both a good American citizen and a devout Muslim.

I saw this approach as beneficial not only to Muslim immigrants but also to the melting pot that is American society. I was then, and am still, convinced that my approach is the right one for safeguarding our identity and religious freedom. In addition, I believe that the teachings of Islam and the cultural achievement of Muslims in the world add to the cultural and religious richness of America.

Based on those convictions, I could not give up my efforts. I had to pursue my dream.

* * *

Several years passed without my being able to put together a team of fellow Muslims or Iranians who believed in the vision and were ready to work for it. In the beginning there were some who were willing to consider the project, but their interest faded and, over time, I grew frustrated and disheartened. Repeatedly I came to the conclusion that my vision and ideas for Islam in America, as worthy as they seemed to me, simply did not appeal to others enough to set them in motion together with me. I told myself that maybe the time had not yet arrived for Muslims in the West to feel secure enough to embark on their long-term planning for the future. There were times when I would decide for a while to abandon my quest, but then I would wake up at night in bed and tell myself, "If I do not do it, who else will?"

In the meantime, I preached the need for community building and developing religious institutions among Muslims whenever and wherever I had a chance. I gave talks in Iranian circles in Seattle and raised the subject with Iranian students at the University of Washington. Except for a few isolated persons, my presentations did not resonate with them. My American friends, however, encouraged me not to give up. In particular, a retired Methodist minister named Fred Owen became interested in my ideas. Fred had made several trips to Turkey and was impressed by Islam. He wanted to explore with me the religious teachings common to Christianity and Islam, and I wanted him to tell me what to do to build our Islamic community in the Northwest.

At his home in Tacoma one day, we were having a lengthy discussion on the subject when Fred sat up straight in his chair and pointed his finger at me.

"Mahmood!" he said. "Why are you whining?"

"I am not whining," I protested.

"Yes, you are," he said. "If you have a dream, do something about it. This is America. You can achieve things if you have good ideas and work hard."

Fred pointed to the example of how the University of Puget Sound was begun. It started as a small house that a few Methodists bought in the 19th century. The founders used it to teach the Methodist version of Christianity they had brought with them from Europe, and today it is a thriving college that has been teaching students for well over a century.

"Don't be afraid," Fred told me. "Start acting."

Fred Owen's pep talk got me moving in spite of the mixed reactions I had been getting from my own community. Soon I met with my attorney, Jim Krueger, who listened to me compassionately and said, "Your ideas are good, but you need money to do what you want to do."

He told me that if I could set aside $30,000 each year, he would establish and register a charitable foundation for my work. I agreed.

We had an interesting dialogue about writing the foundation's articles of incorporation.

"What are your objectives, and what are your strategies to achieve those objectives?" he asked.

"I don't know exactly," I said. I told him I wanted to do something to preserve the Islamic heritage and Iranian culture for my children and future generations of Iranian Muslims. "I want you to tell me what I should do."

He refused to tell me. We talked a few minutes further without getting anywhere.

Finally he said, "Mahmood, it is your money and you must be clear about your ideas. You have to decide what you want to do. Don't rely on others."

This, like Fred Owen's challenge, was another eye-opener for me in the course of learning how to go about community work. My instinctual urge to wait for someone else to take the initiative—an authority, a "big" person—did not fit the context in the USA, where things are accomplished through the proactive energy of everyday people.

Thus was born the American Moslem Foundation (AMF) in December 1988. The next step was to figure out how exactly to go about building community. My own funds would not take me very far. I appealed to others for help, and at first the response was encouraging, as people who knew and trusted me agreed to join the cause by making financial contributions and becoming members of AMF. This support, however, did not last long. People fell away, saying they were too busy to be involved or they didn't have enough money to continue making donations.

Finally I turned again to a few American friends whom I trusted.

I invited Thomas Saddler, my accountant, and Mike McGowan, a respected businessman and fellow Rotarian, to a luncheon meeting. They were supportive of my project, but Mr. McGowan had some important advice for me.

"Mahmood," he said, "your project is a good one, but the reason you are not moving ahead is because you are trying to create a need in your community and get people to respond to the need at the same time. You cannot do both together. You should go to the community and find out what their priority need is. Then try to respond to that need. The rest will follow."

I took Mike McGowan's advice to heart, and as I asked around, I learned a lot about the Iranian and Muslim communities that had not been clear to me before. In the first place, people tended to be primarily concerned about their material welfare, providing for their families and saving up for their retirement. Their social relationships centered on gatherings of friends who shared similar backgrounds, and these gatherings served as a replacement for the community they had left behind in their countries of origin. Members of the Sunni communities with whom I spoke gave me the impression that they were not as much concerned about losing their religious values or their cultural identity as they were concerned about losing their way of life.

There was one subject of concern to most of them, Shi'a and Sunni alike, both practicing and non-practicing Muslims, and regardless of their national origin: their desire to be buried with all the Islamic rituals—and preferably in a Muslim cemetery. That widespread need rang a bell with me: the initial venture for AMF would be the development of an Islamic cemetery, and it would become the first step in what came to be called the House of Mercy project, or HOM. I looked around for a suitable piece of land and found eight acres in what was then an unincorporated area of King County, southeast of Seattle. The

Foundation purchased the land in 1995, and I began developing plans for the cemetery.

Another dream of mine was to establish an Islamic theological school, and while talking about the cemetery one day with Buck Thompson, a cemetery director and fellow Rotarian, I happened to mention the school to him. He asked me about the size of the Islamic population in the Puget Sound area and told me that, based on demography, the eight acres I had purchased was far more than was needed for the cemetery. He suggested, therefore, that I build the school in one area of the same parcel. Thus was the idea of building the Islamic Theological School of Seattle—the second part of the House of Mercy Project—born in a small office at Mountainview Memorial Park. While the cemetery was under planning, I commissioned architectural plans and applied for the building permit. My dream had begun to take shape.

Little did I know how long it would take to realize the first part of that dream. Little did I understand the obstacles we would encounter—the legal complexities, the county land use hearings to answer questions and satisfy the doubts of neighboring communities, and the difficulty of fundraising. By the time I retired from medical practice in 1998 to pursue my dream full time, we had succeeded only in buying the land we needed and putting in place the plans for the cemetery.

To get the process rolling, we had to apply to King County for a permit for building a religious cemetery. The first obstacle came in the form of an organized effort by neighbors who objected to the idea of having an Islamic cemetery—or, indeed, any Islamic institution—in their "back yard." We had to go through an extensive hearing process in which local homeowners expressed their fear and apprehension. One neighbor asked me if "mullahs with their attire" would roam around in the cemetery. Others were concerned that refugees from Islamic countries might be housed in the cemetery at some future time. After a long and arduous process, plus three days of deliberations, the county granted us a conditional use permit for the Islamic cemetery and funeral home. Our legal and other fees came to $18,000.

Then, while we were in the middle of developing the plans, the community of Covington became incorporated as a city. The House of Mercy property was located within the bounds of the new municipality, which meant we had to go through a second permitting process. To my dismay, the City of Covington refused to honor the county's permit and informed me that it had to go through a "reissuing" process. I was on my knees, praying to God for the permit. I had already signed the contract with a contractor to build the cemetery. I was very worried when I returned to the new city headquarters after a few days and met with a member of the city planning commission to inquire about the process.

He looked at the application and told me, "Go ahead and build it, it's okay."

I left the office stunned by the sudden turnaround but relieved at having the city's approval. I'm still not sure what had changed since our first application, but thankfully, the officials of the newly incorporated municipality were by this time satisfied that they had done their duty and were ready to give the project their blessing.

Now we had a permit, but I had no idea how to build or run a cemetery. My good friends in the Rotary Club again came to the rescue. Buck Thompson, the director of Mountainview Memorial Park in Tacoma, asked me if I had ever built or run a cemetery, and I said no. He introduced me then to his top assistant, Jim Noel, a veteran cemetery administrator. Jim gave me a crash course in the technically complicated processes of developing and running a cemetery. He helped us build ours and record it with state and local government offices. On his recommendation, I engaged a specialized architectural company to design the cemetery. I was surprised—and proud—to learn that ours was the first recorded cemetery to be built in King County for fifty years.

Over several years Jim worked with us tirelessly and always with a smile. Most surprisingly, he refused to charge us anything for his services. When I asked him why, he said, "Americans have done a lot of bad things in the world, and this is my way of showing the good side of America." He was always available, and without his help, I don't know how the project would have been completed.

But complete it we did. We broke ground in 1999. The City of Covington made its final inspection in November 2000 and approved the cemetery. We performed our first interment in March 2001. Jim Noel attended, as did several members of AMF. At the end, Jim took me aside.

"You and I have made a great contribution to American religious history today," he said.

I was, of course, very pleased. I hoped the cemetery would catch on, that the Islamic community in the region would accept it as theirs and bury their loved ones in it. I began to feel hope that the cemetery would become the cornerstone for the larger plan of building the community and establishing an Islamic educational center. And indeed, the initial response from the community was encouraging as, during the first two years of operation, 20 families trusted us with the burial of their loved ones.

After the initial wave, however, rumors and misunderstandings began to spread. The first was that the cemetery was intended only for Shi'a Muslims; Sunni Muslims were discouraged by their Imams and the more fanatical Sunnis to use the cemetery. It was not true that the cemetery was only for Shi'ites; our articles of incorporation made that clear, but of course it is hard to stop a rumor once it starts.

A second problem arose within the Iranian community. There is a modest house on the property, formerly a private residence, with a kitchen and some gathering spaces, available for families of the departed to use, but some did not consider it adequate for entertaining the guests at the burials. In other words, they didn't feel that the cemetery facilities would serve the image of their family properly.

Third, and perhaps most importantly, there were those among both the Shi'a and Sunni communities who resented the rules and procedures that had been instituted in the cemetery. For example, they did not understand the necessity of burying their loved ones within a vault (as required by law) or placing a memorial stone on the grave after the burial. And then there were those who thought everything was negotiable—not only the rules and procedures but also the actual services and pricing as well. That is, they wanted to cut corners in the hope of getting a price break.

Cultural factors underlay all of these misunderstandings, and after the initial wave of enthusiasm for the House of Mercy Cemetery, many found their own reasons for not using our services. The number of burials dwindled. Those families who did use the cemetery, however, never failed to express their enthusiasm about the services and the Islamic identity of the cemetery. It seems that once the burial takes place, people understand the reasons for the rules and procedures.

Thus our ambitious plans for establishing the cemetery as an institution serving the entire Muslim community ran up against unforeseen obstacles, and it has been a slow process. We have struggled with the challenge of effective public relations needed to combat false rumors, and we have butted our heads against difficulties arising from ethnic, cultural, and sectarian differences that American Muslims bring with them from their countries of origin.

* * *

Establishing the theological school has proved even more compli-cated. The idea of building a theological school had occurred to me for several reasons. First, there already existed an Islamic school in Seattle offering primary and secondary education, but there was no Islamic institution of higher education anywhere in the Pacific Northwest. There were only a handful of Islamic theological schools in the Western world, and these, by and large, were either "satellites" of established theological schools in the Middle East or unaccredited schools that were not integrated into the broader educational system. In my judg-ment, they did not meet the needs of a growing population of Muslims who faced the challenges of maintaining their religious and cultural values within the secular environment of the West. It seemed clear to me that an American-based school, teaching students drawn from American Muslim families, would produce religious leaders who were culturally closer to our youth and better equipped to identify with them and educate them in their religion. Such leaders would also be in a better position to represent the views of Islam to the American public and act as consultants to the mass media. Building such a school struck me as a logical next step in the activities of the American Moslem Foundation. It was an ambitious step but, in Fred Owen's words, "this is America" and anything was possible.

Thus, while we were going through the permit process for the cemetery, AMF also applied to build a specialized instruction school in the southern part of our property. We contracted with Ronhovde Architects in the nearby town of Kent to design and make architectur-al drawings. Once again, at considerable cost and with a lot of effort we received the county and city building permits. Now we needed the funds to develop the school—a lot of funds.

Our costs were already running high. At the outset, we estimated that we needed about $600,000 to develop the cemetery itself and another $600,000 to $800,000 for the religious assembly hall—what, for us, serves as the funeral home and also a gathering space. In Islamic culture, cemeteries have a special place because the cemetery connects us to the afterlife. There is a traditional visit to cemeteries on Thursday evenings—on any Thursday evening in Iran, you can see a great many people going into the cemeteries to visit graves—and the assembly hall serves their needs. In addition, after a burial, families invite friends to join them in memorial gatherings on the third day, the seventh day, and the fortieth day, and the assembly hall serves these functions as well.

The cost of the building for the theological school would add about $4 million, an estimate that covered not only construction of the school but ongoing maintenance, equipment, library facilities, and so on. In addition, we estimated that we would need $3 to $4 million in reserves to support the school on a temporary basis. We figured the school would lose money for the first five or six years, until enough students enrolled to help cover the costs through tuition.

I was thinking in terms of a four-year program, roughly paralleling those in Christian seminaries and Jewish rabbinical schools. The curriculum of the school would be developed by an expert committee who would draw from traditions in Islamic theological schools and input from the religious leadership in those schools. In order to equip the students for the spiritual demands of modern time, additional subjects would be included in curriculum as seen fit by the experts. At the end of his or her studies, a student would be certified as a competent, newly trained religious leader. To safeguard the continuation of the Islamic traditional teachings in terms of both content and teaching methodology, the school's board of trustees would include a strong contingent of religious leaders, both Shi'a and Sunni. Finally, I envisioned regular exchanges of students and teachers between our school and religious schools in the Middle East.

Perhaps most importantly, I envisioned the school as an interdenominational institution. This would be possible because, unlike in Christianity, there are in Islam no significant theological differences between the various denominations and branches (Sunni, Shi'a, Sufi, and others)—the basics of the Qur'an, the Hadith, and Islamic history are the same. The differences are mainly in the field of Islamic jurisprudence. Thus, it is entirely possible to put together a curriculum that includes general courses for all students and specialized courses for those of the different branches of Islam. There is, in fact, a precedent for such a program at schools in Damascus during the 15th century.

I saw the project as a grand experiment, a kind of laboratory test for what could eventually emerge as a system of Islamic theological schools in the U.S. and Europe, all of them accredited and involved in cooperative programs with various existing colleges and universities. It seemed logical that if we could get American institutions involved, it would be more than likely that both American philanthropic foundations and Islamic donors would be willing to support the project.

But first we needed money to get the project rolling—at least $6 million, according to our initial estimates.

We applied for funding to the Alavi Foundation in New York, a charitable organization that provides funds to schools and other institutions for teaching Persian and Islamic culture. This application did not bear fruit, but while in New York for meetings with the Alavi people, I also met with the Iranian Ambassador to the United Nations, Hadi Nejad-Hosseinian, to ask his advice. Mr. Nejad-Hosseinian felt that, in addition to the money for building the school, we also needed the support of influential leaders in the seminaries of Iran or elsewhere for running the school and supplying teachers. He referred me to some members of the religious leadership in Qum, and upon his advice I journeyed to Iran in 1999 to explore the possibility of getting support and funding there.

My first stop was Tehran, where I had inconclusive discussions with several government officials. My next stop was Qum. Ambassador Nejad-Hosseinian had kindly referred me to Hojatol-Islam Shahrestani, a son-in-law of Grand Ayatollah Ali al-Sistani, now famous as the most prominent Iraqi Shi'ite leader in the post-Saddam Hussein era. I called Mr. Shahrestani from Tehran and made an appointment to meet with him in his office at 8:00 in the morning.

I made the two-hour drive to Qum early on that morning and was received cordially by the Hojatol-Islam. As we sat down, he said, "Let's have breakfast first." We had an excellent meal, and he gave me some gifts. We spoke for some time, and he expressed a certain amount of sympathy for my project. However, he avoided talking in any specific terms about how he might be able to help, and by the time we parted, the expression in his eyes told me he was not in a position to make a commitment to support my plan.

Others whom I met in Qum responded with less warmth and an equal lack of commitment. One of them was Hojatol-Islam Tabatabai, the Dean of a conservative Haghani college in Qum, who was apparently very close to Ayatollah Seyyed Ali Khamenei, the successor to Ayatollah Ruhollah Khomeini as Iran's supreme leader. Tabatabai appeared quite interested at first, but as we continued our discussion and he came to understand that the school would be located on American soil and run by an independent board of trustees, he backed off.

Another man with whom I spoke was Ayatollah Reza Ostadi, with whom a friend in Vancouver, Canada, had put me in touch. Ayatollah Ostadi was a member of the Expediency Discernment Council, the powerful religious body that oversees parliamentary affairs in Iran to make sure all laws passed are in conformance with Islamic precepts. Ostadi was blunt; he looked me in the eye and said, "Who are you to undertake such an important project? What are your qualifications?" He answered his own question by telling me that I was not qualified to undertake such a project—I was not a clergyman and did not have the necessary background in religious training and experience.

And then he said something further that was very revealing: "We are under constant pressure to revise the meaning of our religious tenets with new interpretations in the light of new discoveries in the world. If we cannot even control the interpretation of Islam in this country [meaning Iran], how can we trust you to set up a school in a land so far away?"

I came back to the States empty-handed, but not yet discouraged. Sometime after that, I had an opportunity to meet with Hojatol-Islam Keshmiri, another son-in-law of Ayatollah Sistani. Mr. Keshmiri, who was based in Kuwait, happened to be visiting in the Puget Sound region as the guest of another organization. He visited the site of the House of Mercy project, and I explained my plans for the theological school. Like Hojatol-Islam Shahrestani, he expressed some interest and sympathy but would not offer any support.

"Your idea is very good," he said, "but what if you are not able to raise enough money later on to run the school? I like your project, but I'm afraid you will not have enough money."

Further efforts brought me no closer to my objective. These included a second meeting with Mr. Shahrestani in Qum, and a meeting with a prominent religious leader in Damascus, who promised to secure funds for the project from Arab leaders in Kuwait. Disappointingly, however, we did not receive a follow-up to that promise.

Why didn't the religious authorities overseas want to help? Couldn't they see the need and the potential for strengthening Islam in America? The short answer, in my opinion, is that they were not sure of the outcome and they did not see the immediate benefit of such an institution to their own Islamic communities in the Middle East.

I have always retained faith in the decency of progressive Americans who would side with us and defend the rights of a new religious minority. We had seen the support of Americans in the Northwest during the initial phase of the House of Mercy project; I personally trusted in their continuing good will. The lack of support from the religious authorities in the Middle East, in contrast, has been a great disappointment.

The religious establishment in the Middle East, both Shi'a and Sunni, is nervous about the possibility of an independent Islam in the West. My conversations with those leaders made me understand that it takes an enormous leap for them to accept the intellectual capacity of a secular country, not to mention the thought that they might lose control over the interpretation and teaching of Islam so far away from their base of operations. An independent theological school would be working in an unfamiliar environment, one containing many social and political forces that are beyond their control. Conditioned by recent history, when Westerners were able to use Middle Eastern governments to impose their ideas upon the religious establishment, today's religious leaders are afraid of being overpowered and pushed into a corner where they will have to make compromises.

It was now apparent that AMF would not be able to achieve its ambitious fundraising goals in the near term, and so, after some further consideration, we revised the plan and divided it into stages. We scaled down our first-stage goal to raising $300,000 as seed money to set up a secretariat and recruit qualified people from the U.S., Europe, and Islamic countries for a planning committee. The planning committee would choose a project director and draw up a "bluebook" laying out the detailed plans for developing the school: student body, academic staff, curriculum, finances, and processes for the ordination of candidates. And, of course, to seek funds inside and outside the U.S.

* * *

That is essentially the point at which the story of the House of Mercy project now stands. We look hopefully to the future. We are far from our goal and searching for new ideas and new partners, but we have laid the foundations of a great project and trust that younger and more energetic Muslims will pick up from where we have left off.

We look back upon two decades of struggle during which the obstacles have often seemed overwhelming, but at every turn we have received support and moved forward. We rely strongly on the mercy and guidance of Almighty God. He is the one, for example, who led Jawad Khaki, a vice-president of Microsoft Corporation, to donate a large number of shares of his company's stock, the sale of which helped us greatly in the early development of the cemetery. More recently we have benefited from the generosity of Jameel Hydar, a Microsoft employee who gave us a large contribution to pay for 80 burial sites and services that were earmarked for donation to needy members of the Muslim community in the future. I am proud to mention also my lovely daughter, Dr. Shahrzad Sarram, who has made a generous cash donation to the cemetery.

Many others have contributed with small and large donations and even engaged themselves personally in making improvements at the House of Mercy. For example, I received a phone call one day from Mohammad Sabbaghi, a horticulturist with a landscaping company, who said he wanted to serve the project for the sake of God. Mr. Sabbaghi worked tirelessly to landscape the cemetery; for more than two years he donated and planted trees and shrubs to make it beautiful—without charge to us.

Throughout the years of the cemetery's operation, the traditional religious rituals of body preparation and burial have been free of charge, done for the sake of God, and carried out by volunteers. There has not been any occasion at the House of Mercy when we did not have volunteers to perform the rituals.

And I shall never forget the kindness of Anne-Marie Ianniciello, a Native American woman originally from Faith, South Dakota, who arranged for the burial of her husband, Achilles John, a Muslim living in Seattle. Ms. Ianniciello was so thrilled and thankful for our services and the support of the community that she donated her wedding ring as a gift to the House of Mercy and made HOM the beneficiary of her life insurance.

These and many other acts of kindness and devotion to God have helped our organization pay off most of the bank loan we took out to build the cemetery. They have helped us maintain the grounds and furnish the building that houses the HOM office; in this respect, one particular gift of two Persian carpets by Mr. Raisdana from Wichita, Kansas, is noteworthy. And they have made it possible for us to establish an Endowment Care permanent fund for the cemetery.

Providing for the future of such an organization requires mechanisms aimed at keeping the necessary funds coming in and acknowledging the kindness of those who contribute. To this end, we started offering memberships in the House of Mercy All-Muslim Cemetery Foundation, aimed at recognizing the Foundation's members as the true owners and protectors of the cemetery, whose membership fees support the institution. We encourage Muslims to include the HOM endowment care fund in their will, and we have constructed a board for posting the names of our major benefactors at the HOM religious assembly hall.

In terms of moving further forward, our efforts got a boost in 2007 when two members of the Sunni mosque in Kent, Sajjad Khan and Mohammad Sheikh Shafique, visited the HOM Cemetery and expressed their desire to support the cemetery in any way they can. We were delighted when they both became full members of the HOM All-

Muslim Cemetery Foundation and Mr. Shafique agreed to act as primary contact person between the cemetery and his community. Shortly thereafter, several Imams from Sunni mosques in the Puget Sound area visited and requested that we reserve a section of the cemetery for the burial of Sunni Muslims. We agreed to the request, and soon we began to perform more frequent Sunni burials in the new section. We are encouraged to be gaining acceptance from the Sunni community.

It cannot be denied that we have a very long distance to go before we achieve the goals we have set. For all our efforts, the theological school remains a dream whose only concrete form so far exists in the architect's drawings and the body of preliminary planning documents that we have completed. I still hold onto my dream, and I still have faith in the plans of Almighty God, as well as in the motto "This is America, where you can achieve things if you have good ideas and work hard."

* * *

Community-building efforts invariably encounter opposition to change—not unlike the reactions I had experienced in Iran toward the process of modernization. Especially frustrating for me has been the fact that many Muslims with whom I speak nod their heads in agreement with my assumptions and plans, but when it comes time to take action they drag their feet and clutch their wallets.

Years of experience, reading, and reflection have led me to an understanding of this mindset. Muslim immigrants begin their lives in a new country in survival mode. Physical, material, and economic concerns occupy much of their attention. They must struggle to put their family's financial affairs in order; they must find a good job, a place to live, and the right schools to send their children to. They need cars, household furnishings, healthcare insurance, food on the table, clothing. When they think about the long term, they confront the enormous challenge of knowing that they must accumulate assets for their old age. And along the way, they are concerned with maintaining a good image, vital for their self-esteem and their social contacts with others of their community.

Iranian immigrants have a particular issue when it comes to their religion. Most of them suffered greatly in order to escape the Islamic government, and they arrived in America with, at best, mixed feelings about Islam. They were content with the idea that each family could impart its values to their children within their own home. What they did not foresee was the profound effect of the school environment, peer pressure, and the public media in shaping their children's value system and patterns of behavior. As a result, problems have often arisen between parents and children as the children have drifted away and moved toward their friends, especially during their teen years.

And so it is that my work continues amid many frustrating moments and the occasional thrill of success. I must confess that I am not one of those people who are gifted with the "people skills" usually associated with aggressive fundraising for the realization of big projects. I am an "idea" person who is most comfortable in the background of an ambitious endeavor, not out in the spotlight, but I have been called to serve God in the capacity in which I find myself. Regrettably, the American Moslem Foundation has not yet grown to the point where we can afford a director of development or a public relations staff, and we still have no one on board with deep experience in these areas. As a result, we may have lost some of our early benefactors because we were not able to maintain their interest and involvement.

And yet, I have not lost hope that someday our worthy projects will come to fruition. Someday the House of Mercy cemetery will be a home for an ever-expanding community, Muslims of all denominations and ethnic backgrounds who have gone to meet God, and a ceremonial home for those who mourn them. Someday the Islamic Theological School of Seattle will be a respected institution producing young clergy for our religious community.

And someday, God willing, American Muslims will find in our work an example that will help prepare the way for more efforts toward bringing us all together in a common pride of our religion and the culture that has come down to us through the wisdom of the prophets, the blood of our true martyrs, the knowledge of teachers and seers, and the energies of the faithful in our own times.

I take heart in the words of Jim Krueger, the attorney for our Foundation, who visited the HOM project and the cemetery at a moment when I was questioning its future.

Jim said, "Mahmood, the doors of this institution will not close. This institution will thrive in the future—with you and without you. Most likely you will not see the result of your work in your lifetime. But the history of America shows us that the first-generation immigrants to this country lay the foundations of their institutions and their communities, and the next generation builds on those foundations."

CHAPTER ELEVEN

A Vision for Muslims in America: Understanding Our Heritage

Americans do not always appreciate all the benefits they derive from their freedoms. A person like me who has come here from a very structured environment senses the change in the atmosphere immediately. America is a place where people like Fred Owen and Jim Krueger tell you, "You are important; you have to think for yourself. You have to define your own goals and make decisions to achieve those goals. You have to assert yourself, and you have to go your way even if others don't accept it." It was a strange concept to me, but ultimately, this is the America that I have especially come to value. The atmosphere of freedom and personal responsibility has enabled me to reach a high degree of self-awareness, come to a more profound understanding of my heritage as an Iranian Muslim, and seek ways to share my heritage with other Muslims living in the West.

The first time I was in America, it was temporary; I was here to gain the skills needed for my chosen profession. My home was still Iran, and there was no need for me to assimilate into the society outside the medical complexes where I served my internship and residency. The second time was different. I started a medical practice, brought my family here, and changed my citizenship. My religion, my Iranian heritage, and my personal drive guided me to be productive in society, and I did my best.

And over time, I realized that America has given me much in return. Obviously, it gave me economic opportunity and the freedom to pursue my profession to the best of my abilities. But America gave me something more, something infinitely valuable: an environment in which I could think independently, exercise my capacity to study and reflect, to learn, and to deepen my knowledge of my cultural and religious heritage. In America, free from the distorting influence of rulers with their own power interests and clergy who are beholden to a hierarchy of rulers, I have reacquainted myself with Islam as it was revealed to the Prophet Mohammad *pbuh* and practiced in early Islamic communities. I have developed a better understanding of God amid the light of new discoveries in science, and I have begun to grasp the ongoing miracle of creation through an approach that is both rational and mystical. In short, I have been given the gift of finding myself among the great truths and mysteries of the universe. This precious gift is the first thing I wish to share with my fellow American Muslims.

The second thing I wish to share is a consciousness and pride in our common history, with all its triumphs and failures, promises and challenges. As Muslims who come to America from abroad, we all bring with us some knowledge of our religion; however, it is a knowledge that has been colored throughout the history of Islamic countries by narrow and dogmatic ideas, as well as an overemphasis on ritual. Our religion has come to be confused with the dictates of social and ethnic customs, such as dress codes, and distorted by those whose main concern is protecting their vested group interests. Yet we have not lost the core values of Islam; they have been handed down to us in God's words as they appear in the Qur'an and as they have been meticulously recorded in the historical events and traditions of the Prophet (the Hadith) and the early rulers of Islamic societies. It is my sense that few of us here in America have taken the opportunity to rediscover the richness of these traditions and the core meanings of Islam.

American Muslims need to do this. We need to understand clearly the legacy of the Prophet Mohammad *pbuh* and the essential message of his teachings—the oneness and centrality of God in human existence and the imperative of developing our spirituality as we journey through this life. We need to fully comprehend that, as humans, we are responsible for our actions, and we will reap the rewards or punishments for our actions on the Day of Judgment. Amid all the choices we have for directing our lives, God gives us the opportunity of drawing near to Him by acquiring His attributes—honesty, kindness, love, forgiveness—and employing them in our daily lives. God calls us to be His vice-regents on earth. In this capacity, we are to practice those Godly attributes in all of our dealings with each other. The struggle to realize Godly attributes and live our lives accordingly—this is the purpose of human life on earth. We are like a farmer who sows seeds in this life and reaps the harvest in the life that follows his earthly death.

We are further called to seek social and economic justice for our fellow humans, recognizing that we all stand equally before God irrespective of our sex, race, color of skin, or ethnicity. Our value in His eyes is determined by our faithfulness, discipline, and self-control (*taghwa*)—and not by our worldly possessions or our ability to exercise power over others. These are the basic, irreducible principles of Islam, the religion founded by Mohammad *pbuh*, whose prophethood we acknowledge.

What happened to this great religion over the centuries to make it such a force in the world today? And what has happened that causes so much confusion today among people, including even Muslims, about the true meaning and message of Islam?

Islamic society went through a golden age for several centuries after the death of Mohammad *pbuh*. From the seventh to the twelfth century, Islam spread across a vast stretch of territory until it reached from Moorish Spain and northwestern Africa across the southern Mediterranean, the Middle East, Persia, the lands of Afghanistan and the Indian subcontinent, central and southeast Asia, and all the way to today's Indonesia. Intellectual life flowered as a result of this expansion. Muslim thinkers discovered the scientific, literary, and philosophical achievements of the ancient Greeks, long forgotten by Europeans; many of the classical Greek writings were translated into Arabic and made accessible to Islamic scholars. Arabs conquered the Sassanid Empire in the East and were exposed to the teachings of Zoroaster and the court system of the Persian Kings. Dynamic societies flourished in the territories that the Muslims conquered.

Within a short span of time Muslims gave the world precious gifts in the form of material, scientific, and intellectual achievements. It was in the Islamic world that modern mathematics first developed, the beginnings of experimental astronomy and astrophysics took shape, and scientists made new discoveries about chemistry and optics. Every major Islamic city in the Middle Ages had a hospital, including one in Cairo with more than 8,000 beds and another principal center of medicine in Baghdad. Islamic thinkers made major contributions in philosophy and theology; Islamic scholars and translators kept alive the great classical works of the Greeks and Romans; and Islamic poets and artists produced works of beauty and enlightenment the likes of which would not be seen in Europe until the Renaissance. While most of Europe languished under the political chaos and intellectual torpor of the Dark Ages, cities such as Baghdad, Damascus, Cairo, Isfahan, and Córdoba were alive with the progress of ideas and education. It has been said that in the ninth century the library in the abbey of St. Gall in present-day Switzerland, with 36 volumes, held the largest collection of books in Christian Europe, while the library of Córdoba in Islamic Spain boasted more than 500,000 books.

The Mongol invasion of the thirteenth century brought an end to the dynamism of the Middle Eastern communities, and the Christian reconquest of Spain, culminating in 1492, snuffed out the once-vibrant culture of the Moors. Islam as a religion lived on in most of the lands to which it had spread, but Islamic culture eventually gave way to Europe as the fount of intellectual, technological, and eventually political dominance. Most of the lands in the Middle East came under the rule of the Ottoman Empire during the sixteenth century. The Ottomans were Muslims governing a diversity of peoples, cultures, and religions within their domains, and while they were known for their political, military, and bureaucratic skills, intellectual and cultural development made little progress over the Empire's lifespan of more than 600 years.

About the so-called golden age of Islam, the question for thoughtful Muslims is what was the relationship of the various dynasties' worldly achievements to the message of the Prophet Mohammad *pbuh* and the spiritual essence of Islam? It is important for Muslims today to know about the grand material achievements of Islamic societies, but how important were those achievements compared with the core purposes of Islam, the religion? If we take pride in the outward dimensions of our cultural heritage, do we do so at the expense of our spirituality?

There can be no question but that Islam is a powerful, dynamic religion that has persisted throughout the ages and remains today a major force in the world. But its legacy is more than that. Islam is a part of the great monotheistic tradition that began with Abraham, the first

Muslim (a person who surrenders himself to the will of God), who called followers of Prophet Mohammad *pbuh* as Muslims (Qur'an 22:78), a tradition that was expanded upon and handed down by the ancient Hebrew prophets through Christianity, and finally by the Prophet Mohammad *pbuh*, the last messenger who further developed and purified God's message. Running through the ages and the wisdom of the prophets is the continuous theme of humanity seeking to reach beyond itself toward the ultimate Truth in God. The message in this priceless tradition is one that humans all over the world need today as much as ever. We who are Muslims must embrace the tradition, strive to understand it, and apply it to the vital questions of our lives, both individually and in community.

At the heart of Islam is the human search for oneness with God, a spiritual journey on Earth that takes place in the context of our life among fellow travelers. The Qur'an teaches us that this common human journey requires certain attitudes and behaviors that enable us to live together in dignity and mutual respect—codes of ethics and behavior that were taught by the prophets and took root among Muslims in the earliest years of our history. We shall return to those codes of ethics and behavior later; for now, it is important to understand that they were an integral part of Islam's essence during the Prophet Mohammad's (*pbuh*) lifetime and for some time thereafter, but in subsequent centuries the codes of ethics and behavior became submerged beneath religious interpretations and practices that departed from the core of the original theology.

During the earliest centuries following the Prophet's revelations, clergy had much freedom to interpret the message of Islam based on the understandings of the companions of the Prophet and the knowledge acquired as the community of Islam expanded far beyond Arabia and became exposed to new worldviews. Men of knowledge who had the luxury of devoting their time to the study of the Qur'an and the Hadith began discussing theological questions. Their studies were aided by what they learned from other civilizations (especially the legacies of the ancient Greeks and Persians) about creation and the application of reason to theological and philosophical inquiry.

Influenced in part by such ideas, a number of devout Muslim thinkers developed a rationalist interpretation of Islam, and as they attracted others to their way of thinking they came to be known collectively as the "school" of Mo'tazeleh. Their work in interpreting disputed theological questions captured the favor of the Abbasid Khalif Ma'moon (813–833 A.D.), the son of the famous ruler Haroon-ol-Rashid, to such an extent that theologians who did not subscribe to the philosophy and interpretation of the School of Mo'tazeleh lost their positions in the religious leadership. The Mo'tazeleh scholars made a valuable contribution to Islamic theology; unfortunately, however, the government's overzealous persecution of those who held other ideas provoked a reaction against all rationalist or progressive interpretations of Islam. Conservative religious forces convinced Ma'moon's successors to curb the influence of Mo'tazeleh, and by the middle of the tenth century A.D., a rival religious school arose, that of Asha'ereh (also called Ah-ol-Sunnah). The proponents of Asha'ereh insisted on a strict observance of the "Word" and opposed independent interpretations of the Qur'an. This new school attracted the strong support of the Abbasid Khalif Motowakel (854–869 A.D.).

The Asha'ereh school has had a profound influence upon Islamic theology ever since. Under the influence of Asha'ereh, the productive minds of Muslim thinkers gradually succumbed to the rulings of the government and its religious leaders. It is generally accepted that the twelfth century A.D. marked the start of the decline of major Islamic intellectual achievements, as the impact of Asha'ereh theology spread to the other scholarly disciplines.

Thus there is an irony about Islam's golden age. The material and intellectual triumphs of that era occurred within highly authoritarian political systems in which khalifs became all-powerful and many members of the *Ulama* (clergy), who were meant to serve the people as spiritual guides in the grand human quest for Truth, compromised the essence of Islam to please the powerful and justify the un-Islamic behavior of the elites. Instead of leading the people, those clergy, in essence, became the servants of the rulers. In their hands, the deep spirituality of Islam gave way to an emphasis on form and ritual. For several hundred years, through the Mongol invasions, over the course of the Ottoman period and up to recent times, mainstream Islamic culture lost touch with a vital part of its early religious heritage.

It is important to note that not all members of the *Ulama* allowed themselves to be corrupted. In fact, many resisted the pressures of the political authorities and refused to deviate from their understanding of the truth. We read little about them today and generally do not know their names, but we know that those anonymous *Ulama* acted to safeguard the true Islamic heritage in an uncompromising manner—and that many of them suffered consequences for their courageous stand. We also know that there was not a clear line dividing those who served the khalifs and sultans and those who resisted them. There were many who did their best to seek the truth while also walking the tightrope of loyalty to their rulers. In any event, we who seek the truth in the twenty-first century are indebted to those members of the clergy who kept alive the core resources of Islam, the Qur'an and the Hadith, in relatively unaltered form and passed them down to us through many, many difficult years. For more on the *Ulama* and Islam's basic sources of truth, see Appendix A.

* * *

In Europe, the Renaissance brought a burst of science and technology, built in large part on the foundations created in the Islamic world. Shipbuilding and navigational technology took Europeans everywhere, including the lands of the Middle East. The Westerners arrived in the Islamic lands in pursuit of trade and wealth. They made contracts with the kings and the aristocracies, bypassing the common people. The ruling classes of the Middle East profited materially from their dealings with the West, but their societies inevitably fell victim to the superior power of the Europeans. It was hard to resist the onslaught of Western ideas, Western technology, Western military power, and Western money. The result was colonialism in both its political and economic forms, a system of exploitation that lasted for centuries and carried with it humiliation, a weakening of basic community values, and confusion about Muslims' identity and heritage.

The troubles within the Islamic world today result from a combination of European colonialism's impact and the internal weaknesses of the local cultures. Westerners' image of cunning Arab sheikhs, tribal warriors riding camels and fighting with swords, and unscrupulous rug merchants grew up during the long years of colonialism. Such stereotypes are to some extent still alive, along with the more modern jumble of suicide bombers, bearded clerics, and fabulously wealthy oil princes. Lingering doubts about Muslims seem to dominate the attitudes of Europeans and Americans, and we continue to suffer from the sting of being considered either inferior or dangerous (or both). It is not surprising that Muslims the world over have mixed feelings about the West, and it is no wonder that we find ourselves perplexed and ambivalent about our identity as a community.

In the case of Iran, the country of my origin, the history of our encounter with the West has much in common with that of other Muslim countries, but our past also has its own coloration. Starting from the Safavid Dynasty in the sixteenth century and continuing through the Ghajar Dynasty of the eighteenth and nineteenth centuries, Iran's leadership appeared blind to the intentions of the Europeans and did not appreciate the power of Western ideas to undermine the local culture. Even more so, the Pahlavi Dynasty of the twentieth century failed to understand the full impact of European attitudes upon our people. The Iranian elites believed that the way for our society to modernize and catch up with the West was not only by adopting foreign technology and management techniques but also by assuming the foreigner's way of life, external appearance, and value system, including the West's materialistic worldview. In other words, our secular leaders believed that Iran would become a modern country by imitating the West. It did not matter to them that the Westerners' attitudes and behavior sometimes offended our values, and it did not occur to them that resentment among our people would grow and eventually become focused on our own pro-Western leaders.

When the enthusiasm of the Islamic Revolution gave way to a troubled state at war with its next-door neighbor, Iraq, and cut off from its former American ally, many people left. The first wave of emigration had actually started just before the fall of the shah, as those who benefited from the corruption of the royal system saw the political storm coming on and fled with their families and their wealth. Later, intellectuals and other early supporters of the revolution who were disappointed to see it taken over by the religious leadership and their radical young foot soldiers, became a second wave of emigrants.

Iran's history since has been one of difficult relations with the outside world and a growing tension between hardliners among the ruling clergy and governmental leaders, on the one side, and a disproportionately young population that is once again restless, on the other. The government has come under much pressure from Western countries and the United Nations to abandon its ambitious plans for developing nuclear energy and its efforts to make independent strides toward the future. These pressures have created hardships for the Iranian people and headaches for the government. There is worry that Iran and the West are edging toward war.

Iran is only one country in the Islamic world from which millions of emigrants have chosen to live in the United States and many other Western lands. Each country—Egypt, Lebanon, Syria, India, Pakistan, Afghanistan, Somalia, and others—has sent its children abroad in search of political stability, economic opportunity, and personal freedom. Each family that has come to the West brings along its language, its specific religious customs and practices, its educational traditions, its patterns of community life, its styles of dress, and many other habits and customs. Thus, while it is true that we American Muslims share a common religion and a common ambivalence about the land in which we have settled, there are a great many differences among us that might seem small when seen from a distance but loom large up close.

The combination of our colonialist past and our ethnic and sectarian differences makes it difficult to find the heart and soul of a community to build upon in this country. We understand the importance of having a common religion, but we do not really know each other and find it difficult to see beyond the issues dividing us. In addition, we all come from cultures that have long been organized "from above," by kings and aristocrats and clerics; when we attempt to "do it ourselves"—to build organizations from the ground up—we stumble because we do not have the cultural experience of creating our own institutions and engineering the development of our own communities. Just as I encountered resistance to change among my patients, students, and colleagues in Shiraz and Isfahan, I have found that many Muslim immigrants in America cling to old patterns and shy away from personal initiative. It is hard for them to make their personal and social life compatible with that of their fellow Americans. Cultural values are deeply rooted, local customs are hard to adjust, and new ways are always subject to distrust.

Particularly resistant to change, for example, are our assumptions about time and the nature of reality and truth. Westerners tend to view time as "monochronic," as organizational psychologist Edgar H. Schein expresses it, meaning that time can be divided into sections, but in each section only one thing can be done at a given point in time. In contrast, most people in Islamic countries regard time as "polychronic," meaning that several things can be done simultaneously. On the larger question concerning the nature of reality and truth, the difference has to do with defining (a) what is real and what is not, and (b) how truth is ultimately to be determined, that is, whether one *discovers* truth or whether truth is *revealed*. Westerners tend to the former position, believing that truth has to be discovered, whereas in the Islamic mind truth must be revealed—or at least supported by revelation; truth has a halo of mystery to it, a kind of holiness.

This is ironic in light of the fact that the Qur'an encourages Muslims to study nature and admire the wonders of God in creation, to travel the world and observe what is happening in other countries, and to study history and contemplate the fate of nations in the past. Many chapters in the Qur'an are named after animals—"The Cow," "Honeybees," and "Elephants," for example—and other natural elements such as the sun, the moon, thunder, day, and night. Numerous other chapters are named after the prophets and nations of the past. The Qur'an repeatedly encourages Muslims to "think," use their "reason," and "indulge in, and think about, the meanings" of the Qur'anic verses and revealed truth. In other words, revelation and reason go hand in hand. Thus the methodology of finding the truth through observation, deduction, and rational inquiry are not at all alien to Islam.

Nevertheless, the cultural attitudes and habits that Muslims have built up over the ages persist, and Muslims by and large continue to find certain fundamental aspects of Western culture uncomfortable. Such discomfort with the surrounding American culture contributes to the difficulty of community building among Muslim immigrants.

What are we to do with our backgrounds? Adjusting to a new environment always requires making changes, but must we abandon everything from our past in order to become Americans?

Of course not. Previous immigrants to this country did not leave behind the essential qualities that made them who they were. The history of America since the landing of the first Europeans is one in which each group of newcomers brought their religion, their values, and at least some of their customs with them, formed communities among their fellow immigrants, and kept alive many of the ingredients that made them special within the American melting-pot. German immigrants built churches and formed clubs to celebrate their ethnic backgrounds; Norwegians, Poles, Italians, Chinese, Koreans, and Puerto Ricans did likewise. Many such groups have built their own churches and community centers, held festive gatherings on their national holidays, marched in parades wearing their ethnic costumes, and taught their children to take pride in their heritage.

This is the way of the future for American Muslims. We, too, can honor our past by keeping our great time-honored traditions and our own values alive here in America. We can build our mosques and community centers, pass our beliefs and values on to our children, prepare and serve our foods with pride—and also be good Americans. We can study and learn about the achievements of our past, teach our children our native tongues, and help them develop an interest in the art, music, and literature of our distant ancestors. Above all, we can develop programs to instruct them in the fundamental principles of our great religion, Islam, in an environment that is free from the distortions of autocratic rulers and those in the clergy who serve their earthly masters' interests. We can do all these things while remaining positive about the human values and achievements of the American people, creating a positive attitude within our community about American society and the American system of government. There is no contradiction in this.

In other words, we can encourage each other to think deeply about our heritage, to understand it and take pride in it. And as we do so, we can uphold and strengthen our Islamic way of life within our families and our communities. We can grow confident in the power and beauty of our traditional teachings; we can know that, far from being a handicap, our religion can fortify us as we develop our careers and pursue success.

Becoming Americans—that is, embracing our home in this new country and establishing ourselves within the wider American community—does not require us to stop being Muslims. It does not require us to adapt our basic values or change our behavior to fit the fashions of others around us. We can hold onto what we know to be true and good and righteous. The "American way of life," after all, is not one standardized set of behaviors determined by TV commercials and the questionable role models of celebrities; it is, as the African-American leader Jesse Jackson once described it, a "crazy quilt" of diverse colors and fabrics that make up a beautiful whole. Despite moments in American history when racial, ethnic, and religious minorities have suffered difficulties and hardships, this country has grown and matured in the course of its national experience. My family and I have seen how gracious and kind Americans can be to newcomers from abroad, and I know that, in its collective heart, America accepts and celebrates its diversity. This is a country where, in the long run, we need not be afraid to honor our own traditions even when they seem to set us apart from others. We do not have to compromise our values by adopting the total package of Western behavior. We can be ourselves.

Do we need to conform to certain standards of personal conduct in order to fit into the culture of the American workplace? Do we need to adopt a new set of ethics to meet the touchstone of Western expectations? While being tolerant and accepting toward minorities and newcomers, Americans do expect high standards in work ethics and personal character. We cannot make our way successfully in this culture by lying, shirking responsibilities, failing to deliver on our promises, or relying on others to do what we ourselves are expected to do—patterns of behavior that have been regrettably common among our compatriots back in our homelands for many, many years. We need to make reasonable adjustments to our working habits; for example, if dealing with one thing at a time produces better results in our work, we should abandon our habit of doing several things at once. And, importantly, we should be open to discovering truth through observation and deduction in cases where that proves more effective than relying on tradition.

And here is the good news: the standards that are expected of us in America are not foreign to our traditions. Our ancestors during the golden age of Islam followed the guidance of the Qur'an and made excellent use of observation and deduction as methods of arriving at the truth—not only in science and mathematics, but also in theology and philosophy. And the same positive personal ethics that have given Western society its dynamism—industry, truthfulness, dependability, generosity, and others—are in fact core principles of Islam, expounded in the Qur'an and taught by the Prophet Mohammad *pbuh* and his earliest interpreters.

Since the very beginnings of Islam, there has existed a basic code of ethics meant to guide humans in their social behavior. Centuries of theological misinterpretation by rulers and their obedient clergy caused the original Islamic code of ethics to be obscured and overpowered by the emphasis on form and ritual. However, if one consults the original texts and explores the life and work of early Muslims as recorded in history books, one cannot miss the centrality of the behavioral codes in the fundamentals of our religion.

We touched upon these Islamic codes of ethics and social behavior in the Introduction to this book. They comprise a number of principles that are repeated again and again in the Qur'an, and that are meant to guide our attitudes and actions within our communities:

- We should always tell the truth.
- We should always fulfill our promises.
- We should always fulfill the terms of our contracts.
- We should safeguard all goods entrusted to us by others and return them.
- We should deal fairly with others.
- We should work hard, create wealth, and support our families. At work, we should be focused on the task and produce to the best of our abilities.
- We should give a designated portion of our earnings to the poor and to public welfare projects.
- We should not be hypocrites.
- We should fear no one but God.
- We should participate in the struggle of building our communities and give of our time and our monetary assets to this cause.

These principles may sound familiar. They are, in fact, universal. They are God-given laws of human behavior, and some form or portion of the commandments exists in most known cultures of the world. Importantly, they represent rules of social behavior that facilitate progress, and they are the driving human force behind modernization.

This should encourage Muslims, especially those of us who have left our countries of origin and settled in the lands of the West. It means that our religion and our basic traditional values do not separate us from the fundamental norms of the societies in which we now live. This is a concept that is crucial for us to absorb—and vital for us to send as a message to our neighbors, co-workers, friends, political leaders, and indeed everybody with whom we come in contact within our new homeland.

How do we send such a message? By living out the commandments of the Islamic codes. By being truthful, fulfilling our promises and contracts, dealing justly with others, working hard, being generous—in other words, embodying and practicing in our daily lives the universal virtues that also stand as guiding behavioral precepts of our religion.

By obeying our religious teachings and building our character upon its core ethical principals, we also conform to what is expected of us by those who are outside our religion. This is how Muslims in America can achieve respect and dignity. It is how we can, and must, become a part of the multicultural "crazy quilt" in which we now live.

On the surface, that might seem obvious and simple, but it is not. In the West, the codes of social behavior have grown up together with a set of cultural norms and habits that govern a wide range of human life, from dress codes and tastes in music, for example, to modes of greeting one another, family and friendship patterns, and sexual conduct. Such attitudes and behaviors have evolved and changed over the years, and one can find many different patterns among the societies of the West (and even within any given society). Nevertheless, it is hard for Westerners to separate their more narrowly focused lifestyle qualities from their deeper system of ethics.

It is equally hard for Muslims because we have traditionally looked upon Westerners as a total "package"—that is, we tend to see a Westerner as a person who follows these habits of dress, these patterns of sexual behavior, and these standards of ethics. We do not find it easy to mark the separation between the universal principles of ethical behavior and the specifically Western (or American) customs and habits that Westerners exhibit.

The point is that they are nevertheless separate. Being fair in our dealings with others and always fulfilling the terms of our contracts are qualitatively different from wearing neckties or pant suits, listening to "rap" music (or Mozart, for that matter), and living within nuclear families. More to the point, adhering to the universal codes of social behavior does not require us to have a secular or materialistic view of life.

It is crucial for Muslims to understand this. We can be Muslims and live our lives according to the universal codes of ethics. We can be progressive, hard-working contributors to our wider community and follow the basic tenets of our Islamic faith. We can be "modern," in the basic sense of the word, and still be Muslims. We do not have to choose between our religion and the ethical obligations of our environment. Acting according to the Islamic codes of behavior is practical; it just happens to be an effective means for assimilating smoothly into American society. And as our community takes root here, we will inevitably change; as in other communities where Islam took root in the past, the local culture and ethnic habits will interact with Islamic teachings and, over time, modulate them—a process that will take place in the course of generations.

The existence of universal ethical codes became clear to me only in America, only by reflecting on my professional success here, my personal and business relationships, and the revelations that came from deep reading of books on community building and, especially, books and other documents relating to the meaning and history of Islam. It may seem ironic, but it was in America that I became deeply and intimately acquainted with the religion of my birthplace. This is not to say that I learned nothing of value from my childhood and upbringing, my participation in the religious circle of Sheikh Rajabali-Khayyat, and my conversations with fellow Muslim students in Germany. All of those experiences were important in my religious awareness. But learning is a lifelong process, and my own self-designed program of "continuing education" in the United States took me several degrees beyond the religious teachings of my youth. The atmosphere of freedom in this country made it possible for me to intensify my understanding of the Qur'an, the lives of its early prophets, and the subsequent contributions of scholars and wise men such as Rumi and Hafiz. Here I have been able to visit libraries and purchase books; here I can sit quietly in my study to read and think; here I am free from censorship, whether from political forces or self-imposed, in defining my values and my understanding of Islam.

It was only in America that I learned how universal values enabled the West to succeed in meeting the challenges of modernization—and why the Islamic countries of the Middle East have not done so. For it has dawned on me that any society, religious or secular, can achieve great social progress if the people are bound together—and, crucially, to their government—by a mutually accepted set of social ethics and norms. In contrast, any society lacking such mutually accepted norms and values cannot succeed and invariably falls victim to corruption. As I think back on my experiences in Iran, it becomes clear that there was a longstanding "disconnect" between the people and the government, which translated into a lack of complete trust and honesty among our citizens. Our religious leaders taught us the forms and rituals of our faith, but they did not clearly teach us the fundamental ethical codes of the Qur'an, and so those codes did not become a part of our natural behavioral instincts. We did not learn those behaviors from the foreigners who brought us new technologies because we saw that, in their lives, the positive attitudes and behaviors were mixed together with customs and habits that we found strange and offensive.

And yet, many Muslims whom I have encountered have a sense that there is something right about Americans' behavior. I often hear it said that Americans, through their actions, are better Muslims than we Muslims are. This tells me that as Muslims we do recognize the value of the Islamic codes of behavior, but somehow we have not learned to apply Islamic ethics to our everyday deeds. We place great importance on certain moral principles, such as maintaining the chastity of women, but we do not give equal weight to principles such as honesty, reliability, fairness, and service to the community.

What Muslims living in the West need to learn, and what the societies of the Middle East also need to learn, is how to internalize the Islamic codes of ethics and behavior so that they become natural and normative in our lives. Once we succeed in doing this, we will be able to stand on our feet and move forward with pride—pride in knowing that our own heritage has prepared us for the modern world, and pride in the future that we can create for ourselves.

The Qur'an (for example, 53:38–40 and 74:38, among other passages) teaches us that God hates laziness, hopelessness, apathy, and irresponsibility; God commands us not to shunt our obligations onto the shoulders of others and particularly not to make others pay for our living expenses. God loves hard-working people who live virtuous lives and make positive contributions to their community. These are the aspects of Islam that have been obscured within our legacy; these are the elements of our faith that we must rediscover and apply to all our affairs.

How do we do it? We are talking about cultural change, a serious and difficult challenge. Cultural change does not happen overnight, and it does not come about easily. But there are things we must resolve to do if we are to achieve the goal of internalizing the ethics of true Islam:

1. First and foremost, we have to revive the religious edict of "conjoining the good and discouraging the bad"(*Ameroona bel maaroof wa yanhoona ane-al-monkar*). It is the duty of all Muslims to support and encourage one another to practice good Islamic behavior and turn away from behavior that is un-Islamic. We must create an atmosphere in which Muslims, both individually and as a community, accept good Islamic behavior as a top-level priority in our daily lives.

2. Every Imam in every mosque should consider it his duty to enlighten the community about the importance of observing the Islamic codes of behavior in our personal and social lives.

3. Teachers in both weekend schools and regular Islamic schools should present the importance of adherence to the Islamic codes, and children should be taught to earn the grace of God by acting as good Muslims.

4. At home, parents, too, should teach their children the norms of Islamic ethics and reinforce the lesson by acting accordingly.

5. It is important to teach children (and adults, as well) that God expects able-bodied men and women to care for themselves and not become a burden to others. To this end education, good jobs, and work ethics are of paramount importance to Islamic communities in America. There is a saying from the Prophet (*pnuh*) that "God turns away from His grace the person who places the burden of his life upon others."

* * *

My life has taught me that the social and technological progress of the West, which we call modernity, is a valuable thing; our lives have benefited from giving up donkeys for motor vehicles, we all enjoy longer and healthier lives thanks to modern medical science, and for sure, it is easier to write a book using a word processor than applying ink to paper by hand. Modernity is not something Muslims should fear or abhor. Science and technology are a gift from God, and the human ability to fashion material goods from the materials God gives us—that, too, is a divine gift. Historical circumstances created favorable conditions in the West for developing the knowledge, the work ethic, and the skills to achieve tremendous benefits. Other societies, both in the Middle East and elsewhere, did not seize the opportunity—or, in some cases, were kept from having the opportunity—to do the same hard work and therefore did not achieve what the West has achieved during the past five centuries. This in no way means that the West uniquely deserves the benefits of modernization. In fact, numerous non-Western societies have already begun to make much progress in their own social and economic development. No one would argue that what the West has achieved is wrong for the rest of the world.

And there is no reason to believe that modernization is bad for Islam. On the contrary, modernization is good for Islam. Modernization is not synonymous with moral decay, and it does not require compromising the values of our faith. It does, however, require conforming to those ethical and behavioral standards that have underlain the progress of modernization—the universal principles that also happen to be the fundamental elements in the Islamic codes of behavior.

We Muslims in the world, especially those of us who have emigrated to the West, can become successful only if we abide by those universal codes. And we can do so while retaining our traditional outlook on life and our own, specifically Islamic, value system: our worldviews, our concepts of existence, our understanding of creation, life, and death—the vital ideas that were developed in the earliest years of Islamic societies.

None of this is meant to suggest that Islamic or Middle Eastern values are the same as American or Western values. While there are many points of overlap, there are also areas of divergence. Consider, for example, competitiveness, which is central to Western capitalism and generally understood as a positive human quality. Competition has a mixed connotation in the Islamic context. On the one hand, competition, as it is generally understood in the West, implies that somebody wins and somebody loses. Losing, however, is not an enduring reflection on the whole person or organization; rather, it is seen as the outcome of one specific contest or incident, and it is reversible.

In contrast, Islam values competition in another sense of the word, one that takes the emphasis away from personal gain at the expense of others. Self-gain is permissible as long as it does not glorify and set apart persons or groups in the society, but the main thrust of competition, in the Islamic sense, is on virtuous acts. The Qur'an (2:148, 3:114, 5:48, 21:90, 23:61, and 35:32) advises us, in essence, to compete with ourselves in creating positive works for the welfare of society. The aim is to work hard, use our mind, and do our best to please God with our deeds. The concept is akin to the American slogans "Personal best" and "Be all that you can be."

Thus, Islam rejects competition as a means of self-aggrandizement. The idea is that there should be no losers; some competitors win because they achieve their goals, others because they try and, in trying, give their best effort. A parallel in the West can be seen in the Special Olympics, where athletes with disabilities win by overcoming the odds against them; they all receive honors for showing up and running the race in wheelchairs or playing the game on crutches. Islam values the very act of competing, not necessarily the outcome as seen in the context of winning and losing. All who "give it their best shot" are winners. As it is written, "There is no gain for a human except that for which he struggles." (Qur'an 53:39)

Muslims in America must nevertheless learn to operate within the Western environment of competitiveness. That does not mean we should give up our sense of fairness, but if we are to succeed in the West, we must find some balance that permits us to perform in a way that does not disadvantage us. We do not have to become personally aggressive—a characteristic that is inherently difficult for many of us—but if we focus on our own individual capabilities and strive always to perform according to our personal best, we can succeed while, at the same time, demonstrating to those around us our competence, our capacity for teamwork, and our sense of fairness.

Another difference between Muslims' traditional way of thinking and that of the Western world resides in the political realm, specifically in the concepts of representative government and the rule of law. Throughout history, Muslims have generally been content to trust their religious leaders and their traditional rulers to govern benevolently, and have not felt an urgent need to get involved in the day-to-day affairs of governance. It is only in recent times that Islamic societies have been exposed to the representative mode of governance as it has developed in Western countries, but this has not yet resulted in a deep understanding of the "rules of political engagement." Elections take place at various levels of government but, by and large, citizens' sense of political responsibility more or less ends at the ballot box. The attitude seems to be, "We've done our duty by electing our leaders; now we can go home and let them rule."

In the Western systems, by contrast, when citizens elect people as representative leaders, they take the word "representative" seriously;

they expect their leaders to make policies and enact laws that reflect their ethical standards and deliver benefits to the masses. To this end, citizen groups and even individuals petition and lobby their legislators, expressing their particular interests and demanding concrete results. Many citizens and interest groups contribute money to politicians' electoral campaigns, expecting to be repaid in terms of either special group interests or the wider public interest (as the contributors interpret it).

Whatever a person's partisan beliefs, respect for the law is a powerful force in Western societies. Such sayings as "It is the law of the land," "… because that's the law," or "It's against the law" are potent expressions that affect people's behavior. Laws are drafted, proposed, discussed, and passed by the representatives of the people and therefore command a high degree of respect and obedience by the masses— even laws that are not to the liking of this or that person.

In most Islamic countries today, parliaments and other elected bodies pass legislation, but the people do not completely trust the laws (and may even consider it optional to abide by them) because they feel that their voice is not heard and the laws do not really address their interests. Often this is true; politicians pass laws that ignore the interests of the people, and the masses are unable to express their objections or demand changes.

Traditionally among Muslims, moral codes have played a role akin to the rule of law among Westerners. The moral codes, handed down to the people by the prophets, are presumed to be backed by the power of God and therefore stand independent of society's laws. Whoever transgresses the moral codes is ultimately answerable to God. This contrasts with the presumption in Western cultures, where individuals who transgress the law or the ethical codes are answerable to the people, the law, and the government.

Muslims in America need to understand these fundamental facts of the Western social and political culture. Secular ethics define the dominant norms of personal behavior. The law must be obeyed at home, at work, and at all levels of society. When a social situation calls for a judgment between right and wrong, Muslims must consider not only whether a given action is moral and acceptable to God, but also whether it is ethical and lawful by American standards.

Like other citizens, we Muslims should learn to use the power of the law for individual and collective benefits. We should get involved in the electoral process and make sure that those who campaign to represent us have our interests in mind when we cast our votes, and we should not be hesitant to petition them in office. This is another way in which we can prove our worth, both to ourselves and to our neighbors, and demonstrate that we, like all the immigrant groups that preceded us, deserve our position as first-class citizens of this country. (For more about ethics and morality, see Appendix B.)

* * *

What, finally, can we say to those among us who question the validity or importance of our religion? If we have chosen to leave our countries of origin behind, why do we not just assimilate completely into the world where we now live by either adopting a totally secular philosophy or joining an existing Christian or Jewish faith community? Why should we insist on holding fast to Islam? These are not simple questions, and we cannot answer them persuasively by saying "because it wouldn't be right," or even "because we are, after all, Muslims."

But in fact, we are, after all, Muslims—and that statement, while insufficient in itself, begins to answer the question of why it is important for us to hold onto our faith. Islam is the source of inspiration and guidance that has governed our lives in the past and should continue to do so over the long term. And far from being a dispensable item that we can leave behind, our religion is especially needed when we move from our ancestral surroundings to another place far away.

Human beings are bound by nature to live with each other in social settings. We are born into a family, grow up and go to school with other children, and find our friends in school. We find our partner in marriage and build a new family within a community. We work and conduct business with others in the marketplace, the office, the factory, or the farm. Eventually we die and leave our inheritance to our family. In every step of life we depend upon interactions with others. Local and ethnic customs, cultural norms, value systems, and laws that are rooted in the history of each community determine the rules and norms for these social interactions. Many of these rules and norms are invisible on the surface, but they shape our behavior every day and within all of our relationships. Throughout much of human history and continuing today, human communities have relied on religion to give meaning and form to the rules by which we live, as well as a sense that our lives have a purpose that transcends our mundane affairs.

When an individual or a family migrates to a place that is governed by different cultural norms and a different value system, they face what can be enormous problems of adjustment. Immigrants do not understand the nuances of their new environment, make false assumptions about others, and become distressed when they are not treated with understanding and respect. They have left their familiar surroundings behind, together with the cultural assumptions that held their former communities together, and they may not find religious resources adequate to their need for spiritual support.

Those of us who come from Islamic countries leave behind societies in which most people interact within the framework of large extended families. Throughout our lives we have enjoyed deep loyalties and a sense of trust that comes to us freely and naturally from our family members. As children, we grow up with cousins, grandparents, uncles, and aunts. We have no identity crisis, because we know who we are within the structures of our families. We carry a system of values and an appreciation of how to behave in all situations, based on our upbringing and the multitude of role models surrounding us. We do not have to prove ourselves or explain the way we act or speak; our family and our society accept us as we are. We are rarely conscious of the social structures holding us up, but they are always there.

In our countries of origin, we did not even have to think about what it might mean to defend or apologize for our national identity— or our religion—but in the West, it is quite the opposite. We are foreigners, speaking English less than perfectly and with an accent. We bring with us ideas, customs, and a faith that others find strange— exotic at best, dangerous at worst. Our children especially enter an environment at school where they are immediately identified as different, and they quickly feel the pull of the surrounding culture to be like everyone else, which generally means they are expected to adopt a secular outlook and a materialistic value system. Peer pressure, itself powerful, is reinforced and intensified by the public media. And later, as the children become adults and move into the workplace, the forces tugging at them grow even stronger.

It is not surprising that our children become critical of themselves, their parents, and the culture of the "old country." Yet they love their parents and are constantly in conflict over how to maintain the love in their heart and at the same time distance themselves from their parents' norms and expectations. Many find themselves torn between wanting to be like their classmates, feeling that is the only way they will be accepted, and wanting not to be alienated from their parents. They experience a sense of crisis over their values and their identity; they do not know for sure who they are, to which culture they belong, or how to determine what is good and what is not so good.

The adults, the parent generation, generally realize the nature of the problem, but many react defensively and express feelings that are inconsistent or confused. Their attitudes vary depending upon the degree of their adherence to Islamic teachings, their socio-economic standing, and whether they are disposed to be conservative or liberal. Typical attitudes follow several different patterns:

• Total and pro-active conformity. America is our new country, and it is a melting pot. Our children and their children will eventually accept America's culture, way of life, and value system. This is a normal process, and we should not resist it. Like most American children, some of ours are going to be educated and successful and some will turn out not so successful. We will do our best to raise them according to American standards and teach them decency and good character.

• Total rejection. American culture is ungodly and corrupt. For our own sake and that of our children (especially our daughters), we plan to return to our home country as soon as we get the opportunity. In the meantime, we will shield our children in every possible way from the bad influences of this country.

• Passive conformity. We like America and wish to stay in this country and raise our children here. But we want our children to adhere to our own culture and value system. It seems next to impossible, however. We do our best at home to teach our children our good manners and develop their character as we would want them to be, but we are not sure we can succeed. As for the future, we leave it in the hands of fate and concentrate now on our economic priorities: paying for our home, feeding the family, and providing for the education and welfare of our children.

• Pro-active and constructive adaptation. We choose to stay here because we value the positive aspects of America. We wish to be loyal American citizens, but we are also determined to preserve our religious, spiritual, and moral values. We consider Islam a precious asset for our children and ourselves, and we involve ourselves in organizations that strive to keep our Islamic heritage alive as a guiding force in our families and community.

Among American Muslims, each of these attitudinal patterns exists across lines of ethnicity and national background, whether we are talking about Indians, Egyptians, Lebanese, Iranians, or almost any other group.

From all that has been said in this book, it should be apparent that the last-mentioned approach, pro-active and constructive adaptation, reflects my position, and my vision of the future for American Muslims revolves around the goals implicit in this approach. Those who agree with me strongly believe in Islam, whose basic precepts we endeavor to follow in our daily life. We want our children to acquire a deep knowledge of our faith and become good examples of practicing American Muslims. We believe that Islam is a religion of reason and, as such, is thoroughly compatible with modern science and technology. We enjoy the fruits of modernity and, like other Americans, place a high value on progress. With its wealth of spiritual and intellectual resources, Islam embraces the challenges of modern life and offers its wisdom to guide us along the right path. Islam is an asset to our lives, not a liability.

Even as we value our religious heritage, we also value our freely chosen identity as citizens of the United States of America. We intend to make ourselves known as enthusiastic contributors to our adopted country. We are proactive in preserving our cultural and religious identity, and we refuse to be passive or reactive in the face of discrimination and negative stereotyping which we sometimes experience because of our backgrounds. We do not accept or tolerate any barriers or constraints for ourselves or our children to becoming involved and achieving success in both the private and the public spheres of life in the country that we are now proud to call our home. We fiercely defend our honor as American citizens and, hand in hand with our neighbors, we gladly work toward the common goals of building our community.

My vision for American Muslims, then, is one in which we project our values and pride outward while working diligently in all social and economic spheres of society. In the workplace, we must be exemplary in terms of our honesty, reliability, and industriousness. In our private lives we must be kind, loving, and helpful, doing all things with an eye toward the grace and acceptance of God.

Deep down in our hearts, Muslims feel a sense of honor and dignity, but we do not yet see our neighbors, public officials, and the mass media recognizing this dignity. We are particularly concerned about our image in the mass media. When we turn away from the news reports and look in the mirror, we see that we are not as bad as what we have just seen, heard, and read about ourselves. We are learning that we have to do whatever it takes to earn the respect and honor of our fellow citizens.

And when we succeed in demonstrating that we are useful and contributing members of society, we will also be recognized for who we are on another level. We are Muslims, which is to say, we are people of a particular religious faith carrying the wisdom and spiritual power of our tradition, and as Americans, we bring with us all that we have from our past and present to bear on the challenges our country faces now and in the future. What we have to offer, and what we will gladly contribute, are the work of our hands, the kindness of our hearts, the thoughtfulness of our minds, the richness of our heritage, and the spiritual insights of our religion. To the beautiful crazy quilt of American society, we add our own patch of brilliant color.

Chapter Twelve

A Vision for Muslims in America: Building Institutions for Our Future

How do we realize the vision of community among American Muslims? Through what strategy can we establish ourselves as a cohesive and constructive force in the multicultural landscape where we now make our homes?

Most members of the recent immigrant generations arrive in America from countries where the dominant culture and value system are based on Islam. Living as a religious minority is something new and different, and for many it presents a challenging environment. Add in the fact that the basic political, legal, and social ethics of the United States are secular, and the result can be confusing for many. Most of the immigrants have no prior experience of life in a secular society, where religion and state are separate and operate independent of each other in the public arena.

In the United States, church and state function parallel with each other in a fashion that is sometimes cooperative and sometimes not—but it is always premised on the independence of religious organizations from the state and the principle that religious organizations do not impose their interests on the institutions of public authority. Americans inherited this essentially secular public philosophy from Europe. Although many European countries still maintain connections between the state and religious organizations—such as the Church of England and the existence of government funding for churches in most of Europe—the public value system there, too, is the product of a secularization process that has taken place over the past several hundred years. The framers of the American Constitution were determined to carve an even stronger separation between church and state so as to guarantee that neither would encroach on the rights and purposes of the other. More than two and one-quarter centuries of independence have guaranteed that the separation of church and state is ingrained in the American political culture.

Some Islamic countries, such as Turkey, have also adopted constitutional principles of secularism; by and large, however, Islamic countries have not gone through secularization step by step as a natural process but, rather, they have had secularization imposed upon them by political forces—as in both Iran (prior to the Islamic Revolution) and Iraq, for example. As a result, Muslims are often confused about the margins of separation of church and state in private and public life.

This confusion carries over into Muslims' attitudes about how their religious communities are created and maintained. As we have pointed out elsewhere in this book, ordinary Muslims have a tendency to expect others—the wealthy and powerful members of society—to create their institutions, provide the funding and leadership, and ensure their continuation into the future. We see that happening in the United States today, as many of the mosques that have sprung up in American cities have developed thanks to "petro-dollars" from the Middle East. One must question the wisdom of such reliance on others who live in remote countries and, in many cases, have their own interests. And one must question the overall benefits of such largesse to our communities, for we live here within a wider society that values and promotes self-sufficiency, not reliance on out-siders. If we as American Muslims cannot provide and maintain our own institutions, what does that say about our sense of commitment to them? And what does it say about our ability to find our own identity as full-fledged Americans capable of making our maximum contribution to our country?

We need to build our own religious institutions, then, first of all because we need to establish our sense of identity separate from the powerful forces we have left behind in our countries of origin. My efforts toward establishing an Islamic theological school have had that aim all along. Only through an independent effort can we develop the religious leadership we need to interpret our religion and guide our faith in ways that are thoroughly conscious of our realities as Muslims living in America.

A second reason for creating our own institutions grows out of conditions discussed in Chapter 11, namely the loss of the social support systems that we left behind when we came to this country. Some of us may have brought along a portion of our extended family, but none of us have brought the entire web of family relationships, let alone the network of wider social relationships and customs that grew up over many centuries on the basis of complete family and kinship systems. Here, in emigration, we become aware of what we are missing. As an influence on their children's development, nuclear families do not have nearly the strength that extended families have. Our system of support and role models cannot stand up to the power of the surrounding culture, with its materi-alistic values, peer pressure, and media appeal.

In this environment it is not surprising that, little by little, Muslim parents lose control over the direction that their children take in life. In far too many cases, their children become strangers to them, and by the time the children grow up, they have become deeply influenced by their world at school and by the public media. Sometimes parents are too quick to throw up their hands in defeat, admitting that the society has more influence over their children than they have. One often hears the comment from parents, discouraged by the trends among their children, that "we should have stayed in our country" instead of immigrating to the U.S. They are suffering—and their children, who may or may not be willing to admit it, are also suffering because a wall has grown up between them and their parents.

What we have lost in terms of extended-family networks, we must replace with strong religious institutions that will serve to educate our children in their faith and help them develop the strength to live as dutiful Muslims within the surrounding social environment. Such institutions must be built by our hands from the resources of our own pocketbooks, and led by persons who are not only well trained in the elements of our faith but also familiar with the circumstances of our lives here in secular America.

In addition to mosques and seminaries, we must also build Islamic community centers, which can further help us raise our children in our faith. I have in mind places of gathering where children associate regularly with other Muslims, young and old, and learn from them. Community centers can serve some of the functions of the extended family as children meet role models among successful adults. They can also gain strength by making friends with other children who have the same values and outlook in life. This is not to say that the community centers would in effect segregate our children from non-Muslim children, but rather, our children would find reinforcement for their religious faith and our moral values. Such reinforcement would help our children understand that they are not alone when they interact with children from other religious (and secular) backgrounds, and therefore they need not feel "weird" or marginalized among their non-Muslim friends and schoolmates.

Another reason for building strong community institutions pertains to adult Muslims in the American workplace. Many Muslim immigrants arrive in the United States without the education or skills required for good jobs. As a result, their ability to support themselves and their family is limited. It is not uncommon to find Muslim families on welfare, receiving food stamps. They work mostly in service industries and operate in survival mode. They have hopes for a comfortable dwelling place and adequate food and clothing for their families, but it is hard to break out of the cycle they are in because they do not have the time or the financial means to seek new jobs or gain the training they need for a better position.

There are, of course, many successful and contented Muslim immigrant families in the U.S. Their children have become successfully educated and gainfully employed, and they enjoy happy family relations, for the most part. These better-off Muslims can serve as a valuable resource for those who are less well off, but the Muslim community does not have effective institutions for bringing people together and communicating needs. In the old country, kinship ties and related social support systems tend to look out for those who face economic hardship, but here in America, we need new mechanisms of career networking and support in order to care for our own.

Still another need concerns the elderly members of our population. In the old country, the elders in the extended family enjoy a position of respect; their children look after them and make sure they do not live in poverty and loneliness. One of the sad realities in the United States is that a great many elderly people are left to fend for themselves even as they become incapable of earning a living, and they do not receive sufficient financial and medical benefits from public sources. Poverty and loneliness are epidemic among America's elderly.

To our shame, the problem has begun to occur among Muslims in this country. The custom for Muslims to socialize and relax with friends at evening parties becomes more difficult as people grow older and less mobile. Many sit at home and expect others to visit them, but this does not always happen. Their old friends die one by one or are similarly unable to get around easily; their children are busy with their own lives and do not feel obligated to go out of their way to visit their parents. Boredom and depression may set in. The elders look forward with fear to the day when they are put up in nursing homes.

Thus, the elderly among us represent yet another urgent condition within our Muslim community that cries out for institutions capable of responding to the need. Certainly our traditional values tell us that we must raise our children according to the teachings of our faith, assist those among us who need help making their way in life, and provide loving, generous care to our elders. We are not lacking in the financial means or the compassion to take on these challenges. So far, however, we have been lacking in the will and the imagination to do so.

And just as it is important for Muslims to remember our basic obligations to each other, it is also important to instruct and remind Muslims of those virtues and practices that constitute the Islamic codes of ethics and behavior. We need educational programs in community centers and preaching in the mosques to urge our fellow Muslims to adopt the codes as a strict guideline for their lives.

Mosques, schools, community centers, and cemeteries … obviously, we are talking about money, commitment, time, and energy. Such institutions cannot be created and maintained without personal and community sacrifices. And they cannot achieve their purpose without the wisdom and the ongoing support of activists among us who are willing to "carry the ball" and hand it off to subsequent generations. We are talking about buildings and physical properties, yes; but we are also talking about a vigorous effort on the part of many individuals, beginning now and extending into the future farther than any of us who are alive today can see. I am aware that what I am asking is not easy and will not come about overnight, but it is vital to the survival and, indeed, the soul, of the American Muslim community.

We only have to look at examples around us to get a picture of the possibilities. This land has accepted immigrants since the earliest European settlers arrived. America has been called a melting pot, but in fact the many national, ethnic, and religious groups who have formed this society have brought with them specific group identities. Many new immigrant groups have faced some form of discrimination or even outright hostility, but they all find a way to become accepted. In time, they take advantage of the chance to prove themselves and show that they are good citizens. During the early years of the twentieth century, for example, it was not uncommon to see shops and factories with signs that read, "Help wanted—Irish need not apply." It was not until well after World War II that Chinese and Japanese came to be accepted as the equals of white Americans, and it was only then as well that Jews were welcomed into the elite universities, corporate board rooms, and country clubs. But today, nobody blinks an eye at members of these groups occupying responsible positions in business, medicine, politics, education, and every walk of life across our country.

Traditionally, new immigrants have found solidarity by banding together to preserve their cultural identity, and America has allowed and even encouraged them to do so as long as they stay within the law. In their public dealings, however, they are all expected to follow the norm and abide by laws and behavioral codes that apply uniformly to everyone. Over a period of time, the newcomers create a public image for themselves as a group; Italian-Americans, Polish-Americans, Hungarian-Americans, Japanese-Americans, Chinese-Americans, Mexican-Americans, and so on—these "hyphenated" Americans find their way into the mainstream without losing their group identities. As Muslims in America, we have not yet established such a positive public image for ourselves. We are not yet hyphenated.

One of the ways the American public builds an image of immigrants is by noticing the extent of self-help each group and its institutions achieve. An immigrant group is more respected if its members are organized and able to help themselves, particularly if they take care of the weak and needy members of their group. Muslims in America should take a lesson from this. By creating institutions in which the members of our community come together and help each other achieve a productive and honorable life, we not only serve the individual and family interests of our own people, but we also develop a positive public image of ourselves.

American Muslims can take comfort from the fact that the history of immigrant groups in America and how they have entered the mainstream is not only about ethnic, national, or racial groups. Certain religious minorities have had to establish themselves within the mainstream, as well. Jews, Catholics, and Mormons have encountered discrimination in their times; indeed, as recently as 1960 many Americans voted against John F. Kennedy for the presidency simply because he was a Catholic. Religious minorities in America have always recognized the importance of their faith communities as a source of strength in times of hardship and social prejudice. Once again, American Muslims can take a lesson.

Religious communities in America are usually built around churches, synagogues, and temples. Each of these words denotes both the faith organization itself (the congregation) and the physical building that houses the organization. Thus, for example, a person might say, "I am a member of Saint John's Church (or Temple Beth Shalom)" and also "I attend worship services at Saint John's Church (or Temple Beth Shalom)." Each member of a faith community feels responsible for the support and maintenance of the community. When money and manpower are needed for a task in the community, everyone is expected to help—there is no "free lunch." Thanking others or offering prayer does not substitute for giving money and helping with the tasks; all know that they have to contribute to the community if they expect to receive from it. Everybody is aware that the community must be built first and become financially strong before it can help its members.

In a typical American church, families send their children to Sunday school from the time they are small. Children go to the daycare and kindergarten that are organized and run by the church. Teenage children and youth are taken to church services regularly. They join other youth in the church for group activities, sports, and summer camps. Young adults often find their marriage partners in the church community and take up the work where their parents have left off. The most faithful adults attend religious services each week. They attend additional church functions, such as community meals, and meet other families who have common goals and values in life. They participate in adult religious education, and they serve on the governing councils and committees of their congregation. In many church communities, members find economic opportunities as prospective employers and job seekers, professional people and potential clients, get to know each other within the church.

The United States may be the most religious country in the industrialized West. It is said that over 40 percent of all Americans belong to a church, temple, or other religious organization and that, on average, each family contributes $1200.00 to $1500.00 to its faith community every year. Some give many times that amount. Traditionally, the payment to the church is based on the concept of tithing, a practice from Judaism, where in ancient times each person or household was required to pay 10 percent of its gross income to the religious community. This concept is still taken seriously by many Jewish families and some of the Christian denominations, for example, Seventh-day Adventists and Mormons. Other denominations tend to leave the amount of member contributions to the discretion of the individuals, or they may suggest (but not require) certain levels of giving as a goal.

A majority of the Christian churches in the United States are small, and most of them struggle to meet their annual budgets; however, there are also a significant number of very large, wealthy, and highly visible churches and synagogues that are able to afford beautiful buildings and generous programs of assistance to the poor, both in their own locality and around the world. Muslims observe such large churches, sometimes, with a sense of despair, realizing that the new church building going up in their neighborhood costs millions of dollars while their own (Muslim) community seems unable to raise enough money to build a small mosque.

In light of this negative comparison, we have to ask ourselves who is responsible for our problems and hardships. Is it America's fault, because Americans tend to see us as alien or untrustworthy? We know that, despite the successes some of us have enjoyed in our professions, suspicion and bigotry toward us exist among many of our neighbors. As a community, Muslims in the United States today—not just since 9/11/2001 but also before that horrible moment—must struggle to overcome prejudices and stereotypes not unlike those that Italian, Jewish, Irish, Polish, and other immigrant groups faced in earlier times. Will we overcome these prejudices over time? And over how much time? Or are we a special case? Does our religion lie too far outside the mainstream of American culture?

I do not believe so. Muslims may face greater difficulties than other immigrant groups have faced, but I believe America holds wonderful opportunities for us. We must assume some of the blame ourselves for not having the foresight to come together and present a coherent, positive group identity. There is still time for us to do this. We are a young group, as immigrant communities go, and we have not been a noticeable part of this country's population for nearly as long as those earlier groups who struggled and won their rightful place in society. But it is time to gather our forces and begin the task of developing community institutions.

Some have succeeded in taking small steps forward. In the Seattle area, for example, several organizations have grown up among both Shi'a and Sunni communities. One such organization is IMAN-WA, established by Muslims of the Khoja-Shi'a, consisting of members who have mostly emigrated from countries in East Africa. The organization holds religious services in its center in Kirkland, a Seattle suburb, as well as an active Sunday school for children. Another Shi'ite institution is the Islamic Educational Center of Seattle (IECS), which has regular Friday- and Saturday-evening meetings that include both parents and children. In addition, IECS devotes Sundays to activities for children and youth. Seattle and its suburbs are also home to several Sunni mosques, including the Idriss Mosque in Seattle, Kent mosque, Northside Mosque, the West Seattle Masjid, Jama'at Al-Ikhlas, and Masjid Abu Bakr, as well as the Seattle Islamic School, an elementary school for Muslim children.

These are only a handful of many local institutions that have sprung up around the U.S., each centering on its own community and having purposes that vary somewhat. They represent a good start, but for the most part they remain small organizations focused on specific Muslim populations. All of them, Sunni and Shi'a alike, face financial challenges rooted in the longstanding habits of Muslims to rely on outside forces for funding and leadership. And so far, the general tendency of the existing institutions has been to serve their own denominational or sectarian communities and to resist cooperation across sectarian lines, for example between Sunni and Shi'a. As a result, there is little sense of unity among the many groups and congregations, and not much momentum toward building a public image that presents American Muslims to the wider society in a way that gains us the honor and respect we crave.

But in this light, I must mention a promising organization that has begun to develop. One Nation is a foundation whose mission, in its words, is "to bridge the divide [between Muslims and other Americans] by integrating the voices and viewpoints of the American Muslim community into the national conversation, including their stories, their faith, and their contributions to American society." One Nation has developed a website, www.onenationforall.org, that aims to promote a national conversation about common values all Americans share. One Nation stands as an interesting, and potentially vital, type of organization that is much needed by both Muslims and non-Muslims across this land.

But what will make the broad effort work? What is required for realizing the vision of understanding and preserving our heritage, communicating our true character to the American public, and firmly establishing our place in the social landscape of this great country?

If Muslims in America wish to achieve these goals, we must first come to an understanding that doing so requires:

• Strong, lasting institutions.

• The committed, active, generous participation of the majority of American Muslims, who must be the main providers of money and manpower for building and running effective institutions.

• That we all make this a top priority in our lives—as important and, indeed, mandatory, as paying our mortgage or buying groceries.

It is easy for me to write about these requirements, but meeting them will call for more than just words. To realize the vision, we Muslims in America will need to make a colossal paradigm shift in our attitudes, a change that will require persistent and effective educational efforts by our civic leaders and the Imams in our mosques. It is up to us to take responsibility for building and maintaining Islamic institutions. We must stop hoping for wealthy benefactors from other countries to provide the financing, and we cannot expect the government—any government, American or foreign, national or local—to step in and do the work. We can work to build philanthropic organizations to lead the way—but the proper emphasis must be on the fact that *we* build the philanthropic organizations. To create and maintain *our* institutions, *we* must assume the responsibility. *We* must be willing to make the sacrifice. *We* must get involved.

There will be no lack of difficulties. Our ethnic and cultural differences are great; whether we are Arab or Iranian, Pakistani or Indian, Somali or Nigerian or African-American, we find it hard today to reach across the boundaries and cooperate with other Muslims. Similarly, we face the deep-rooted historical and political chasm between Sunni and Shi'a. Perpetuating these divisions is not in our interest. We have to understand that for Americans, government as well as society, there is only one Muslim community in the United States. We are not seen as ethnic groups or denominations; we are seen as Muslims, and whatever one of us does, we all are identified with it. The image we project to the wider public is that of Muslims, not as Sunni or Shi'a, and not as Arab, Pakistani, or Iranian.

And yet, the reality among ourselves is that we have not yet succeeded in establishing effective means of communication across our various communities. There seems to be very little personal contact between Muslims in one locality and those just a few neighborhoods away, let alone across the country. We desperately need dialogue, discussion, and regular exchange of information among the many mosques and Muslim communities in the U.S. We need conferences and meeting forums. We need a sense of oneness.

And we need to break through our obsession with *image*. Image plays too big a role in the minds of Muslim individuals and families. People (especially the wealthy among us) judge each other by the face that they show to the community. All too often, the social functions surrounding events such as marriage, death, and burials become showcases for people to display their family image through the number of guests in attendance, the lavish venue, and all the material excess that goes into the ceremony.

When all is said and done, our obsession with image becomes a way of separating ourselves from each other. We define ourselves not as a united community working together for the common good, but as individuals and families who wish to divide our community by creating hierarchies of wealth and status. We must learn to focus on what binds us together, not what divides us, for ultimately, we will succeed in reaching our larger goals only to the extent that we function together for the common good. In other words, we should be concerned about our image *as a community of Muslims*, not our image as individuals and families in competition with each other.

The basic requirements for realizing our vision through institution building boil down to money, manpower, and organizational skills. With respect to the first of these elements, money, we can turn to our own Islamic traditions for an ample number of models and means for raising revenues. Throughout the centuries, Islam has developed a number of concepts and practices through which people make monetary contributions to the cause of community projects: *Zakat, Khoms* (a specifically Shi'a practice), *Sadaghah, Enfagh, Ithar,* and *Waghf* are all terms referring to forms of giving or paying dues. In addition, Muslims (like Westerners) also have the tradition of benefiting religious and public institutions through their wills. In Islam, religious dues do not constitute an act of charity; they are an obligation for those able to give, and an entitlement for those whose personal circumstances make them recipients—and among the recipients that are entitled to receive the benefits of religious dues are religious and community institutions in need of financial support. For a further explanation of Islamic concepts and practices of giving, see Appendix C of this book.

I do not believe that American Muslims are less capable of giving than members of other religious groups. However, our community needs to undergo a process of education and trust-building in order to pull together financially. Enlightened, persuasive leadership will be a crucial factor in this process. Muslim religious leaders must be willing to emphasize the importance of giving in Islam. Muslims are generous by nature; our ancestors supported good public causes throughout earlier centuries of Islam, and I believe that when those of our own day see the benefit of a strong community for themselves and their children, they will generously contribute to it.

As for manpower, we again can draw upon past traditions to inspire our contributions for the future. Traditionally, Muslims have always considered themselves brothers and sisters in faith. Islamic codes of behavior encouraging cooperation and teamwork are repeatedly mentioned in the Qur'an (for example, 3:103 and 22:78) and Sunnah (the religious acts of the Prophet Mohammad *pbuh* and his companions during his ministry). In early times protecting the borders, fighting enemies, and doing charity work were valued highly, and Muslims volunteered for those tasks as a part of their religious duty and for the sake of God. Unfortunately, during the many centuries of centralized governments these virtues gradually became corrupted and shunted to the background. In the Islamic societies of today the traditions have been preserved on the surface, but their spirit and meaning have become greatly distorted.

Organizational skills, the third requirement for realizing our vision, are something that we have yet to learn—and must learn well. Americans have developed skills and practices in leadership, group-building, and organizational management that are unsurpassed in the world, and we will benefit greatly by applying them to our own institution building. From the beginning of our efforts we should make the best use of the available knowledge; we should not be too proud or hesitant to seek expert advice, and over time we, too, will become experts as we develop our own approach and find our own solutions to our particular organizational management needs.

The organization and management of religious institutions are culture-specific, and American faith communities tend to run themselves in ways that reflect their broader social surroundings. I am particularly impressed by those Christian churches and denominations (mostly Protestant) that function on the basis of self-governing through the democratic approach, but even the churches that are based on hierarchical governance structures, such as the Roman Catholic Church and the Episcopal (Anglican) Church, have powerful lay committees on the local level that play a vital role in the lives of their congregations.

It may be tempting for us, as Muslims, to import the traditional forms of organization and human relations that are standard in the Middle East, but that is something we should avoid at all costs. We should model our institutions on the ways that other religious institutions in America are run. This means that we must all think of ourselves as active members in the Muslim community, and we must be actively involved in the governance of our religious institutions. We must have truly representative, democratically elected boards of directors who are in fact—not just in name—the managers of our institutions.

By no means does this vision of our institutional life exclude clergy. We absolutely need qualified religious leaders trained in Islamic seminaries to guide us in spiritual matters, religious ethics, the study of our sacred texts and traditions, and as public spokesmen for our communities. However, our active role as lay members must always be the backbone of our institutional governance.

* * *

Cultures are resistant to change, and when they change they generally do so through gradual, organic processes that have a life and momentum of their own. However, there are occasions when rapid cultural change takes place, usually as the result of a major environmental event. The large-scale immigration of Muslims that we have seen in recent decades, involving sudden exposure to a vastly different culture and worldview, might be seen as such an event. Under the impact of this event, changes in our culture are capable of jarring loose the foundations of the community. Confronted by a powerful and inescapable new culture, we can too easily be intimidated into a state of passivity and gradually succumb to the pressures of our new environment. Instead of holding onto our traditions and reinforcing our identity, we can take the path of least resistance and try to blend into the surrounding culture.

It would be a tragedy if American Muslims suffer such a fate—if we lose our religious identity, forget our cultural heritage, and disappear into the landscape without a trace of our past and without a firm sense of our true identity. If this were to happen, we would lose—and America would also lose. That is why it is so important to act now: to build the structures we need to preserve our community identity, to reaffirm our true sense of who we are, and to stand tall amid the multicultural forces of our new homeland.

To do this, we must face up to several realities:

• We have to accept the fact that we are in the United States to stay. This is our country. It is the birthplace of our children or grandchildren. Most of us will not return to live and die in our countries of origin, and we must give up the fantasy of doing so; such nostalgic ideas will only hold us back and prevent us from making sensible, long-term life plans.

• We are a religious minority in a secular, pluralistic society. As such, we come face to face every day of our lives with the temptations and challenges of the surrounding culture. We must of course live in, and accommodate ourselves to, that surrounding culture, but we must also hold onto the truth of who we are, for the sake of our own sense of identity and for our souls, and we must pass that truth on to succeeding generations of our families.

• As a community of souls united by Islam, we must create and sustain institutions that further our spiritual awareness, guide us in our behavior, educate us and our children in the fundamental values of our faith, and help us grow continuously closer to God. Both as a community and as individuals, we must generously give of ourselves and whatever wealth we have to provide for the institutions that will nourish us in these ways.

We owe America a debt for giving us a home, economic opportunity, and freedom. The best way we can pay back that debt is by keeping the wealth of our heritage alive—our history, literature and poetry, philosophy, and above all, our religion—and offering these great gifts to our fellow Americans as resources. We bring with us the beauty of a long, proud past, together with much wisdom about the eternal questions of life, birth, death, and the purpose of life on earth. We can share that wisdom with others.

And while we are thinking about our gifts, we should remember that our life itself is a gift from God—a magnificent gift that comes to us with the guidance of God and the Prophet *pbuh*, the guidance of reason, and the internal compass, or *Fetra*, that every human possesses. God wants us to be good people, worthy of His companionship, and these gifts are ours to use as we find our way in the world, whether we leave our place of birth for distant lands or stay in our home village until we die.

We who have been transplanted from afar have an obligation to put in place institutions that will safeguard our heritage and allow our Muslim community to realize its possibilities here in America. We must act to maintain and strengthen the core of our religious tradition as we strive to play our role in the surrounding society. We must ensure that our great-grandchildren will think of us and say, "Our great-grandparents brought us to this country, gave us a home here, fed us, clothed us, and helped us get an education. But most importantly, they made it possible for us to fully experience our Islamic religion and celebrate our cultural heritage."

It is a big challenge, but we can do it. As Prophet Mohammad's (*pbuh*) son-in-law Ali, the Fourth Khalif, said, "Caravans that travel by night reach their destination early in the day." That is, they set forth when the times seem dark and difficult so as to arrive in the brightness of the morning. This is our challenge: to work together through the difficult times, to work against the odds, and to reach our goal at the dawning of a glorious new day.

Appendixes

APPENDIX- A

The Role of the Ulama and the Sources of Truth in Islam

Over the centuries when kings, sultans, and khalifs enlisted the clergy to interpret Islamic doctrine for the benefit of the rulers, many members of the clergy, or *Ulama*, resisted the pressures and refused to deviate from their understanding of the Truth. Although they often suffered severe consequences for their actions, those courageous individuals made it possible for us to understand the true message of Islam in the twenty-first century. There were others who managed to walk the tightrope of loyalty to their rulers while still working behind the scenes, so to speak, to help keep alive the main sources of Islam. The rulers and the forces of their environment invariably influenced the latter, but they, too, made a positive contribution. Thanks to all of their efforts, the Qur'an and the Hadith were preserved in their original form and handed down to subsequent generations.

I consider myself one of the benefactors of what those great men have bequeathed us. I have spent many hours reading books about the early history of Islam and the traditions of the Prophet Mohammad *pbuh* and his disciples. I have studied the historical and political events that conditioned the rise and spread of Islam throughout the centuries. And I have pored over the pages of the Qur'an, grateful to have it in its pure form as a resource with which to discern, to my own satisfaction, the truth about Islam as it was revealed to the Prophet and practiced in early Islamic societies. I have not had formal education in the great religious centers or theological schools and cannot claim to be an expert, but I am a product of a Western education that taught me how to think systematically. Thanks to the existence of the primary sources, my ability to think, and the freedom I have in America, I have learned a great deal about my religion that I might not have discovered had I stayed forever in the country of my birth.

The Sources of Truth in Islam

The authentic sources of knowledge to which Muslims, both religious leaders and laypersons, have referred throughout history in their search for truth are the following:

1. **The Qur'an, or Koran.** The Qur'an, which comes to us directly from the Prophet Mohammad *pbuh*, is the undisputed source of truth for Muslims, and its content is accepted as the undisputed word of God. The content was revealed to Prophet Mohammad *pbuh* over a period of 23 years. Mohammad *pbuh* could not read, but he recited the verses of the Qur'an to his companions and they memorized them. Muslims gathered and wrote down the Qur'an within a few years following the death of the Prophet and put it in the form of a book that has been kept unaltered for 14 centuries.

2. **The Hadith, or Traditions.** The traditions of the Prophet Mohammad *pbuh*, his sayings and his actions, have been major sources of knowledge for Muslims. It is important to know that the khalifs forbade Muslims to write down the tradition of the Prophet for about

100 years after his death for fear that it would interfere with the content of the Qur'an. However, these traditions were kept alive in the memory of the Prophet's compatriots and transferred orally during the first few generations after Prophet Mohammad's (*pbuh*) death. Finally, during the second and third centuries after the death of the Prophet, these traditions were collected, critically examined, and written down in the form of books. Muslims have referred to these texts, over the centuries, as a means of finding the truth.

Among Sunni Muslims these books are called *Sehahe Setteh*, or the Six Correct Books, and they are titled *Sahihe Bokhari* (dated 194–256 H.Gh.), *Sahihe Muslim* (202–261), *Sonane Abudawood* (202–275), *Sonane Ebne Majeh* (209–273), *Jame'e Tarmazi* (209–279), and *Sonane Nesai'* (–302). In each of these books there are many thousands of "Hadith," and the authors admit that they have tried to select the most correct ones among many more. They caution that all of the reported Hadith may not be authentic and free of error.

Among Shi'a Muslims there are four reference books, namely *Al-Kafi* by Koleini (–328), *Man La Yahzoroh-ol-Faghih* by Sheikh Sadoogh (–381) and Al-Tahzib and Al-Estebsar, both by Sheikhe Toosi –460). In Shi'a, those Hadith are considered to be authentic and reliable when they are confirmed by one of the Imams (11 successive progenies of Prophet Mohammad *pbuh* who lived among Muslims until 260 H.Gh.).

Because of the possibility of errors in the Hadith books, both Sunni and Shi'a *Ulama* insist that the content and meaning of each Hadith must be accepted only if it does not contradict the Qur'an.

Among Sunni and Shi'a Muslims and their *Ulama*, the content of these books has been used to justify their interpretations of Islam and in teaching students in religious schools throughout the centuries. Since these reference books contain different and sometimes contradictory statements about the same subjects, elaborate methodologies have been developed to identify the correct Hadith and interpret the meaning. It is reasonable to assume that the human element—factors such as vested interests and human weaknesses— have influenced the interpretation of the Hadith in Islamic religious centers throughout history, beginning with the Ommiad (Umayyad) and Abbasid Khalifs.

Often the *Ulama* in Islamic countries, both Sunni and Shi'a, have limited their rulings to the meanings of the words (literal interpretation) that they have found in the Hadith. In addition, the *Ulama*, especially during the 17th to 19th centuries, have resisted including new discoveries made in Western countries. It is only during the past century that Muslim *Ulama* have been widely exposed to the achievements of the West and have been increasingly making use of the new knowledge in their interpretation of the Hadith and their understanding of the Qur'an.

Ethics versus Morality in Islamic Societies and among Muslims in America

I n Islamic societies, it is generally accepted that anything moral is at the same time ethical. Of the two concepts, people speak more about morality than about ethics. The moral codes governing personal and social behavior are backed by the independent power of God and handed down to the people by prophets. Ethics, as understood in the Western societies, on the other hand, find justification in the collective understanding and acceptance by the masses, and are expressed through the laws of the land.

In Islamic societies, if one transgresses the moral codes, one is ultimately answerable to God for the transgressions. In contrast, when someone in the West transgresses the ethical code, he or she is answerable to the people, the law, and the government.

In my opinion, Muslims in America need to understand the importance of ethics as they exist in the collective mind of Americans. When defending our rights, we must take care to do so in terms of Western ethics rather than our traditional sense of morality. When confronted by a situation or considering an action, we should first think about whether it is ethical and lawful—and then, at some distance, consider its morality and its acceptance by God.

Appendix- C

Islamic Concepts
and Practices of Giving

The following are means and concepts of giving that have developed within the Islamic context and are applicable to the fundraising objectives of today's Muslim communities:

ZAKAT. *Zakat* (alms, or tithing) is the backbone of public finances in Islam. As originally conceived, *Zakat* was assumed to apply to any income, but in the early days of Islam in Arabia, the only sources of income were a few agricultural items and precious metals—and these have remained the only items that are considered to be subject to *Zakat* payments in modern times. With the vast expansion of sources of income in manufacturing and service industries, it stands to reason that all sources of income should be subject to the payment of *Zakat*. We should remind ourselves that, according to Islamic teachings, a certain part of our personal assets, earnings, and income in life belongs to God and we must pay that amount back to the community in order to "cleanse" the rest of our income. In most verses of the Qur'an that instruct Muslims about practicing *Salat* (ritual prayer), Muslims are also instructed to pay *Zakat*. Abu Bakar, the first Khalif, fought fiercely against those Muslims, known as *Ahle Raddeh*, who reverted back to idol worshiping after the death of the Prophet Mohammad *pbuh* not because they did not pray, but because they refused to pay *Zakat*. Ali, the fourth Khalif, used to go to Yemen himself to collect *Zakat*.

The percentage of income required to be paid as *Zakat* differs according to denomination. Most Sunni Muslims set the percentage at 2.5% and more according to the nature of one's income. Among the Shi'a, there is some confusion as to the percentage of income subjected to *Zakat*, and the exact percentage required appears to be determined by the religious authorities.

KHOMS. Khoms is a form of giving that applies specifically to Shi'a Muslims. It is assessed at the end of the financial year at the rate of 20% of net income, that is, after the payment of an individual or family's household expenses and work expenses. This amount is paid directly to the head of the religious hierarchy.

Khoms is divided into two equal portions: half goes to descendants of the Prophet Mohammad *pbuh* who are in need of financial support and the needy progeny of the Prophet. The other half is to be paid to the grand ayatollah, the religious head of the Shi'a community, or his designated agents. He can use this half at his discretion for religious education and public works. It appears that not all Shi'a pay their *Khoms* regularly and, even if they pay, they do not generally pay the full 20%.

SADAGHAH. In the Qur'an, *Sadaghah* is used interchangeably with Zakat to describe a means of giving to the religious community. However, the meaning of *Sadaghah* is wider, applying to any voluntary payment of alms made by the wealthy to the needy for the sake of God. The Qur'an and the Hadith repeatedly recommend *Sadaghah* payments as a good deed, promising high rewards from God to the giver.

The meaning of *Sadaghah* and its use have changed gradually over the past centuries, and today it is customary for Muslims to consider *Sadaghah* a form of disaster relief, paid (usually in small amounts) to the poor at a time of calamity and disease in their family.

Another form of voluntary alms, closely related to *Sadaghah*, is the concept of *Enfagh*, which tends to be more narrowly defined for special situations of varying types.

ITHAR. *Ithar* (altruism) is the selfless giving of money, food, or services to the needy at a time when a person is himself in need of those resources. It is an act of charity that only exceptional personalities can perform. The rewards are of course commensurately high.

WAGHF (ENDOWMENT). *Waghf* is the major financial source for establishing and maintaining public charity work in Islamic countries. Large pieces of agricultural lands and many buildings in cities in Islamic countries are traditionally bequeathed, as an act of *Waghf,* to charities with well-defined causes.

WILL. Each Muslim is allowed to make a will and allocate one-third of his inheritance to any cause he wishes. The resources given to them in the will of dying persons have built many public institutions in Islamic countries.

These concepts and traditional practices of giving make it clear that there are ample vehicles in Islam for funding public religious projects.